Cambridge Companions to Music

The Cambridge Companion to the Clarinet

The Cambridge Companion to the Clarinet

Edited by
COLIN LAWSON
University of Sheffield

CAMBRIDGE
UNIVERSITY PRESS

Published by the Press Syndicate of the University of Cambridge
The Pitt Building, Trumpington Street, Cambridge CB2 1RP
40 West 20th Street, New York, NY 10011–4211, USA
10 Stamford Road, Oakleigh, Melbourne 3166, Australia

First published 1995

Printed in Great Britain at the University Press, Cambridge

A catalogue record for this book is available from the British Library

Library of Congress cataloguing in publication data

The Cambridge companion to the clarinet/edited by Colin Lawson.
    p.   cm. – (Cambridge companions to music)
  Includes bibliographical references and index.
ISBN 0 521 47066 8 (hardback) – ISBN 0 521 47668 2 (paperback)
    1. Clarinet. I. Lawson, Colin (Colin James) II. Series.
ML945.C36   1995
788.6′2–dc20   94–47624 CIP MN

ISBN 47066 8 hardback
ISBN 47668 2 paperback

Contents

Illustrations

The contributors

JOHN ROBERT BROWN is a member of staff at Leeds College of Music, where he is currently Postgraduate Course Leader and Head of the External Relations Unit. His published transcriptions include *Jazz Clarinet 1* and *2*, *Pure Wynton Marsalis*, *Pure David Sanborn* and *Pure Courtney Pine*. His published compositions include *Quintet for Brass* (1994).

MICHAEL BRYANT trained as a metallurgist, but switched to broadcast engineering and has worked for the BBC World Service for over twenty-five years. Having taken a special interest in rediscovering forgotten and unpublished chamber music for the clarinet, basset horn and bass clarinet, he has provided advice on rare repertoire and research methods to students, collectors and professional players.

NICHOLAS COX is Principal Clarinet of the Royal Liverpool Philharmonic Orchestra. As a soloist he has appeared at Britain's most important festivals and concert halls, and several composers have written him commissions, including Hugh Wood, Richard Rodney Bennett, Jonathan Lloyd and Andrey Eshpay. Solo tours and masterclasses have taken him to Europe, the Far East and Russia.

GEORGINA DOBRÉE   From early in her career, Georgina Dobrée took an interest in the more unusual members of the clarinet family, and in 1951 the firm of Henri Selmer undertook to make a basset horn especially for her. This instrument accompanied her summer visits to Darmstadt, where for almost ten years from 1953 she gave performances of new music. In recent years the repertoire written especially for her has increasingly been specifically for the basset horn and has been premièred in Britain, the USA and what is now the Czech Republic.

MICHAEL HARRIS is principal bass clarinet with the Philharmonia Orchestra. He also pursues a vigorous freelance career in orchestral and chamber music, appearing regularly with groups such as the Nash Ensemble, the London Sinfonietta and London Winds. He has developed a keen interest in early clarinets and is professor of classical clarinet at the Royal College of Music.

PAUL HARRIS studied clarinet, composition and conducting at the Royal Academy of Music and music education at the University of London. He has now established a reputation as a teacher, composer, writer, performer, examiner and adjudicator, with well over one hundred publications to his name, many of which deal primarily with stimulating and helping young players to develop their musical skills. Paul Harris has also undertaken research into specialist music education for the highly talented – an interest that has taken him to many musical institutions around the world.

ROGER HEATON has worked closely with many leading composers, including Feldman, Bryars, Volans, Ferneyhough and Henze, and has performed with the Arditti and Balanescu Quartets, Ensemble Modern, the London Sinfonietta, the Gavin Bryars Ensemble and many other groups. Since 1982 he has been Clarinet Professor at the Darmstadt Ferienkurse für Neue Musik and was Music Director of Rambert Dance Company, 1988-93.

COLIN LAWSON has played principal clarinet with most of Britain's leading period orchestras, notably The English Concert, The Hanover Band and the London Classical Players. He has given period performances of concertos by Mozart, Weber and Spohr at a number of international venues, including Carnegie Hall and the Lincoln Center, New York; he has also published widely on various aspects of historical performance practice. His writings on the history of the clarinet include *The Chalumeau in Eighteenth-Century Music.* He is currently senior lecturer in music at the University of Sheffield.

JO REES-DAVIES's life has been fairly equally divided between the worlds of libraries and of music, the latter as performer and teacher. She has been librarian of the Clarinet & Saxophone Society of Great Britain since 1984 and is currently editor of the society's quarterly magazine. Her clarinet repertoire lists, translations and compilations cover most of the countries in Europe.

ANTONY PAY was born in London, studied at the Royal Academy of Music and read Mathematics at Cambridge University. He has been principal clarinet of the Royal Philharmonic Orchestra, the London

Sinfonietta (of which he was a founder member) and the Academy of St Martin-in-the-Fields, and a member of several chamber ensembles. Since 1984 he has concentrated mainly on solo playing and conducting, recording Spohr concertos and period performances of Mozart, Weber and Crusell concertos on specially reconstructed instruments. He currently plays in the Orchestra of the Age of Enlightenment.

NICHOLAS SHACKLETON is a Fellow of the Royal Society with a long interest in the clarinet and its history; his interest in the acoustics of the clarinet helped him elucidate the cause of ice-age cycles. He has examined clarinets in virtually all the major collections of musical instruments in the world. He has played on a wide range of instruments and advises Daniel Bangham on making replicas of historic clarinets. He has written several authoritative articles on the history of the clarinet.

BASIL TSCHAIKOV was successively a member of the London Philharmonic and Royal Philharmonic Orchestras and then became a member of the Philharmonia (1958-79), where he played clarinet and E♭ clarinet. A former Professor at the Royal College of Music, he was Director of the National Centre for Orchestral Studies for ten years from 1979. He is currently editor-in-chief of the journal *Musical Performance*. His numerous publications include the chapter 'Performance and audience' for *How Music Works.*

PAMELA WESTON began her career as a clarinet soloist and was a professor at the Guildhall School of Music and Drama for eighteen years, before turning to writing about the history of the instrument and its players. She travels widely as lecturer and broadcaster, and is the author of books and articles on clarinet virtuosi past and present. A prolific contributor to *The New Grove*, she holds honorary membership of clarinet societies worldwide.

Preface

The chapters which make up this volume were commissioned from various friends and colleagues, all experts in their respective fields. Our purpose has been to stimulate constructive, penetrating thought about the past, present and future of the art of clarinet playing. Our survey includes a great deal of historical information, including discussion of the clarinet's structure and development, its fundamental acoustical principles, its chief exponents and its repertoire, as well as discussion of its role in jazz and on record. A particular focus of attention has been the relevance of our material to the individual player, reflecting the performing skill and experience of several of the authors. The chapters relating to the early clarinet and to the contemporary clarinet contain a deliberately practical bias, as indeed do the sections pertaining to individual members of the extensive clarinet family. Chapters on the mechanics of playing the clarinet, the professional clarinettist and on teaching the clarinet contrive to combine in varying degrees a practical and philosophical approach. I believe that this special combination of historical perspective and professional experience has not been attempted on such a scale in any previous book relating to the instrument. Overall, we have sought to encourage the kind of performer – much valued throughout musical history – for whom mental agility complements digital dexterity.

In this sense the book is intended as a true 'companion'; it is not, however, a 'compendium'. Comprehensiveness would require a volume many times the size of this. My contributors and I have therefore had to be selective in our essays and overall scheme, and in our illustrations, music examples and bibliographical references. But this has been balanced by the opportunity for each of us to address our subjects from a personal viewpoint, and this policy has been actively encouraged, subject to reasonable editorial constraints. As a result I am hopeful that the book will provoke thought, discussion and even argument about the world of the clarinet, as it reaches out to some unaccustomed (as well as more conventional) branches of the subject.

There are one or two conscious omissions (such as extensive investigation of the continuing role of the clarinet as a 'folk' instrument), but we have aimed to investigate most significant areas relating to the instrument. As editor, I must of course take full responsibility for the volume's overall proportions and various subdivisions, which were devised to comply with the understandable limitations of length imposed by the publisher. Our text is intended for all who have an interest in the clarinet – 'amateurs' as well as students and professional musicians. Exhaustive lists of repertoire or pedagogical literature have not been attempted, though our appendix lists early tutors and relevant sources available in facsimile, as well as a selection of modern teaching materials. In general, references have been chosen for inclusion where they have some special bearing on practical considerations.

It is a pleasure to acknowledge the help given so willingly by so many in the preparation of this book. I am indebted to all my contributors for their co-operative attitude and prompt response to various problems and queries. As can readily be imagined, the circle of performers and writers whose advice has been sought is much more substantial than the mere list of contributors might imply, and this book would have been much poorer without their unstinting help. I am especially grateful to my wife Hilary for her encouragement throughout the project, since its development has entailed long periods of absence at the word-processor, even throughout normal bouts of concert preparation and frantic searches for a playable clarinet reed. Lastly, I must extend my sincere thanks to Penny Souster and her team at Cambridge University Press, for their helpful advice and firm but unobtrusive guidance in bringing the book to fruition.

Colin Lawson

Acknowledgements

Acknowledgements for kind permission to reproduce illustrations and music examples is due to the following:

Illustrations

Bayerisches Nationalmuseum, Munich: Fig. 1.1
Clive Barda, London: Fig. 5.4
Germanisches Nationalmuseum, Nuremberg: Figs. 1.2, 2.1
Archiv der Gesellschaft der Musikfreunde, Vienna: Fig. 1.3
International Music Publications: Fig. 11.2
The Merlin Company: Fig. 11.1
Mühlfeld family collection: Fig. 5.1
Österreichische Nationalbibliothek, Vienna: Fig. 8.5
Sächsische Landesbibliothek, Dresden: Fig. 1.4

Clarinets from the Shackleton collection in Figs. 2.2–2.5 were photographed by Dona Haycraft

Fig 3.1 is reproduced with the consent of the publishers from *The New Grove Dictionary of Music and Musicians* ed. by Stanley Sadie, 20 vols. (*c* Macmillan Publishers Ltd, London, 1980)

Music examples

Boosey and Hawkes: Exx. 3.3 and 3.10
Breitkopf & Härtel: Ex. 10.3
Chantry Publications: Ex. 3.14
Peters Edition: Ex. 10.1
Universal Edition: Ex. 10.2

Abbreviations, fingering and notation

The following books are identified in the text only by their authors' surnames:

ANTHONY BAINES, *Woodwind Instruments and their History* (London, 1957; 3rd edn, 1967)

JACK BRYMER, *Clarinet* (London, 1976)

OSKAR KROLL, *The Clarinet* (tr. Hilda Morris, ed. by Anthony Baines, London, 1968)

GEOFFREY RENDALL, *The Clarinet* (London, 1954; 3rd edn rev. by Philip Bate, 1971)

Clarinet fingerings are assigned the following digital indicators: Lth, L1, L2, L3 and L4 (left hand thumb and four fingers); Rth, R1, R2, R3 and R4 (right hand).

Pitch registers are indicated in the usual manner: middle C just below the treble staff is indicated as c', with each successive octave higher shown as c'', c''', c'''' etc. and the two octaves below shown respectively as c and C. Under this scheme the lowest written note of the clarinet is represented as e and the top of the clarinet register as c''', the extreme high register extending to c'''' and beyond.

1 Single reeds before 1750

COLIN LAWSON

Introduction

The remarkable and eventful history of the clarinet continues to prove an endless source of fascination amongst players and listeners alike. A wealth of new research relating to the clarinet's origins and development has been stimulated by an increasing recognition that historical instruments and performance practices have a great deal to teach us about both the art and craft of music. The earliest years of any instrument's life inevitably reveal varied patterns of acceptance, and only gradually is any coherent picture of the early eighteenth-century clarinet beginning to emerge. However, any lingering doubts about the clarinet's vigorous career in the two generations before Mozart's birth have now at last been conclusively laid to rest.

It is the special acoustical make-up of the clarinet which seems to account for many particular features of its history. For example, during the first half century of its life it really existed as two instruments; the essence of the baroque clarinet was its upper register, whereas its close relative the chalumeau was restricted to a range of a twelfth in its fundamental register. Only during the classical period did it become possible to manufacture an instrument in which both registers were relatively satisfactory and in tune. Although the baroque clarinet engaged some important composers such as Handel and Vivaldi, the repertoire for chalumeau is actually much more wide ranging in scope and deserves to be far better known.

Origins and birth of the clarinet

Remarkably, there is no evidence of clarinet-types in art music until just before 1700, and this accounts for the clarinet's reputation as the youngest member of the orchestral wind section. In fact, the baroque flute, oboe and bassoon had been developed not many years before, and were featured in the orchestra by Lully (1632–87); however, their immediate antecedents were rather more closely related to them both in design and musical usage. Most clarinet histories have begun by tracing single-reed instruments back as far as *c.* 3000 BC, whilst identifying examples of folk instruments and bagpipe chanters until 1700 AD and beyond. A recent listing of these instrumental sources[1] has as its earliest item the Egyptian double pipe, or 'memet', with its reed cut in a separate tube, inserted in the top of the pipe and taken entirely into the mouth. Pipes with idioglot reeds (not separate pieces of cane, but cut in the tube itself) have been identified from later civilisations, for example the Greek aulos and the Sardinian launeddas. Such instruments also occur in a variety of pictorial evidence from the Middle Ages onwards and survive today in folk culture. None the less, it is highly significant that no single reed instrument, with the exception of the regal organ, is mentioned in any of the instrumental treatises by Virdung (1511), Agricola (1529), Luscinius (1536) or Praetorius (1619).[2]

Before proceeding to examine evidence for the birth of the clarinet, we should note that in French sources from the twelfth century onwards, the term 'chalumeau' and a host of related words deriving from the Greek *kalamos* via the Latin *calamus* were in frequent use – as generic terms for *any* simple pipe. For example, in *Harmonie universelle* (Paris, 1636) Mersenne describes several different reed-pipes as chalumeaux, among which are two simple instruments with idioglot reed. He also mentions various parts and reeds of the folk bagpipe – the *chalemie* or *cornamuse* – illustrating two single idioglot reeds and one double reed next to the tubes in which they were inserted.[3] The double-reed chanter or 'chalumeau' of this type of bagpipe was sometimes pulled out of the skin and played as a small instrument in its own right. Such definitions of the chalumeau are also found in at least one contemporary treatise and even as late as the first half of the eighteenth century.

Who invented the clarinet, and at what date? The starting point for any account of the clarinet remains J. G. Doppelmayr's *Historische Nachricht von den Nürnbergischen Mathematicis und Kunstlern* (Nuremberg, 1730), with its biography of the maker Johann Christoph Denner (1655–1707) containing the celebrated statement:

Finally his artistic passion compelled him to seek ways of improving his invention of the aforesaid instruments [recorders], and his praiseworthy intention had the desired effect. At the beginning of the current century, he invented a new kind of pipe-work, the so-called clarinet, to the great delight of all music-lovers, discovered again from ancient times the already well-known stick or rackett bassoon, and at length presented an improved chalumeau.

It has been observed that Doppelmayr is elsewhere a not wholly reliable source, that he tended to exaggerate the achievements of local craftsmen and that he failed to assess the contributions of other makers to the development of the chalumeau and clarinet.[4] But the most serious problem is his failure to make clear the relationship of the two instruments and Denner's involvement with each. Nevertheless, no evidence has emerged to contradict Doppelmayr's claim, which finds support in other sources such as Bonanni's *Gabinetto armonico* (Rome, 1722), Walther's *Musicalisches Lexicon* (Leipzig, 1732) and Majer's *Museum musicum* (Schwäbisch Hall, 1732).

Appended to Bonanni's chapter on the oboe is a description of an instrument called the *scialumò*, a simple pipe similar in length to the recorder, with a thumb-hole and six finger-holes. More sophisticated is his *calandrone*, with two keys at the mouthpiece end covering diametrically opposite holes; one may deduce from other evidence that this instrument had by now a separate ('heteroglot') tied-on reed. Majer identified a family of soprano, alto or quart, tenor and bass chalumeaux which were hard to blow because of their difficult embouchure. Musical sources indicate that Majer's four chalumeaux corresponded in size to sopranino, descant, treble and tenor recorders, though sounding an octave lower on account of the acoustical properties of the cylindrical stopped pipe. Majer notes that the fingerings closely resemble those of the recorder, though its range is not much more than an octave; if one can play the recorder, the chalumeau is quite easy. Such comparisons of the two instruments, as well as their physical similarity, lend credence to the hypothesis that the chalumeau evolved from the recorder, perhaps during attempts to increase its dynamic range. The general classification of wind instruments on the basis of the number of finger-holes rather than more scientific criteria was entirely characteristic of eighteenth-century writers. A volume of music for the mock trumpet − an instrument probably identical with Bonanni's *scialumò* − was content with the simple instruction 'Put the Trumpet in your Mouth, as far as the Gilded Leather, and blow pretty strong . . .'.

Bonanni's clarinet (*clarone*) was two and a half palms long, terminating in a trumpet-like bell three inches in width, and with a further differentiating feature from the chalumeau − its two key-holes were no longer diametrically opposite, but with the thumb-key hole further towards the mouthpiece (as with the modern speaker key). On Bonanni's evidence, it would be possible to take Doppelmayr's ambiguous statement at face value; perhaps Denner introduced a separate reed and extended the range of the chalumeau, and then proceeded to develop the clarinet by means of a smaller mouthpiece and resited speaker key, projecting its upper register via a bell rather than a mere recorder-type footjoint. Bonanni described its sound as high and vigorous, whilst significantly Majer and Walther observed that from afar it sounded like a trumpet, a characterisation nicely reflected in the earliest clarinet repertoire.

Walther and Majer ascribed the invention of the clarinet to a Nuremberger 'at the beginning of this century', information which patently derives from Doppelmayr, and suggests an air of uncertainty even in the 1730s. There is also a long tradition of writings which specifically mention the date 1690 or thereabouts, an early example being C. G. Murr's *Beschreibung der vornehmsten Merkwürdigkeiten in Nürnberg* (Nuremberg, 1778). Recent research has unearthed various references to the chalumeau from this time; for example, in his 1976 catalogue of the wind instruments at the Bachhaus in Eisenach, Herbert Heyde has shown that 'Ein Chor Chalimo von 4. Stücken' was purchased from Nuremberg in 1687 for the Duke of Römhild-Sachsen.[5] Usage of the chalumeau in Germany is documented from shortly afterwards in an anonymous collection now in Darmstadt, dated 'Hannover 1690' and entitled 'XIIe Concert Charivari ou nopce de village a 4 Violin, 2 Chalumeaux 3 Pollissons et un Tambour les Viollons en Vielle'. Mattheson's biographical sketch of the composer Telemann observes that during his early career at Hildesheim (1697– 1701) he became acquainted with the oboe, flute, 'Schalümo' and gamba, amongst other instruments. Whilst at Hildesheim, Telemann established contact with French musicians of the Brunswick court, who may have been responsible for introducing him to the chalumeau.[6] At this period the German nobility slavishly copied their French contemporaries, adopting their language, clothes, food, furniture, dances and music, as well as their instruments.[7] It is significant that in 1696 J. C. Denner and the woodwind-maker Johann Schell successfully petitioned the Nuremberg city council to be recognised as master craftsmen and to be granted permission to make for sale the '... French musical instruments ... which were invented about twelve years ago [i.e. in 1784] in France'. Whilst the document specifies only recorder and oboe, it is surely not unreasonable to surmise that the single-reed chalumeau was also one of the new instruments.[8]

Denner's surviving instruments include a tenor chalumeau (Munich, SM, No. 136) similar in length to a treble recorder (500 mm), with three joints and two keys (Fig. 1.1). Its headjoint comprises a mouthpiece and a lower section which forms a base for its two keys. Their design clearly indicates that the instrument was intended to be played with reed uppermost. An alto chalumeau by Liebau and two tenor chalumeaux by Klenig are extant in Stockholm, and at least four more instruments have been identified as chalumeaux, though with varying degrees of certainty.[9] To the tiny list of known chalumeau-makers have recently been added the names of Philip Borkens, Jeremias Schlegel, Jan Steenbergen and Andrea Fornari, none of whose instruments is known to survive. Early eighteenth-century documentary evidence of

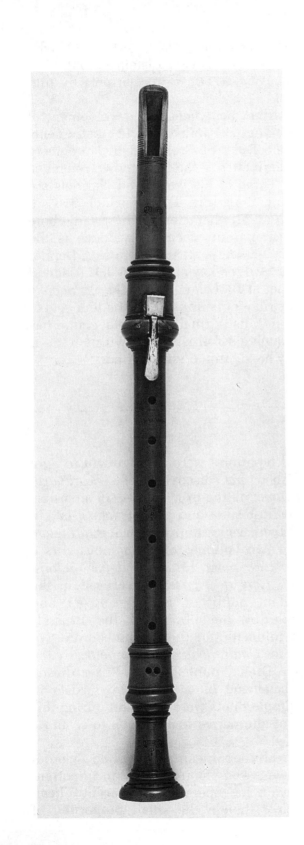

Figure 1.1   Tenor chalumeau by
Johann Christoph Denner, Munich,
SM, No. 136

the instrument centres around Denner's son Jacob (1681–1735), who received orders for chalumeaux from Schleswig-Holstein (1708), Nuremberg (1710) and Göttweig Abbey (*c.* 1720); only clarinets by him survive.

The earliest evidence of the clarinet post-dates the development of the chalumeau by some years. The 1710 invoice for instruments ordered from Jacob Denner for the Duke of Gronsfeld in Nuremberg includes besides chalumeaux '2 clarinettes' – the first known reference to the instrument in any source. Three of his two-keyed clarinets are extant in Berlin, Brussels and Nuremberg (Fig. 1.2), of which two are pitched in C and one in D. They are all characterised by a large bore and wide mouthpiece. Another important piece of evidence is the incomplete three-keyed clarinet in Berkeley, attributed to J. C. Denner and described by Eric Hoeprich in 'A three-key clarinet by J. C. Denner' and 'The L. C. [*sic*] Denner clarinet at Berkeley' in the *Galpin Society Journal* of 1981 and 1984. The instrument is unusual for its four sets of double holes (for L3, R1, R3 and R4). Its (virtually illegible) stamp has caused particular controversy, though a scroll is visible with a letter D underneath, which can reasonably be identified with Denner.[10]

Reception and repertoire

The chalumeau

The beginnings of the single-reed repertoire were first brought to light by Thurston Dart, who published his discovery of *The Fourth Compleat Book for the Mock Trumpet* dating from 1706–8 in an article of 1953.[11] It is regrettable that the little solos and duets (range *g′–a″*) in this volume have scarcely found their way into print since that time.[12] Contemporary with this book are two volumes of anonymous *Airs à deux Chalumeaux, deux Trompettes, deux Haubois, deux Violons, deux Flûtes, deux Clarinettes ou Cors de Chasse*, advertised in the 1716 catalogue of the Amsterdam publisher Estienne Roger and recently reproduced in facsimile by the library of the Brussels Conservatoire.[13] More obviously idiomatic for the chalumeau are two earlier volumes of *Fanfares pour les Chalumeaux & Trompettes* by the Parisian flautist Jacques Philippe Dreux, published by Roger during 1703–4 and advertised in his catalogue of 1706; a copy exists in Wolfenbüttel. Such volumes of simple duets were common during this period, as was the specification of alternative instruments to secure a wider sale for the publisher.

Contemporary with this historically significant but simple material comes the establishment of the two-keyed chalumeau as an important orchestral and ensemble instrument. Its repertoire has recently been the subject of extensive research,[14] though the small proportion of

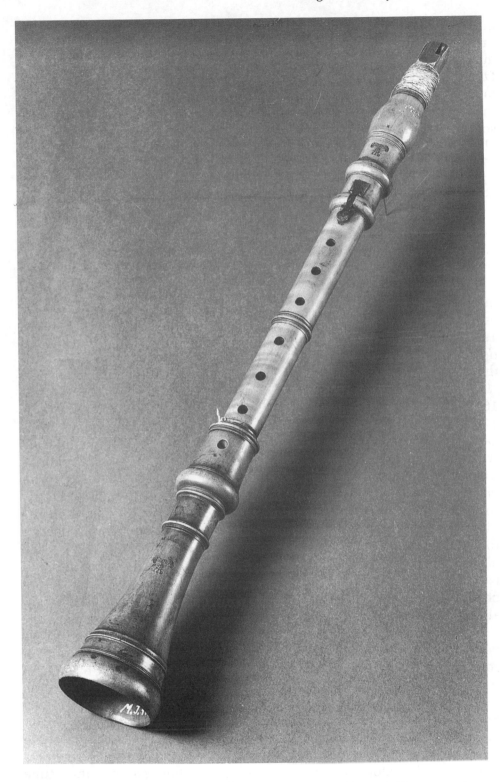

Figure 1.2   Two-keyed D clarinet by Jacob Denner, Nuremberg, GN, No. 149

music available in modern editions has so far not achieved for the instrument the prominence it deserves. Amongst the most celebrated musical contexts with chalumeau are the Vienna versions of Gluck's *Orfeo* (1762) and *Alceste* (1767), works which in fact form part of a long tradition of writing for the instrument in that city, dating back to the beginning of the century and extending as far as the 1770s. The soprano chalumeau (range *f'–b♭"* or *c'''*) soon became a favourite obbligato instrument, notably in operas and oratorios written between 1708 and 1728 by the court Kapellmeister Johann Joseph Fux (1660– 1741).[15] The chalumeau generally appears as an alternative to the oboe in pastoral or love scenes, either in pairs or with the flute or recorder; such contexts nicely anticipate Mozart's treatment of the clarinet in *Così fan tutte*. Significantly, Köchel's biography of Fux (Vienna, 1872) cites two references written by the composer in 1718 and 1721 for court oboists who also played the chalumeau.

In modern times scores of several relevant works by Fux have been published, including the operas *Julo Ascanio* and *Pulcheria*. Furthermore, an appendix to J. H. Van der Meer's biography of Fux (Bilthoven, 1961) contains numbers with chalumeau from *Julo Ascanio* and *La decima fatica d'Ercole*. Regular obbligato appearances from 1706 until the 1730s in the works of contemporary composers such as Ariosti (1666–1729), Bonno (1711–88), A. M. and G. Bononcini (1677–1726, 1670–1747), Caldara (1670–1736), Conti (1681–1732), Porsile (1680– 1750) and Reutter (1656–1738) remain largely unknown today. Some cantatas by Conti in modern facsimile contain parts for chalumeau, whilst two of Giovanni Bononcini's arias have been published in a transcription with clarinet, together with an aria originally with chalumeau obbligato written by the Emperor Joseph I (1678–1711) for insertion in Ziani's opera *Chilonida* (1709). In 1707 an amusing vignette finds a place in the libretto to Bononcini's *Etearco*, written for the Vienna carnival that year. During Act III, an exchange takes place between two comic characters, in which the remark 'I'll try to find both bassoons and oboes' is met by the retort, 'I'd like there to be chalumeaux as well'. Thus the chalumeau was perceived as an attractive novelty, to be distinguished from the traditional woodwinds.

No evidence of the chalumeau in Vienna during the 1740s and 1750s has yet come to light, so the circumstances of Gluck's revival remain something of a mystery. The list of court players compiled by Köchel reveals the survival into old age of oboists who must have known the instrument and perhaps were in a position to enthuse their pupils. Repertoire with chalumeau from the 1770s includes ballets by Aspelmayr (1728–86) and Starzer (1726–87), as well as Gassmann's late opera *I rovinati*. The first appearance in Vienna of the clarinettists Johann and Anton Stadler was in 1773, but around this time divertimenti with chalumeau were still being composed by Dittersdorf

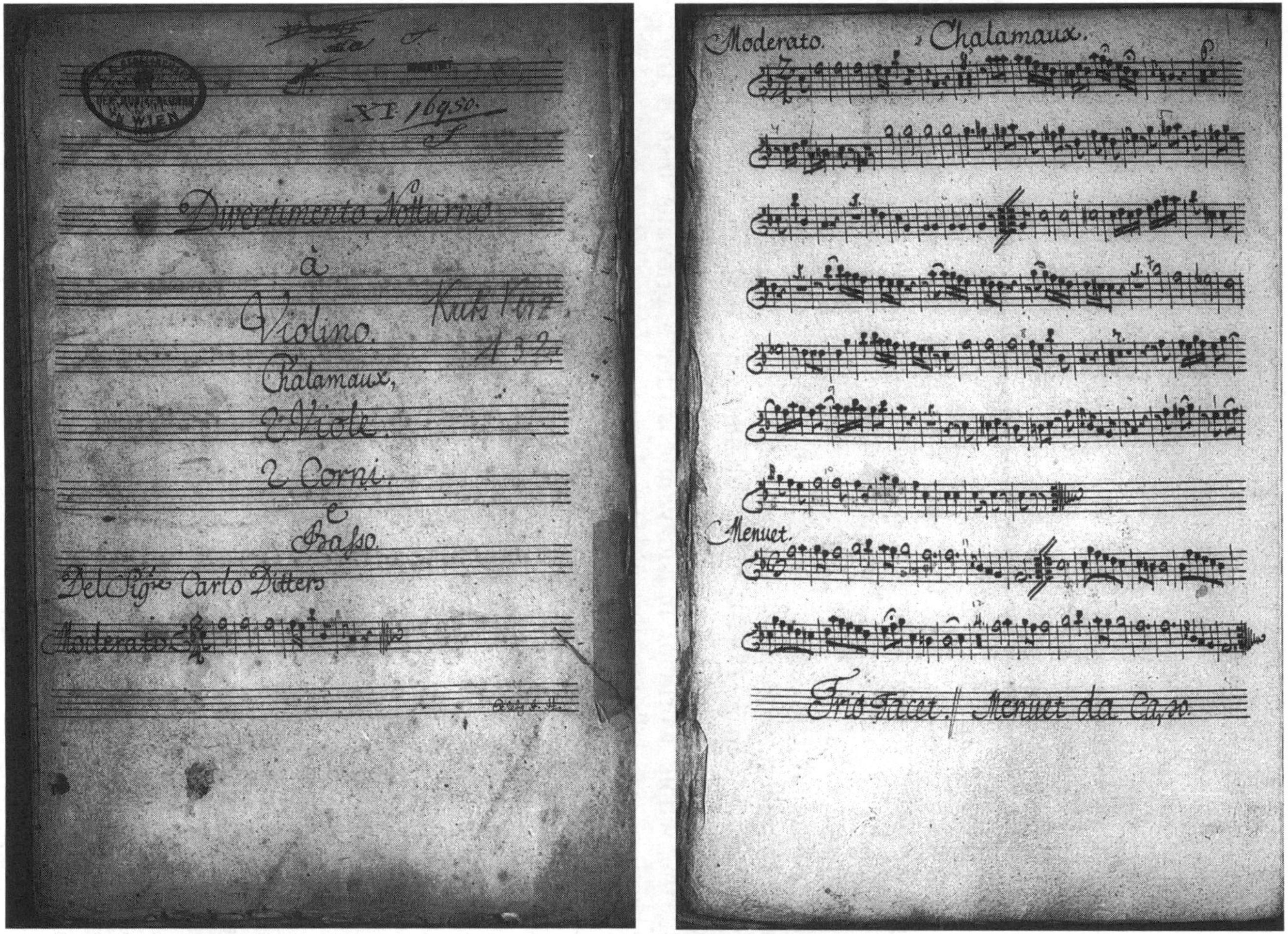

Figure 1.3   Title page and excerpt from the chalumeau part of Dittersdorf's *Divertimento Notturno*

(1739–99) (Fig. 1.3), Gassmann (1729–74) and Pichl (1741–1804). Above all, the concerto by Hoffmeister (1754–1812) testifies to the ability of a virtuoso even at this late stage. Especially significant historically is a 'Musica da Cammera' by Starzer, scored for two chalumeaux or flutes, five trumpets and timpani. The dedication 'alla Regina di Moscovia' suggests Starzer's St Petersburg period (1760–8) as the date of composition; not long afterwards Leopold Mozart copied out all five numbers, specifying only flutes for the upper parts. He added arrangements of operatic numbers by Gluck and the entire sequence was subsequently attributed to Mozart *fils* as K187 (later 159c); its correct identity was revealed only in 1937.[16] However, Starzer's music did inspire Mozart's own identically scored Divertimento K188 (240b), and the whole episode offers more than a suggestion that Mozart was at least aware of Fux's favourite obbligato instrument, if only as a curiosity. Viennese enthusiasm for the chalumeau at the threshold of the classical period has never yet been fully explained, but is confirmed in a magnificent if belated tribute by Daniel Schubart, whose book on aesthetics *(Ideen zu einer Ästhetik der Tonkunst)* written in 1784–5 but published only in 1806 observes: 'its tone has so much interest, individuality and an endless pleasantness, that the whole world of music would suffer a grievous loss if the instrument ever fell into disuse'.[17]

Of German solo works, the concerto for soprano chalumeau by Fasch (1688–1758) has recently been published, and this work alone might well justify the commissioning of a reproduction instrument. Dating from the period 1727–34, the music makes virtuoso but idiomatic demands (Fig. 1.4); it was probably intended for the bassoonist and chalumeau player J. C. Klotsch, who was employed by Fasch in Zerbst, and left in 1735 to work for Christoph Graupner (1683–1760) in Darmstadt. Fasch writes in a transitional style, his baroque structures already infused with some classical elements. Apart from this concerto and a quartet (with oboe, bassoon and continuo) by Hasse (1699–1783), the German repertoire is surprisingly distinct from the Viennese in preferring the lower sizes of chalumeau – especially alto and tenor in combination. Graupner, second choice after Telemann for Bach's post at Leipzig, was the most prolific composer for the chalumeau, including it in over eighty cantatas during 1734–53, and in eighteen instrumental works.[18] The cantatas display an acquaintance with all four sizes (though no more than three are ever used together), whose combination helps to overcome the instrument's inherent limitation in range. The chalumeau is often associated with delicate tone-colours such as the recorder or viola d'amore. Two suites for alto, tenor and bass chalumeaux have been published, as has Graupner's unusually scored trio for bass chalumeau, bassoon and continuo. Unpublished triple concertos include a work with bassoon and cello, and indeed

Figure 1.4 Opening page of the solo part of the chalumeau concerto by Johann Friedrich Fasch

Graupner is well worth investigating for his vivid exploration of colour, even if this is not quite sufficient compensation for a lack of fluency in phrase-structure by comparison with Telemann. Graupner notates music for the upper sizes in treble and soprano clefs, but makes no distinction between the lower two (except for range); they employ the bass clef, sounding an octave lower than written, anticipating Mozart's treatment of the low register of the basset horn.

Telemann (1681–1767) continued to use a pair of alto and tenor chalumeaux long after he had first employed the clarinet in a cantata of 1721.[19] Parts for both chalumeau and clarinet occur in a serenata of 1728, where their roles are clearly differentiated. Telemann often reserves chalumeaux for poignant dramatic moments, for example in the passion-oratorio *Seliges Erwägen*, where they are combined with muted horns, bassoons and muted strings at the beginning of the eighth meditation 'Es ist vollbracht' ('It is finished'). Three of Telemann's important chalumeau works have been published in modern times – the fine D minor Double Concerto, featuring an unusual degree of unaccompanied chromatic writing à 2, the Suite in F for two chalumeaux and/or violette and continuo, and the extraordinary *Grillen-Symphonie*, scored for flute or piccolo, oboe, alto chalumeau, two double basses, strings and continuo.

A complete listing of chalumeau repertoire (not all of it surviving) would also include other works by a variety of composers, such as J. L. Bach (1677–1731), Harrer (1703–55), Hasse, König (1671–1758), Mića (1694–1744), Molter (1696–1765), Schürmann (1672/3–1751), Steffani (1654–1728), Werner (1693–1766), von Wilderer (1670/1–1724) and Zelenka (1679–1745). Handel composed a very fine pastoral aria with two soprano 'chaloumeau' parts for his opera *Riccardo Primo* (1727), though it is uncertain whether this number was actually included in performances. Chrysander published it in an appendix to his nineteenth-century collected edition, and so the score remains relatively accessible. The *Daily Courant* in 1726 shows the names of two German clarinettists, Freudenfeld and Rosenberg, who gave benefit concerts in London in 1726 and 1727; these may have been Handel's players.

Though the entire history of the chalumeau is characterised by single events and works whose very isolation is puzzling, it seems inexplicable that so little French evidence survives. Almost contemporary with the Handel example is a rare mention in the *Mercure de France*; at a Concert Spirituel of 21 February 1728, 'they played a concerto for chalumeau with the accompaniment of the symphony, who formed the choruses. This instrument, which is greatly used in Germany, imitates the oboe and the recorder. The whole thing had a singular effect and gave great pleasure ....'[20] But by the time the instrument was described in the *Encyclopédie* (volume III, 1753), it was no longer used in France.

At the Ospedale della Pietà in Venice, a German oboist taught the chalumeau from 1706, and Vivaldi subsequently used it in a total of five works. The obbligato for the soprano size in the oratorio *Juditha triumphans* (1716), in an aria concerning the lament of a turtle dove, suggests Viennese influence. Of the three concertos with parts for tenor 'salmoè', two (RV558 and RV579) imply a close relationship with the oboe solo, whilst RV555 features pairs of recorders, theorboes, mandolins and violini *in tromba marina* as well as chalumeaux. The Sonata RV779 for violin, oboe and organ has an optional part for tenor chalumeau doubling the bass line. In the absence of much Italian evidence of early single reeds, a 'Concerto per clareto' (1733) by the Paduan composer Guiseppe Antonio Paganelli (1710–*c*. 1763) assumes some importance, its idiom clearly suited to the soprano chalumeau rather than (as has been suggested) the clarinet.

With the advance of recent research and more precise identification of early instruments, Adam Carse's assessment of the chalumeau in *Musical Wind Instruments* (London, 1939) as 'this will' o' the wisp among wind instruments' can now be revised. Also no longer tenable is Rendall's view (p. 66) that '... there would seem no reasonable doubt that for the first two or three decades of the century the clarinet was in Germany, and in Austria even later known as the *chalumeau*'. But even with the establishment of the chalumeau as a truly independent voice rather than a poor relation of the early clarinet, some problems remain, not least the contrast between the delicacy of the musical contexts involving the instrument and its rather unflattering critical reception. Bonanni wrote of the *calandrone* that 'it renders a raucous sound that is not pleasant' (*Gabinetto armonico*, p. 68), whilst Walther (*Praecepta der musicalischen Composition*, 1708, p. 43) stated that it gave 'a sound similar to when a man sings through his teeth'. Mattheson (*Das neu-eröffnete Orchestre*, Hamburg, 1713, p. 272) remarked, 'the so-called chalumeaux may be allowed to voice their somewhat howling symphony of an evening, perhaps in June or July and from a distance, but never in January at a serenade on the water'. The *Encyclopédie* mentions the instrument's tone-quality as disagreeable and savage, but only when played by an ordinary musician rather than an expert. None of these remarks reflects Schubart's enthusiasm for the instrument, which the repertoire richly endorses. Instead these writers were perhaps reacting to a versatility of sound rivalling later clarinets, more powerful than the recorder, with a strong outdoor playing tradition.

The clarinet

Rice's list of baroque repertoire numbers twenty-eight works by as many as thirteen composers. Nevertheless the focus of attention for today is likely to remain Handel, Vivaldi and Molter, even though orchestral C and D clarinet parts have been found in the works of Caldara (1718), Conti (1719), Faber (1720), Telemann (1721, 1728) and Graupner (final cantata, 1754). Of material as yet generally unavailable, two concertos by Valentin Rathgeber (1682–1750) are for C clarinet, and like most of the orchestral contexts listed above, cultivate a clarino style of writing. Ferdinand Kölbel wrote a trio for clarinet, horn and 'basso' (perhaps from the 1740s), which employs a consistently high tessitura to g'''. In mid-century the transition to a more classical approach was then led in France by such composers as Rameau (1683–1764) and Johann Stamitz (1717–57), whose work introduced a wider range of differently pitched clarinets. Stamitz's own orchestra at Mannheim was influential in establishing the clarinet as an orchestral and solo instrument from the 1750s, exploring its developing potential in an imaginative way; this inevitably rang the death-knell for the chalumeau.

From the previous decade, the Handel *Ouverture* for two D clarinets and horn illustrates yet another association of the two instruments. (It seems that clarinet and horn were played by one musician in Telemann's cantata *Wer mich liebet, wird mein wort halten*.) The *Ouverture* has often been associated with the Hungarian horn-player Mr. Charles, who also played the clarinet and chalumeau and toured through Britain and other parts of Europe with his wife and son. The tonal characteristics of recordings of the work since 1950 raise the question of whether open-air performance was originally intended.

Two of Vivaldi's concertos RV559 and RV560 are scored for pairs of C clarinets with oboes and besides a lively appreciation of the upper register, show a delight in exploiting the lugubrious qualities of the lower register. This difference in timbre between registers was subsequently noted by the German author Jacob Adlung (*Anleitung zu der musikalischen Gelahrtheit*, Erfurt, 1758): 'The clarinet is well known. In the low register it sounds differently from the high range, and therefore one calls it chalumeau.' But no other composer before Mozart realised the distinction quite so effectively as Vivaldi. A third concerto, RV556 'per la Solennità di San Lorenzo', combines aspects of the solo concerto with the concerto grosso, incorporating a large wind section with recorders, oboes, clarinets ('clareni') and bassoon. The second movement in the first of its two versions is scored for violin solo with a bass line played by five instruments including unison 'clarini' (clarinets). The later version reduces this bass line to a mere cello, with the clarinets removed from the outer movements as well. Unfortunately, the Ricordi edition adopts neither version, but combines them in a rather unsatisfactory way. Michael Talbot has suggested that RV556 was written for Rome rather than Venice, taking as evidence a typical use of lute continuo and the labelling and idioms of the two violins 'di concertino'.[21] Investigations into Vivaldi's connection with the Roman court of Pietro Ottoboni have revealed a repertoire including two (as yet unpublished) double clarinet concertos, one anonymous and one by the Florentine composer Giovanni Chinzer (*c.* 1700–after 1749).

Vivaldi is one of a select group of composers to have written for both chalumeau and clarinet – others include Handel, Molter and Telemann – but he is the most significant, since he continued writing for chalumeau even after discovering the full range of the clarinet, whose low register must have been less even and more veiled in sound. Comparisons of the two instruments are rare, though Garsault in *Notionaire, ou mémorial raisonné* (Paris, 1761) noted the similarity of embouchure. The principal sources of playing technique relating to the two-keyed clarinet are Majer (1732) and Eisel (*Musicus Autodidaktos*, Erfurt, 1738), both of whom include fingering charts. One of Eisel's questions relating to the clarinet is 'What type of clef is used for the clarinet? One usually uses the G clef, in which case the instrument is treated in the clarino or trumpet style, yet sometimes the soprano and alto clefs are found, in which case the clarinet is handled like a chalumeau.' This nicely reflects Vivaldi's aesthetic, if not his actual practice.

2 The development of the clarinet

NICHOLAS SHACKLETON

Introduction

The clarinet may be defined as a woodwind instrument with a predominantly cylindrical bore and a single reed that overblows at the twelfth. The term 'woodwind' does not preclude the instrument being made of a material other than wood; indeed, at least one of the few surviving very early clarinets is made of ivory. As regards overblowing at the twelfth, the assumption that one can use identical fingering in the chalumeau and clarinet registers has rather less validity on earlier clarinets than modern ones. With these reservations, the clarinet can be traced back to the beginning of the eighteenth century, when it is generally believed to have been invented by Johann Christoph Denner in Nuremberg, as outlined in Chapter 1. Instruction tutors for the clarinet go back more than 200 years, and almost from the beginning the tutor has normally opened with a brief history of the instrument. Originally this was not regarded as having much importance, nor are these brief histories very reliable. My presumption in this chapter is that it will be read by people interested in how the clarinet they know today evolved, or in playing or listening to earlier clarinets, and I will bypass aspects of the history of the instrument that seem to me less interesting from this point of view. This is a major restriction, because many of the fascinating and ingenious inventions that have been applied to the clarinet seem to have had no significant effect either at the time, or subsequently.

Despite the fact that one can learn something of the history of the clarinet from music written for the clarinet, from patents, from concert reviews and from other written sources, the primary resource from a playing point of view has to be surviving instruments. For that reason it is appropriate to pause and to consider how surviving instruments may bias one's impressions. If a twenty-first-century organologist were accurately to reconstruct the changing sounds of the English clarinet in the mid-twentieth century, it would be important that he/she should find a good pair of Boosey and Hawkes 1010 clarinets and a good pair of Buffet R13s – yet the most abundant instruments to survive will probably be made of ebonite or plastic and may well show signs of severe maltreatment followed by neglect. The most abundant surviving early twentieth-century clarinets were probably used in military bands. Many Viennese instruments from the time of Mozart and Beethoven were in use for most of the nineteenth century with new keys added, broken keys removed and the holes blocked up, cracks glued, new mouthpieces added, as they were used successively in orchestras, town bands, dance bands and bars. I have attempted to discuss and illustrate instruments that I believe at least to be characteristic of what was being used by good professional orchestral players and soloists, on the basis that our primary objective in playing historic instruments is to gain a better feeling for what classical music actually sounded like when it was first heard in favourable circumstances.

The earliest clarinets

The earliest clarinets were nearly all built with two keys and pitched in C or D, although early two-keyed instruments in F and G also survive. The two keys of these instruments are equivalent to the A key and the speaker key of the modern clarinet. However, such a set-up would appear to leave no possibility of a *b♮'*. The addition of a third key provided a low *e* and its twelfth *b♮'*, but there is evidence that two-keyed clarinets may have been tuned so as to give a *b♮'* with the two keys at the top of the instrument open, rather than *b♭'* as on the modern instrument.

We really have very little idea what the very earliest clarinets were used for, although it is known that some were provided to monasteries. It is noteworthy that the majority have relatively large bores and wide mouthpieces and are probably better suited to the pieces by Vivaldi (for C clarinet) and for some of the other early literature rediscovered by Rice[1] than to the Molter concertos. Handel's piece for two clarinets in D with horn exemplifies the trumpet-like characteristics of these earliest instruments and comes off well when played on copies of the instrument by Jacob Denner that survives in Nuremberg (Fig. 1.2, page 7). The earliest good concertos we know are those by Johann Melchior Molter and are written for the D clarinet; all six use the clarinet and extreme registers almost to the total exclusion of the chalumeau register. There is a good two-keyed D clarinet by Zencker preserved in Nuremberg with its original mouthpiece (Fig. 2.1). The bore of the instrument is quite narrow, as is the mouthpiece; this seems to be among the best surviving instruments for Molter's concertos, since it is capable of playing the extreme register with fluency.

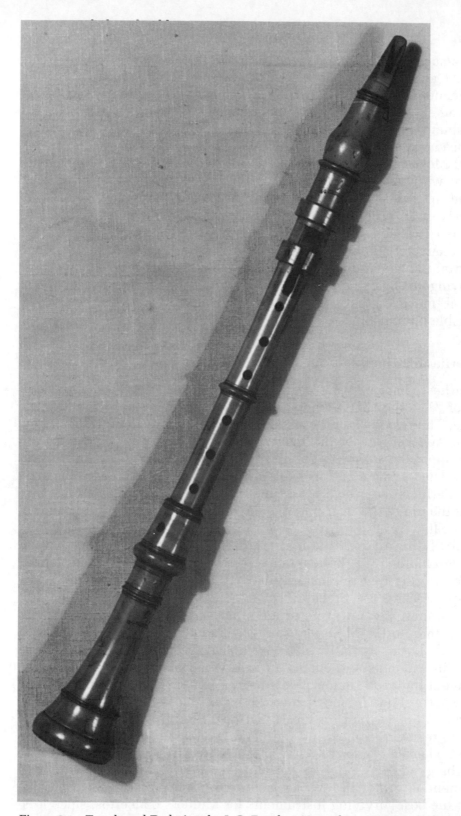

Figure 2.1   Two-keyed D clarinet by J. G. Zencker, Nuremberg, GN, No. R424

Early clarinets in B♭ and A

There are extremely few clarinets in B♭ or A known from before about 1770. A few exist with three keys (the third being the *e/b♮'* key) and a handful more with four keys (the fourth being either the *a♭'/e♭"* key for R4, (e.g. Fig. 2.5a) or (in France) the *f♯/c♯"* key for L4). The earliest identified English instrument is actually dated 1770 and has five keys;[2] several clarinets by distinguished makers after that date have fewer than five keys, but there is no surviving five-keyed instrument that shows evidence of being earlier than 1770. Thus if the concerto attributed to Johann Stamitz was indeed composed by him before his death in 1757,[3] it may have been intended for a three- or four-keyed clarinet. It is interesting to note that while on three-keyed clarinets the third key was usually an *e/b'* key operated by the right thumb, several surviving instruments have been converted so that the key could be operated by L4 instead. In the clarinet register *f"* is produced by closing R1 and R3, and *f♯"* by closing R2 and R3. In the chalumeau register *b♮* using R2 and R3 is very sharp, while using R1 alone is very flat. The Johann Stamitz concerto contains (once) the chalumeau register *b♮* that gives so much trouble on early classical clarinets. It is curious that the only clarinet known to me that has a twin hole for R1 (as is found on some recorders and oboes in this position), producing a *b♮* when only one of the pair is covered, is the much earlier but somewhat controversial instrument surviving in Berkeley, California (already mentioned on page 6) that was probably made by Johann Christoph Denner himself.[4] A few early basset horns have a twin hole in this position, perhaps implying that a well-tuned chalumeau register was regarded as being more important in relation to the basset horn than the clarinet.[5] It must, however, be said that oboists used the technique of half-holing (partially covering a tonehole) at this time, and it may be that this was the solution envisaged by Johann Stamitz, as well as by Carl Stamitz, Mozart and numerous others who used this note freely and unhesitatingly at a time when the majority of clarinets were not built to play it accurately.

The five-keyed clarinet (Fig. 2.2a) is the stage best regarded as the 'standard classical clarinet'. Despite the fact that there is ample evidence that some individual players chose to have additional keys on their instruments, these were chiefly regarded as being for trilling, rather than for improving the intonation of difficult notes. Thus several English B♭ instruments dating to the last decade of the eighteenth century have six keys, the sixth being a key for trilling on *a'* and *b♭'*. The importance of the five-keyed instrument as the basic classical clarinet is suggested by an article by the celebrated maker Heinrich Grenser (1764–1813), who stressed that however many keys an instrument was built with, the maker's primary responsibility was ensuring

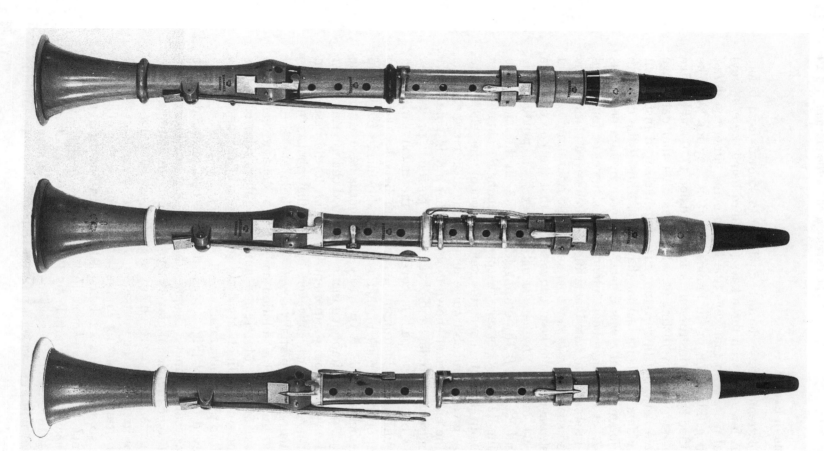

Figure 2.2 (a) Clarinet in C by Heinrich Grenser (Dresden, *c.* 1810). Boxwood, five brass keys.
(b) Clarinet in B♭ by Heinrich Grenser (Dresden, *c.* 1810). Boxwood, ten brass keys. This may be regarded as a five-keyed instrument with additional keys. The cross key for b♭/f′ (R1, R2, R3k) also produces an acceptable b♮ (R1, R3k) but is not well positioned for use in fast passages. The composer-clarinettist Bernhard Crusell used a similar clarinet by H. Grenser.
(c) Clarinet in B♭ by Jacques François Simiot (Lyons, *c.* 1815). Boxwood, seven brass keys. The side key for b♮/f♯″ (R1, R3k) is well placed for either the second joint of R3, or for R4. There is also a well-made c♯/g♯″ key for L4.

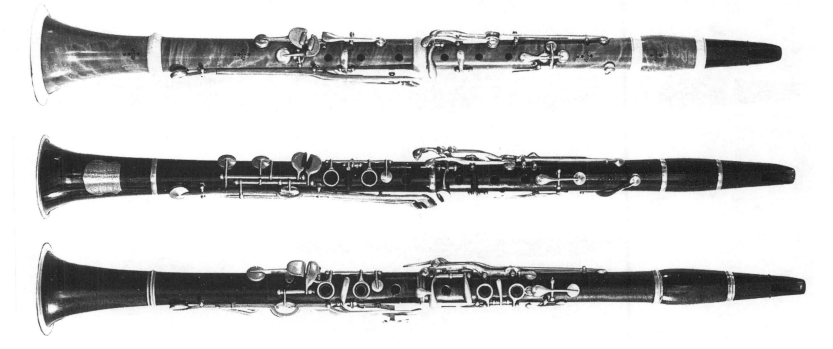

Figure 2.3   (a) Clarinet in B♭ by François Lefèvre (Paris, *c.* 1835). Boxwood, thirteen silver keys. Following Iwan Müller's proposals many makers produced thirteen-keyed clarinets despite the resistance of the Paris Conservatoire.
(b) Clarinet in A by Eugène Albert (Brussels, *c.* 1860). Rosewood, thirteen silver keys. Formerly the property of the celebrated English clarinettist Henry Lazarus (1815–95); instruments of this type were ubiquitous well into the twentieth century (popularly known as 'simple system' in Britain and as 'Albert system' in the USA).
(c) Clarinet in A by Wilhelm Hess junior (successor to Georg Ottensteiner) (Munich, *c.* 1870). Baermann system, virtually identical to the instruments played by Mühlfeld.

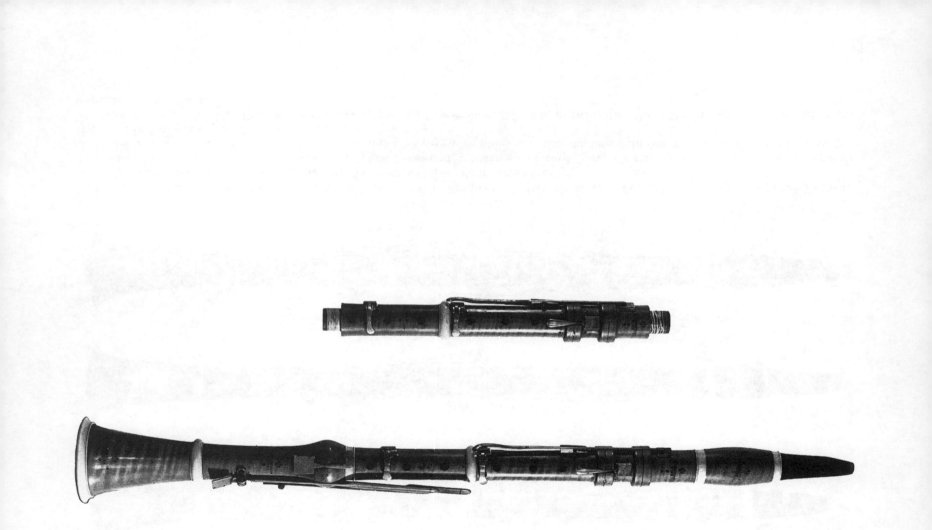

Figure 2.4   Clarinet in A with (left) alternative joint in B♭ by Johann Baptist Merklein (Vienna, *c.* 1810). Boxwood, eight brass keys. A typical classical Viennese clarinet with larger toneholes at the bottom of the instrument favouring the chalumeau register.

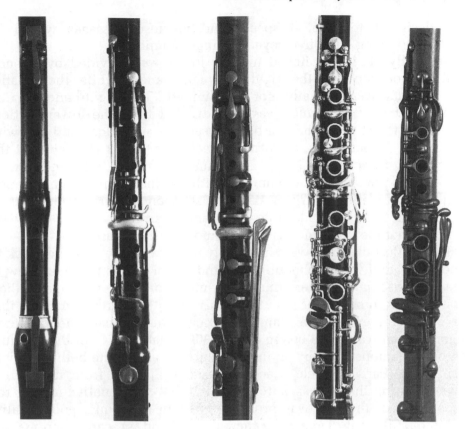

Figure 2.5 (a) Clarinet in A by Godfridus Adrianus Rottenburgh (Brussels, *c.* 1760). Stained boxwood, four brass keys. As on all early clarinets the small hole for R4 that sounds f/c″ is closer to the mouthpiece than the larger keyed hole that sounds a♭/e♭″; the maker has made no effort to shape the touchpiece.

(b) Clarinet in B♭ by Stephan Koch (Vienna, *c.* 1825). Ebony, twelve silver keys. An elegant Viennese Romantic instrument with delicate, well-designed keys. The relative positions of the R4 toneholes are unchanged but the a♭/e♭″ touchpiece is well designed so that R4 can slide from the tonehole to the touchpiece.

(c) Clarinet in B♭ by Richard Bilton (London, *c.* 1840). Boxwood, fourteen brass keys including the f/c″ for R4. Rollers on e/b′ and f♯/c♯″ touchpieces for L4. The touchpieces of the cross keys for b♮ (R1, R2k) and for b♭ (R1, R2, R3k) are carefully shaped so that it is possible for the fingers to slide on to them.

(d) Clarinet in A by Oskar Oehler (Berlin, *c.* 1935). The modern German clarinet follows Sax's fingering but has additional vents to render the tone more even but in consequence the interconnections in the keywork are much more complex than on the Boehm-system instrument.

(e) Clarinet in C by Auguste Buffet *jeune* (Paris, *c.* 1850). Following Theobald Boehm's approach to the flute, Klosé and Buffet revised the rings to provide b♭/f″ (R1) and b/f♯″ (R2) and devised a system of keywork that has survived almost unaltered to the present day.

the quality of the basic design.[6] Thus a good Grenser instrument (Fig. 2.2*b*) may be regarded as a classical five-keyed clarinet, with added keys that facilitate trilling and enable the player to produce certain notes with better intonation and tone-quality. However, the keys are not designed for use at speed, and virtuoso passages would be performed using basic five-keyed clarinet techniques.

Generally clarinets pitched in C or lower were divided by a tenon and socket between the right and left hands, while the smaller instruments were usually not so divided. The right-hand section carrying three finger-holes was also divided from the lower section, known as the stock. Usually a player used the same stock and bell with alternative upper joints, or *corps de rechange* (Fig. 2.4) to convert the instrument from B♭ to A (and, less commonly, from C to B♮, and from E♭ to D). This practice came to an end with the increasing mechanisation in the nineteenth century. A standard set then comprised clarinets in A, B♭ and C in a fitted triple case, and it is only in the twentieth century that the C clarinet has fallen into relative disuse.

The earliest clarinets were invariably made with the bell and stock in one piece, and with the mouthpiece and barrel in one piece. In view of the fact that most owners (including museums) generally claim their instruments to be earlier than they truly are, it is worth remarking that as a general guide one should assume that no instrument with a separate bell was made before about 1800. That this is not the absolute cutoff is demonstrated by an instrument with a separate bell by Michel Amlingue (Paris), which is accompanied by a note from its original owner stating that it was purchased in 1794.[7] The motivation for the separation of the bell was probably entirely economic; good quality wood of sufficient diameter for the bell was (and is) scarce, and making the whole stock-bell from such a piece is wasteful.

The division of the mouthpiece from the barrel came one or two decades earlier. Eric Halfpenny demonstrated that in England this may first have arisen after makers were asked to repair mouthpieces with broken tips, and chose to reuse the original barrel.[8] However, the change undoubtedly had other benefits. First, it enabled the maker to use a more resistant wood for the mouthpiece (imported blackwood instead of local boxwood). Second, it enabled the maker to work on the interior of the mouthpiece from both ends, and made it more practical to modify the bore in the mouthpiece and the top of the barrel for tuning purposes. Lastly (in England and America), a long tenon on the mouthpiece was used for tuning.

The dimensions of the clarinet mouthpiece have changed considerably during its history. The very earliest clarinets have disproportionately broad mouthpieces, but from the mid-eighteenth century they were considerably narrower than they are today. On classical clarinets built around 1800 the mouthpieces were broadest in England and northern Germany, and narrowest in France (where they became broader from the early nineteenth century) and in Austria and adjoining areas (where very narrow mouthpieces survived longest). It is rather surprising that Viennese instruments, which were designed to generate a good tone in the chalumeau register, did so with such a narrow mouthpiece. It goes without saying that the width of the reed was dictated by the width of the mouthpiece, but because few early reeds survive, there is not a great deal of information on changes in their design. As a general rule the lay on earlier mouthpieces was relatively long, and the tip opening relatively narrow, so that it resembled the modern German lay more closely than that usually associated with Boehm-system clarinets.

Keywork in the nineteenth century

The additions and modifications to the keywork of the clarinet that were made during the nineteenth century had several distinct purposes. First (starting in the late eighteenth century) keys were added solely to facilitate certain trills that were otherwise virtually impossible. Second, keys were added to enable complex chromatic passages to be played more fluently and/or with better intonation. Third, keywork was designed to render the tone of adjacent notes more even. Fourth, keywork was designed to enable the instrument to play more loudly.

A major objection to additional keys was the increased likelihood of unintended leakage. Until the 1830s the keys on the majority of clarinets sealed by means of a piece of soft leather attached with sealing wax to a square metal flap; this seated on a flattened area surrounding the tonehole. In London, James Wood patented (in 1800) an alternative whereby the tonehole was lined with a brass tube with a polished outer end, and the key carried a polished brass disc that sealed on the tube by close brass-to-brass contact. Aided with a drop of oil these keys seal well but make an aggravating clicking sound. In France the well-known flute-maker Clair Godefroy *aîné* used cork pads sealing on the end of a silver tube that lined the tonehole. However, the invention by Iwan Müller of the stuffed pad and the raised rim round the tonehole was the most significant improvement in the seating of the pads. At first the stuffed pad was almost spherical and fitted in a semicircular ('saltspoon') cover (Fig. 2.5*e*); towards the end of the nineteenth century this was replaced by the flatter card-based pad in a flatter cup that is in use today. To this day the pads of German clarinets are covered with white kid leather, while elsewhere the pads of the majority of clarinets are covered by thin fish bladder ('skin pads').

The majority of classical clarinets had springs of tempered brass riveted to the key and bearing directly on the wooden body. (On earlier instruments the spring was generally mounted on the body and bore on the metal of the touch-piece.) Well made, these springs can be extremely satisfactory, especially if the key is reasonably long; on very short cross keys they are generally less satisfactory. Early Viennese makers favoured blue-steel clock springs similar to those that are used today. The needle spring was invented by Louis Auguste Buffet (his earliest version of the Boehm-system clarinet had only four needle springs, and one of the few changes that it has undergone is their gradual increase; a typical Boehm-system clarinet today has eleven needle springs). The last factor controlling the reliability of the keywork is the pivot. On early clarinets the keys were pivoted on a wire pin between blocks protruding from the body of the clarinet. Some makers mounted optional keys in brass saddles with somewhat thicker screwed pivots (e.g. Grenser, Fig. 2.2*b*) while others retained carefully sculpted wooden blocks (e.g. Simiot, Fig. 2.2*c*). Those keys on Grenser's instruments that were mounted across the body are generally more reliable than the equivalent keys on English instruments (Fig. 2.5*c*), because Grenser mounted each key in a brass saddle so constructed that the spring worked on the base of the saddle instead of abrading the wood as it moved. Generally the move to stuffed pads was associated with a change to an axle mounted between two pillars that were either mounted on a base plate, or screwed directly into the wood as is done today. A separate metal insert was provided to take the end of the spring. Point screws were introduced for longer pivots parallel to the body such as the low *e* and *f* keys on the Boehm-system clarinet.

The contrast between the keywork of the ten-keyed Heinrich Grenser clarinet and the twelve-keyed Stephan Koch clarinet (Figs 2.2*b*, 2.5*b*) exemplifies the contrast between keys that might be primarily conceived for trills and for occasional notes interpolated in a technique built around the five-keyed clarinet (Grenser) and keywork designed to be fully integrated in technique designed for the twelve-keyed clarinet (Koch). Instruments designed like the Koch instrument are very successful in Romantic music at a relatively low dynamic level. This particular instrument is part of a set comprising instruments in A, B♭ and C. The next major step was taken by Iwan Müller, whose main innovation was the addition of the key for *f/c″* (Fig. 2.3*a*). The importance of this addition was that it gave the maker the flexibility to design an instrument with larger and more even-sized toneholes in the lower half of the instrument, whereas this was impossible so long as the open hole sounding *f/c″* and controlled by R4 was closer to the mouthpiece than the keyed hole sounding *a♭/e♭″*, contrary to acoustical logic. Thus this single innovation heralded a general increase in tonehole diameter, giving a warmer sound at a louder dynamic level. Müller's other innovations, levers that enabled the right thumb to control the L4 *f♯/c♯″* and the R4 *a♭/e♭″* keys, were less popular, although they do draw attention to two areas where technical difficulties arise on this model of clarinet.

Müller promoted his clarinet as 'omnitonic' in the sense that it could play in all keys. In Paris his instrument was at first strenuously resisted on the grounds that it eliminated the desirable distinctions between clarinets in different keys. In Paris at this time it was usual for serious players to have both an instrument with alternate joints in A and B♭, and a second one with joints in B♮ and C; at least three such sets survive.

The move to larger toneholes exacerbated acoustical problems on the right hand: in the chalumeau register separate keys were needed for *b♭* and *b*, and even in the clarinet register the forked *f♯″* (R2, R3) was less satisfactory than it had been on smaller-holed instruments. Thus the addition by Adolphe Sax[9] of rings that allowed the three fingers R1, R2 and R3 effectively to control four toneholes (Fig. 2.3*b*) was the step that freed makers to continue the trend towards even larger toneholes. During the rest of the century the only major change that was made to Sax's instrument outside the German areas was the so-called 'patent c♯' key, a device that provides an easy *e–f♯* and *b′–c♯″* transition. This invention was claimed in 1861 by the English player Joseph Tyler,[10] who sold the idea to S. A. Chappell for use by E. Albert, although Simon Lefèvre had patented an almost identical mechanism some years previously in Paris.[11] The importance of this device, which revolutionised the fluency of the clarinet in music with more than a single sharp in the key signature, is indicated both by its prominence in advertising material and by the fact that towards the end of the century a slightly different (and less reliable) mechanism was promoted by Chappell with 'new patent C♯' engraved on a key cover as a selling point.

Excellent instruments based on this model were manufactured by Eugène Albert and then by his sons in Brussels and were imported into England in large numbers first by the impresario Louis Jullien and then by S. A. Chappell. Boosey and Co., and Hawkes and Son also made similar instruments in London; they were very widely used until after the Second World War.

In Germany the instrument continued to develop. Mühlfeld, for whom Brahms composed his four clarinet works, used Baermann-system clarinets which were in essence Müller's model with a number of additions.[12] On the right hand the rings have the same function as Sax's, while the rings on the left hand improve both *f♯′* and *c♯‴*. A lever for the right thumb opens the hole for *f♯/c♯‴*, but the cover is articulated so that trills *e–f♯* and *b′–c♯″* can be made with L4. Two additional levers for L4 provide an alternative *a♭/e♭″* and *b♭/f♮″*. On the left hand there are additional touch-pieces but no additional toneholes. It is notable that it is only recently that theoretical understanding has been gained of the disadvantages of designing an instrument with an excessive number of toneholes.

The modern German clarinet

During the early part of the twentieth century a number of further modifications were made by Oskar Oehler (1858–1936), a clarinettist who in 1888 turned to instrument-making in Berlin. The Oehler-system clarinet that is used almost universally in Germany today (Fig. 2.5*d*) has only minor differences in fingering from the Baermann system, but has considerably more toneholes (twenty-nine as compared with twenty-four for the standard Boehm system) to provide a complex network of additional venting on both halves of the instrument. On the right hand there is the 'patent *c♯*' device discussed above, but with a movable lug so that the mechanism can be disconnected. A thumb key is fitted to full professional Oehler-system instruments; this controls additional vent holes that raise the pitch of low *e* and *f♮*. Although it is possible to design Boehm-system clarinets so as to bring the sound closer to that of the Oehler-system instrument, the differences between the two schools are perceived to be so important that advertisements for openings in German orchestras still (in 1994) almost invariably specify Oehler system.

The Boehm-system clarinet

The instrument that we know today as the Boehm system was devised by the clarinettist Hyacinthe Klosé with the maker Auguste Buffet *jeune*, and was first exhibited in 1843. The Boehm-system clarinet (like the Boehm-system flute) requires a major change in fingering, as the basic *c″* major scale of the instrument is played by raising successive fingers whereas on instruments from the earliest times up to and including the Oehler system a forked *f♮″* (R1, R3) is needed. The other important advance was the complex set of interlocking levers for L4 and R4 that greatly reduces the frequency with which it is necessary for these fingers to slide from one key to another.

Another radical change in fingering required by the Boehm-system clarinet is the elimination of the standard forked *e♭′/b♭″* (L1, L3) and its replacement by the so-called 'long' fingering (L1, R1) which is a reflection of Boehm's desire to avoid the reduced venting that arises from forked notes. During the late nineteenth century at least three different methods were used to reinstate the true forked fingering without reducing the venting, of which one survives on the so-called 'full Boehm' clarinet as well as on the Schmidt Reform-Boehm instrument.

Bore and tonehole design

As mentioned at the outset, the clarinet is defined by having a bore that at least behaves acoustically as if it is cylindrical. In practice the acoustical ideal (each fundamental overblowing at a true twelfth) is achieved by means of several departures from a true cylinder. Since most deviations from a cylinder would be made by a craftsman by first making a cylindrical bore, and then enlarging parts of it, it is convenient to specify the diameter of the bore in terms of the diameter

Figure 2.6 *Bore characteristics of some representative clarinets*

maker	city, date	key	no. of keys	main bore	bore at f hole
Roberty	Bordeaux 1780	B♭	5	14.6	16.1
Bernard	Lyons 1790	C	5	13.8	15.8
Hale	London 1790	B♭	6	14.2	14.2
Hale	London 1790	C	5	13.6	13.6
Kusder	London 1780	D	5	12.9	12.9
H. Grenser	Dresden 1810	B♭	10	14.4	14.5
H. Grenser	Dresden 1810	C	6	13.7	13.75
Gentellet	Paris 1820	B♭	6	15.0	16.2
Gentellet	Paris 1820	C	6	14.3	16.3
Simiot	Lyons 1810	B♭	7	15.1	16.4
Simiot	Lyons 1810	C	7	14.2	16.9
Simiot	Lyons 1820	B♭	7	14.7	15.8
Milhouse	London 1820	B♭	5	14.5	15.2
Milhouse	London 1820	C	5	13.9	14.8
Lefèvre	Paris 1840	B♭	13	14.6	15.9
Lefèvre	Paris 1840	C	13	14.2	15.1
Koch	Vienna 1830	B♭	12	14.4	14.9
Koch	Vienna 1830	C	12	13.2	13.5
Hess	Munich 1840	B♭	12 2r	14.4	14.4
E. Albert	Brussels 1860	A	14 2r	15.0	17.6
Ottensteiner	Munich 1870	B♭	Baermann	15.0	15.3
Ottensteiner	Munich 1870	A	Baermann	14.8	15.0
Oehler	Berlin 1930	A	Oehler	14.8	14.8
F. Wurlitzer	Erlbach 1939	B♭	Schmidt-Kolbe	15.2	15.2
H. Selmer	Paris 1930	B♭	Boehm	15.0	17.5
B. & H. '1010'	London 1930	B♭	Boehm	15.2	17.2
B. & H. '926'	London 1950	B♭	Boehm	15.0	17.0
Buffet	Paris 1930	B♭	Boehm	14.9	18.7
F. Wurlitzer	Erlbach 1950	B♭	Ref. Boehm	14.65	14.7
Buffet	Paris 1960	D	Boehm	13.3	14.5

of the narrowest cylindrical portion (generally in the lower part of the upper joint). In poorly preserved instruments it is not easy to make this measurement without an appropriate tool because the tenons are usually found to have contracted noticeably (sometimes by more than 1 mm) as a result of continual pressure from the socket on the lower joint. A complete survey of the history of clarinet bores is beyond the scope of this chapter (and has never been attempted) but Figure 2.6 has been assembled to give an impression of the range encountered in important categories.

It may be seen from Figure 2.6 that there has not been a uniform trend in bore diameter. There was a rather rapid widening of the bore around 1800 in many areas; this was associated both with the separation of the bell, and with the insertion of a flare in the bottom of the instrument except in Germany. Subsequently, in the mid-nineteenth century, narrower instruments became more fashionable, after which nearly all regions saw a return to a bore close to 15 mm. In England the designer and acoustician David James Blaikley, working for Boosey and Co., promoted an even wider bore diameter, 15.2 mm, that became associated with the 'English School' of clarinet playing through the 1010 model that was made by Boosey and Hawkes from about 1930 and was used by the majority of the leading English players. In Germany Ernst Schmidt and Louis Kolbe developed the so-called Schmidt–Kolbe variant of the Oehler-system clarinet, also with a very wide bore of 15.2 mm. Excellent examples of this model were made by Fritz Wurlitzer in Erlbach, Vogtland, but today both of these large-bore variants have fallen from fashion.

There are four types of departure from the cylinder. First, not only does the bell have a wide flare, but the bore generally makes a transition that may be a gradual expansion starting several centimetres above the bell tenon (the so-called French bore) or may be much more sudden (the so-called German bore). Second, the maker may expand the bore at the barrel or in the upper part of the instrument using one or more conical reamers. Third, the bore may be made of two or more sections that are cylindrical but of different diameters ('poly-cylindrical bore'). Fourth, the maker may enlarge the bore at selected points ('chambering').

The purpose of the expansion at the lower end is to mitigate the otherwise very wide twelfths on *e* and *f*, but at a sacrifice in terms of the tone-colour of these notes. These notes may be up to 40 cents flat on an instrument with no flare; the magnitude of the difficulty is indicated by the provision of a vent key on modern Oehler-system clarinets to raise low *e* and *f*. This key raises the pitch of each of these notes by about 20 cents.

In general one observes that toneholes have become gradually larger as the mechanisation of the instrument increased. However, the design of the toneholes has also varied from minimal to very heavy undercutting. In general more undercutting will increase the flexibility of the instrument. Of the instruments listed in Figure 2.6 the most marked undercutting is on the narrow-bored romantic instruments by Stephan Koch (Vienna) and Wilhelm Hess senior (Munich); of the instruments from the 1930s the Buffet–Crampon is the most heavily undercut.

Clarinet designs for various uses

The development of the clarinet has been to a large extent driven by the demands of Western 'classical' music, but throughout most of its history a range of models has been available to suit a far wider range of players. In nineteenth-century Denmark the making of five-keyed clarinets by wheelwrights and other part-time makers, for popular music, is well documented. Although this practice must have existed elsewhere it is also the case that at least to the end of the nineteenth century several major manufacturers and suppliers offered clarinets with only five or six keys for popular and dance music. The jazz era began at a time when the majority of available instruments in America were 'Albert system' with many variants that were inspired by French or German influences. Of these it was the simpler French models with fairly large toneholes and no extraneous keywork that proved to be most suited to jazz, and many players still favour these instruments. The same characteristics have made this the favoured model for twentieth-century popular music in most other regions where the clarinet has a special place (in B♭ and C in most regions; exceptionally in Turkey the clarinet in (low) G is used). It is only recently, as the commercial aspect of music has spread worldwide, that major manu-facturers of the Boehm-system clarinet have set out to design different models for the jazz, wind-band, chamber and orchestral markets.

The basset clarinet and basset horn

The concept of using the right thumb to extend the lower range of an instrument is of course standard for the bassoon, where the tube is folded so that the right thumb covers a tonehole (and the left thumb, several keys). An early bass chalumeau using the same principle survives in the Salzburg museum; it was made by an undocumented maker named W. Kress, probably during the early part of the eighteenth century. The range of the basset horn is generally extended without a fully doubled-up bore; instead, the bore is extended by a section inside which the bore travels down, up and down again. The basset horn is generally believed to have been invented in Passau in 1770. Most early examples are in F or G but one example in D is known.

The basset clarinet can be regarded either as a basset horn in A or B♭, or as a clarinet with extended compass. Several surviving examples are constructed like basset horns and have only recently been recognised as basset clarinets; one is curved, some have angles in the barrel, some between right and left hands; one has the flat thrice-bored box typical of Viennese basset horns. On the well-known photograph of basset horns preserved in Hamburg,[13] the instrument with a globular bell by Strobach of Carlsbad is pitched in A and should be regarded as a basset clarinet, and two others in approximately this form are known. This instrument may have been made during the lifetime of Mozart's clarinettist and may be the closest we have to his own instrument.[14] On the other hand an instrument by Bischoff from the 1840s[15] (pitched in B♭) closely resembles a clarinet with a straight extension, as do basset clarinets made today. This instrument has a fully chromatic extension as did Anton Stadler's.

As regards the basset horn, we may be confident that during Mozart's lifetime, the parts he wrote for the instrument were generally played on instruments made by Theodor Lotz or by Raymund Griesbacher, whose instruments are almost indistinguishable.[16] Surviving instruments by these Viennese makers have eight keys and are equivalent to five-keyed clarinets with a key in place of the small hole for R4, and with thumb keys for low *c* and *d*. Presumably Anton Stadler had additional keys on the basset extension, and perhaps elsewhere on the instrument. (The majority of the surviving basset horns by Lotz and Griesbacher have additional keys that were put on during the early nineteenth century, but the added keys do not include those for low *c♯* or low *e♭*.)

The alto, bass and contrabass clarinet

Bass clarinets (an octave below the soprano in B♭ or C) were made from the 1770s onwards. The majority of early examples (before 1820) were extended to written low *C*, and several models were devised in bassoon form, probably for use in military bands. The American Catlin may have been the most prolific maker of the early bass clarinet. Alto and bass clarinets with the same range as the normal clarinet emerged in the 1820s; their design was dramatically improved by Adolphe Sax, who enlarged the bore, enlarged the toneholes, redesigned the keywork and enlarged the mouthpiece. Sax's instruments were pitched in E♭ and B♭ rather than in F and in C. It was the B♭ bass clarinet that became a member of the orchestra from the mid-nineteenth century; instruments in A were also in use at least in areas under the German influence.

The contrabass clarinet (in E♭ an octave below the alto, or in B♭ an octave below the bass) has only become widespread in the last fifty years. A few makers made examples in the late nineteenth and early twentieth centuries and certainly the model patented by Adolphe Fontaine Besson in 1891 had a measure of success.

3   The clarinet family
Introduction: clarinets in B♭ *and A*

COLIN LAWSON

No other instrument can lay claim to quite such a large and diverse family as the clarinet (Fig. 3.1), and even the player's basic equipment of a *pair* of instruments serves to distinguish him from other instrumentalists. The B♭ clarinet has reigned supreme for some 200 years, even though Mozart, Brahms and a host of other writers of orchestral and chamber music have ensured that the A clarinet also remains absolutely indispensable. Almost as familiar within the orchestra are the E♭ and bass, whilst the basset horn has a further specialist role, notably in the works of Mozart and Richard Strauss. The scope of even this select group of closely related instruments is unmatched by any other woodwind category, though in fact the clarinet family extends a great deal further – to as many as twenty-five different instruments. The tiniest is the scarcely known clarinet in high C, more than an octave higher than the normal clarinet; in increasing order of size there are then piccolo, sopranino, soprano, alto and bass clarinets ranging down to the B♭ contrabass.[1] Least familiar are perhaps those clarinets smaller in size than the E♭, though there are also some shadowy larger representatives, such as the *clarinettes d'amour* in A♭ and G (pitched just below the normal A clarinet) from the latter half of the eighteenth century. An especially significant member of the family is the soprano C clarinet, the only one sounding at written pitch, whose prominent role within the repertoire positively demands its widespread revival.

The special character of clarinets past and present accounts for the evolution of such a large family. During the early years of the eighteenth century, the two-keyed baroque clarinet was virtually confined to music within its home key, and gradually the earliest instruments in C and D were supplemented by 1764 to a total of seven, pitched in the keys of G, A, B♭, C, D, E and F.[2] As further mechanism was added, composers gradually felt able to be more adventurous, though in the 1780s Mozart advised his composition pupil Thomas Attwood to write clarinet parts only in C and F.[3] By this time the normal orchestral instruments consisted of clarinets in A, B♭ and C, which amongst them could cover a substantial portion of the tonalities then in common use. It became significant that from an early stage observers recognised the difference in tone-quality of the various sizes. A famous illustration occurred at the Paris Conservatoire in 1812 when Iwan Müller presented his thirteen-keyed B♭ clarinet to a panel of judges, which included the composers Cherubini and Méhul. As Nicholas Shackleton has observed in Chapter 2, Müller claimed that his new invention could play in all keys and would thus render the A and C clarinets redundant, but the panel preferred the continued use of various sizes of clarinet, not merely on technical grounds (though Müller's clarinet could hardly claim to be genuinely omnitonic), but because the exclusive use of a single instrument would deprive composers of an important tonal resource.

The Paris adjudicators differentiated clearly between the sound of the B♭ ('propre au genre pathétique') and the A ('propre au genre pastoral'), and this was a viewpoint widely echoed in contemporary tutors, which tended to regard the A clarinet as gentle, melancholy and even rather dull. Every clarinettist recognises the difference in response between the two instruments, the B♭ tending to brilliance, the A towards mellowness; not all would agree whether there is actually a difference in tone-quality discernible either to player or listener. Likewise, composers seem to have varied in their perception of the two instruments. Dvořák, for example, simply selected the clarinet most appropriate to his tonality, and proved this in his Wind Serenade Op. 44, where the main theme of the first movement recurs in the finale, transposed from B♭ to A clarinet. He would doubtless have agreed with the observation in Cecil Forsyth's *Orchestration* (London, 1914), p. 255, that '... the difference between B flat and A clarinets is less than that between a Brescian and a Cremonese violin ... not even an expert Clarinettist can tell (from its tone-quality) whether a passage is being played in the concert-room on the A or the B flat instrument'. This accords with comments by the celebrated English clarinettist Henry Lazarus in his tutor of 1881: '... those various pitched clarinets (A, B flat, C) are made so as to avoid writing music in keys which would render the fingering extremely difficult were there only one clarinet, and not for the change of timbre, as many think'. Baines (p. 119) was more cautious, remarking that '... there is a small difference in tone-quality between the two instruments, the slightly darker sound of the A being most noticeable in the lower part of the upper register'. Brymer, p. 97, claimed that one could prove scientifically that the sounds of both instruments were identical, but the analysis of clarinet tone in Jürgen Meyer's book *Acoustics and the Performance of Music* (Frankfurt, 1978) suggests the contrary. Meyer noted a lower intensity for the harmonics contained within the sound in certain parts of the range of the A clarinet, especially the lower register. Clarinet sound in general is characterised by the predominance of odd-numbered over even-numbered harmonics, but on the A clarinet the latter are even more subdued. Despite this, Baines observed that in countries such as Italy and Spain the A clarinet has often been dispensed with, some players exclusively using a B♭ clarinet furnished with an extra semitone to reach the A clarinet's bottom note. A celebrated exponent of this practice was the Spaniard Manuel Gomez (1859-1922), a founder member of the London Symphony Orchestra. He attracted criticism from the conductor Sir Henry Wood: 'Personally, I think he made a great mistake in playing everything on the B flat instrument, and I always missed the particular quality of the A instrument with its added low notes [*sic*]'.[4]

Less radical is the common practice among orchestral players of occasionally interchanging the two instruments on technical grounds (see page 161), a procedure which has scarcely been documented in print.[5] The extent to which this damages a composer's intentions is bound to vary from one context to the next, a situation which extends also to the relationship of E♭ and D clarinets, as well as to bass clarinets in B♭ and A. Berlioz, for example, reckoned that the choice of clarinet should always be the responsibility of the composer, and he found support for this from among some celebrated players. Occasionally, composers have ventured to combine B♭ and A clarinets for technical reasons. Balakirev's Second Symphony, with D minor and D♭ major as its main tonal centres, specifies two B♭ clarinets and a third in A; this allows all the principal themes to be executed in convenient clarinet keys, and also provides the bottom note of the A clarinet (sounding d♭) as a useful pedal. Other composers have clearly regarded the B♭ and A as quite distinctive colours, Stravinsky marking the first two of his *Three Pieces for Clarinet*, 'preferably Clarinet in A' and the third 'preferably Clarinet in B flat', though at least one commentator has dismissed these indications as redundant.[6] Poulenc's *Sonata for Two Clarinets* in B♭ and A makes an obvious distinction between the two instruments which can scarcely be ignored. Acutest of all the great composers in relation to clarinet timbre was perhaps Richard Strauss, who during the course of his opera *Salome* felt the difference between A and B♭ to be important enough to use pairs of each simultaneously, the A clarinets having primarily melodic material, the B♭ clarinets brilliant figures and ornaments. A similar situation occurs in the *Symphonia domestica*, whose clarinet scoring is for D, A, two B♭s and bass. Thus in Strauss's Oboe Concerto the temptation to use the A rather than B♭ for any of the highly demanding E major clarinet figuration might ideally be resisted.

(a)   (b)   (c)   (d)

Figure 3.1

(e)   (f)   (g)   (h)

Figure 3.1   The modern clarinet family (Boehm system except (b)): (a) sopranino in E♭;
(b) soprano in B♭ (Schmidt-Kolbe system; note that the reed is tied on with twine); (c),
(d) sopranos in B♭ and A; (e) alto in E♭; (f) basset horn in F; (g) bass in B♭; (h) contrabass
in B♭; all by G. Leblanc, Paris, except (b) by Fritz Wurlitzer, Erlbach

The C clarinet

COLIN LAWSON

The C clarinet's relatively low profile during the twentieth century is highly regrettable, since the instrument has been specified by a vast range of composers and can bring its own special musical rewards. Its long-term inability to compete with the B♭ is easy to understand, since around 1800 the latter was already acquiring a warmth of sound (particularly in the chalumeau register) at a time when the harder tone-quality of the C continued to attract comment. None the less, its individual characteristics achieved some recognition, and the Paris Conservatoire judges in 1812 made a positive assessment of its tone as 'brilliant and lively'.[7] Nowadays, its quick response and relative ease of articulation remain among its most attractive features, and its extra brilliance need not be achieved at the expense of its own distinctive sweetness of tone. Composers have left us C clarinet parts in a wide variety of musical contexts – chamber music, solo sonatas and concertos, together with much orchestral repertoire, including opera. C clarinets traditionally required a different mouthpiece from the B♭ and A, since its bore was somewhat smaller, but in recent times preference for a wider bore has meant that a B♭ mouthpiece can be used. However convenient this may be in practical terms, the result may well be a certain lack of tonal focus. C clarinets tend to have something of a reputation among players as difficult to play in tune, but this is rather unjust, since few clarinettists take the trouble to accustom themselves to the noticeable differences in response from the B♭. In particular, those parts of the compass requiring only a small column of air (such as the throat notes) inevitably demand particular control and acuteness of pitching.

Is the C clarinet ever an absolute necessity? The extent to which one believes that composers used it for reasons of colour, rather than merely a matter of technical expediency, is bound to affect one's answer to this question. The situation is in fact extremely variable and somewhat complex. Strauss often featured the C clarinet in combination with the B♭ or A, and insisted that it was quite indispensable.

Classical composers expected a certain range of orchestral colours in each key, so that it is virtually impossible in the music of Mozart or Schubert to differentiate considerations of tone-quality and technical necessity. As a result, revival of the C clarinet in these contexts is unquestionably desirable. Only on very rare occasions can we be confident that a composer has introduced the C clarinet purely on technical grounds; for example, in Mendelssohn's overture *The Fair Melusine* the first clarinet changes briefly from B♭ to C for a G major statement of the arpeggiated main theme – a passage which would have been impossible on the B♭ clarinet of Mendelssohn's day, but which is of no great difficulty on the Boehm system.

Mozart differentiated the various tonalities by a variety of orchestral means, and his delicate balance can easily be upset by the wholesale transposition of his many C clarinet parts. Where the key of an aria is C or F major, for example in *Don Giovanni* and *Così fan tutte*, he is not afraid to make prominent use of C clarinets; their presence is as vital a dramatic element as the very choice of tonality. Outside opera, C clarinets appear where C or F major has been selected principally to suit another instrument, as in the oboe concerto fragment K416f and the fragment K580b for C clarinet, basset horn and string trio. For E major numbers in *Idomeneo* and *Così fan tutte*, Mozart introduces the closely related but extremely rare clarinet in B, for which (as we observed in Chapter 2) a C clarinet with longer alternative middle joints (*corps de rechange*) would have been used.

As late as *c.* 1803 Backofen's tutor (whilst recommending the B♭ clarinet) noted that the C clarinet was favoured by the French, and this is certainly borne out by the twelve sonatas contained in Lefèvre's contemporary tutor for the Paris Conservatoire, which indicate the possibility of transposing down the accompanying bass line to accommodate the B♭ clarinet as an alternative (Fig. 3.2), a practice preferred in modern editions. In Germany the C clarinet also maintained some profile outside the orchestral wind section, for example in one of the concertos by Carl Stamitz and in two of the three duos for clarinet and bassoon once attributed to Beethoven; the C clarinet also tended to be selected where alternative solo parts for other instruments were published simultaneously, as in the case of Pleyel's Concerto. The florid obbligato in Schubert's *Offertorium* D136 ('Totus in corde lanqueo') may be another example.

Beethoven's clarinet notation often reflects the difficulties brought about by his wide-ranging approach to tonality. A variety of motives seems to have prompted his choice of the C clarinet within the orchestra, and these are now difficult to distinguish. Remembering Berlioz's advice, we should perhaps be more willing to retain the C clarinet even when tonality seems the principal reason for its presence, for example in the C minor solo in the Agnus Dei of the *Mass in C*,

Figure 3.2   Allegro moderato from the first sonata from *Méthode de Clarinette* (Paris, 1802) by J. X. Lefèvre

which occurs shortly before a modulation to the major. The *Leonore* Overtures Nos. 2 and 3 present similar cases, with a C clarinet solo in Ab major in the introduction preceding a principal Allegro in C. More surprising is the C clarinets' appearance in the central movement of the Violin Concerto, where A clarinets could have easily been retained from the outer movements. The use of C clarinets in the scherzo of the Ninth Symphony seems unquestionably a matter of timbre, and clearly something is lost if they are substituted. A watershed was Beethoven's 'Pastoral' Symphony, which although written in the key of F, features Bb rather than C clarinets; within the Austro-German tradition the C clarinet was henceforth virtually confined to its home key. Schubert continued to regard it as part of his normal palette within the key of C, even though in the scherzo of his Ninth Symphony his clarinet parts modulate several degrees both to the flat and the sharp side. The C clarinet should certainly be used as part of the characterisation of the

Variation movement of the Octet. We can only speculate on the extent to which symphonic parts were actually played on the C clarinet, including those contained in Bizet's Symphony in C, dating from some fifty years later. In French opera of the classical period (but not elsewhere in Europe) there was a unique tradition of publishing scores with clarinets notated in C, even where instruments in A or B♭ were to be used, and Saint-Saëns noticed this during the preparation of his edition of Gluck's *Orphée.* This may be an important consideration for the performance of Cherubini's C clarinet parts.

As the clarinet acquired greater mobility during the nineteenth century, the necessity for the inconvenience of maintaining an orchestral set of three instruments diminished. Symptomatic was Mendelssohn's tendency within C major contexts in his symphonies to prefer the option of A clarinets notated in three flats rather than C clarinets in their natural key. Scoring for C clarinet was then increasingly a matter of colour, and this needs to be respected in works such as Berlioz's *Symphonie fantastique.* A great champion of the C clarinet, Berlioz wrote for it in as many as four flats in *Les francs-juges,* featured it over a wide compass in his *Waverley* Overture, and took advantage of its special tone-quality in the *Requiem.* It played an important part in Liszt's orchestral music, such as the Faust Symphony and the symphonic poems *Les Préludes, Prometheus, Festklänge* and *Hunnenschlacht,* all written in Weimar in the 1850s.[8] During the following decade he included C clarinets in the Hungarian Coronation Mass, even within remote tonalities such as A or E. Though Wagner abandoned the C clarinet after *Der fliegende Holländer,* Carl Loewe in 1850 published his three *Schottische Bilder,* a very rare set of character pieces for C clarinet and piano written for his son-in-law, an amateur player. Awareness of its potential must have continued even later, since Brahms specified the instrument in the scherzo of his Fourth Symphony at a stage in his career when mere convention could not have had any further influence on its presence.

In Italy and Eastern Europe the C clarinet retained an important role in the nineteenth century in both outdoor and popular music. Rossini wrote for the orchestral set of three instruments detailed in Chapter 2, and the sheer vitality of his C clarinet parts seems perfectly to match the character of the music. This tradition was continued by Verdi, whose C clarinets venture into relatively remote tonalities and therefore also seem to be a matter of colour. Whilst by the end of the century there may have been players using a single clarinet for B♭ and A (as well as C) parts, there was also a highly conservative streak amongst Italian players; when Ferdinando Busoni (the composer's clarinettist father) wrote his tutor as late as 1883 he was still advocating playing with reed-above embouchure, a technique which in Vienna had been abandoned for a century or so! Custom and practice were doubtless highly variable with regard to all aspects of clarinet technique and equipment. In Bohemia Dvořák was happy to opt for the C clarinet when musical context demanded; in his Slavonic Dance Op. 46 No. 1, for example, that instrument's sound and articulation are as much part of the conception as the contribution of the F trumpets and the carefully calculated percussion effects. Smetana's overture to *The Bartered Bride* is a further context where C clarinets are clearly indispensable and evidently specifically intended, since some of the later operatic numbers in keys sympathetic to the C clarinet are scored instead for the B♭. In other parts of Europe (such as England) the abandonment of the C clarinet was almost complete by 1900, and it was around this time that Mahler and Strauss revived it as a special tone-colour. In Mahler's Sixth Symphony, for example, the C clarinets are an essential dramatic resource. Throughout Strauss's operas his various clarinet sections are astutely chosen and idiomatically treated, the C first appearing in *Der Rosenkavalier* and then recurring in *Die Frau ohne Schatten* (whose score has five clarinets – E♭/D; two B♭ doubling C; basset horn and bass clarinet both doubling C), *Die ägyptische Helena, Arabella, Friedenstag, Daphne, Die Liebe der Danae* and *Capriccio*. A favourite Strauss combination familiar from the late wind sonatinas became C, B♭/A, basset horn and bass. However, it is perhaps significant that his *Duett-Concertino* prefers the B♭ clarinet as soloist; even Strauss's enterprising espousal of the C was restricted to its use in ensemble.

With such a wide-ranging background, the C clarinet is bound to exert some influence on the musical life of every clarinettist, and not just for historical reasons. At least one well-known jazz player has made it a speciality, whilst from time to time contemporary composers continue to succumb to its distinctive qualities. As Baines remarks, it also retains to this day a particular niche within the café bands of central Europe. Furthermore, its advantages in size and technical mobility within an educational environment can provide yet another incentive for its espousal.

The high clarinets

BASIL TSCHAIKOV

Introduction

In general, the large family of *little* clarinets – in all there are nine, though several are no more than ghosts – has been rather neglected in books and dictionaries about the clarinet. The octave C, B♭, A, and the sopranino E, have been referred to by several authorities and it is possible that instruments may have been made, but they have never had any real musical existence, since music written to be played on them has yet to be discovered. However, for the first half-century of its existence the D clarinet was predominant, and, with the E♭, has continued to have a considerable solo, chamber music and orchestral repertoire. The other high clarinets – in F, G and A♭ – have been used in the past, though to a much more limited extent.

Playing the high clarinets

Playing any of these smaller clarinets will normally be undertaken by those who are already reasonably proficient on the B♭ and A clarinets. Indeed, it is important that the player should already have a fully developed embouchure. It is not that the music written for the E♭ and D clarinets is written to any extent in its highest register – it is infrequent that the written notes are above f'''. However, if one plays written e''' on the B♭ clarinet it will sound a tone *lower*, d''', whereas if one fingers the same note on the E♭ it will sound g''', a minor third *higher*; to sound g''' on the B♭ one would need to play a'''. It is probably this difference in pitching which causes beginners on the E♭ to tighten their embouchure too much. Remember that the E♭ is a *small* clarinet rather than a *high* clarinet – the French call it *petite clarinette* and the Italians *clarinetto piccolo*. The extracts from the orchestral repertoire, quoted below, show how composers have understood the unique characteristics and timbre of the instrument.

When purchasing any of the high clarinets, or reeds for them, look for the same qualities as when making these choices for the B♭ or A – good, manageable intonation (especially from c''' to f'''), equality of tone throughout the range of the instrument and well-made keywork. A reed is required that will allow one to play throughout the dynamic range (especially *ppp* in the upper register), both in legato and staccato. There are no study books or tutors for the high clarinets, and the collections of orchestral extracts are so limited as to be of little value. It is for this reason that a selection of compositions worth practising is provided at the end of this chapter. It is not always the solos that need most attention; in many E♭ parts, to an even greater extent than in those for the B♭ or A, the *tutti* passages are frequently the most difficult. Since the E♭ often carries the top line (in unison with the piccolo, first violins or solo), and the music is often technically demanding, these exposed passages can be very dangerous. Often they require more practice than the solos! The repertoire will provide ample material for practice.

The D clarinet

It has already been noted in Chapters 1 and 2 that the D clarinet was the most often employed in the first half of the eighteenth century. However, until the 1750s 'clarinettists' (relatively few in number) were all multi-instrumentalists, as 'session' clarinet and saxophone players are today. The *Ouverture* for two clarinets and horn by Handel is the first work with demanding parts that we can be reasonably certain was written for the D clarinet. The first major works for solo clarinet that we know were written for the D clarinet are the six concertos by Molter already mentioned on page 17. There have been suggestions that two of them might be trumpet concertos, as neither has a title page that designates them as being for clarinet, but it is now generally agreed that their musical content makes this unlikely. Four of the concertos were published in 1957 in an edition by Heinz Becker.[1] All six represent a major technical advance and still remain the best solo music written for D or E♭ clarinet. The slow movements in particular exploit the distinctive, delicate lyricism of the D clarinet (Ex. 3.1).

Of course, these concertos will have sounded very different in Molter's day; the mouthpiece, lay and reeds, as well as the construction of the instrument itself producing the 'clarino' style and sound that contemporary writers likened to the sound of the high trumpet.[2] It is very different from the sound we now associate with the D clarinet. As has been noted elsewhere, these early D clarinets were unsatisfactory in the chalumeau register, so that their effective range was really only *c″* to *f‴* or *g‴*. Once the lower register had been improved and satisfactory B♭ and A clarinets with their more mellifluous tone became increasingly available, both the D clarinet and the chalumeau gradually disappeared from the scene. For a time the D clarinet maintained its

Ex. 3.1 from J. M. Molter, Clarinet Concerto in G major, second movement

place in military bands, but after about 1780 it was increasingly replaced by the clarinet in F, which was itself subsequently replaced by the E♭ clarinet from about 1815 onwards.

The D and E♭ clarinets

In his celebrated book *Orchestration* (London, 1914), p. 279, Cecil Forsyth wrote:

The great advantage of the E♭ clarinet is its distinctive tone-quality. This, especially in its upper register, is preternaturally hard and biting.... In particular the psychological range of the 'E♭' is much narrower (than the B♭). It is almost confined either to passage work of a hard mechanical kind, or to a special sort of mordant humour, such, for instance, as is found in Strauss's *Till Eulenspiegel*.

In fact, with the psychological insight granted to great composers, Strauss chose the D clarinet, not the E♭, to represent Till (Ex. 3.2*a*). The famous arpeggio, which represents poor Till being hanged, takes the D clarinet up to a♭''', a higher and a less easily obtained note than the g''' required on the E♭. Till is not a hooligan. He is a cheeky, impudent young scamp who just goes a bit too far. The D, with its rather warmer, but piquant tone is ideally suited to bring out that characterisation; it should not sound either *hard* or *biting* (Ex. 3.2*b*).

This quite false representation of the musical characteristics of the E♭ and D clarinets has been echoed by a number of writers, including Norman Del Mar. In *Anatomy of the Orchestra* (London 1987 p. 149) he writes: '... its quite individual tonal character, its shrill, hard quality giving pronounced drama and incisiveness to the wind band, as in the *Sunday Morning* opening to the second act of Britten's *Peter Grimes*'. Yet in performance it does not sound *shrill* or *hard*.

The first, and perhaps best-known, orchestral solo for the E♭ is in the *Symphonie fantastique* by Berlioz, written in 1830 (Ex 3.4). After 1845, when Wagner used the D clarinet in *Tannhäuser*, the D and E♭ clarinets were employed by an increasing number of composers, especcially in Germany and Austria. It is difficult to find examples of music to justify the unpleasant characteristics incorrectly ascribed to

Ex. 3.2a, 3.2b from Richard Strauss, *Till Eulenspiegels lustige Streiche*

Ex. 3.3 from Benjamin Britten, *Four Sea Interludes from Peter Grimes,* 'Sunday Morning'

Ex 3.4 from Hector Berlioz, *Symphonie fantastique,* 'Witches' Sabbath'

Ex. 3.5*a* and 3.5*b* from Gustav Mahler, Symphony No. 1, third movement

these piccolo instruments. Indeed, when composers have used them for solo passages in the orchestra or in chamber music, they have mostly taken advantage of their special qualities in the way that Molter did. They have also made use of their rather mysterious and haunting quality of tone in *piano* and *pianissimo* and their ability to produce a particular dramatic, exciting and proclamatory 'silver trumpet' effect.

Mahler, Strauss, Stravinsky, Schoenberg, Ravel, Shostakovich and Britten provide the backbone of the E♭ clarinettist's orchestral opportunities. Each of them understood the capabilities of the instrument and exploited them in their own individual way. Mahler's First Symphony at once demonstrates how well he understands the small clarinets (Ex 3.5*a*–*b*). In Example 3.5*a* he uses two E♭s in their lower middle register to produce a totally different effect than could be achieved on the B♭. Example 3.5*b* is in the light-hearted, devil-may-care style, the cheeky scamp beloved by Strauss. In his Ninth Symphony Mahler, with his remarkable insight into the personality of every instrument, uses the E♭ in so many different ways. In the first and last movements he demands

Ex. 3.6 from Richard Strauss, *Also Sprach Zarathustra*

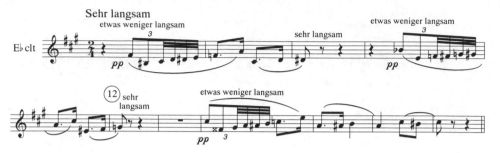

pianissimo between *g″* and *c♯‴* – a waif quietly musing – then in the second movement a complete change of character, exuberantly racing up to a high *a‴*. In the Rondo Burleske it is back to the young scamp again.

A few years later, in 1895, Strauss wrote probably his best-known part for the little clarinet – *Till Eulenspiegel*. As we have noted, this is for the D clarinet, though many think of it as being for the E♭, (including Rendall, p. 129), perhaps because outside Germany and Austria it is usually played on the E♭. Whether it makes a great deal of difference to the average audience is arguable, but to the player who has performed it on both the D and E♭ there is no question of which is more satisfactory. It is not really possible to produce the fuller tone the music requires on the E♭.

In *Ein Heldenleben* the E♭ characterises the spiteful critics: here the crisp, short staccato the E♭ can achieve can be 'biting', but not vicious! In *Also Sprach Zarathustra* Strauss makes effective use of the E♭'s often neglected chalumeau register (Ex. 3.6). Strauss frequently wrote important parts for E♭ and D in his operas; those in *Salome, Elektra,* and *Der Rosenkavalier* are particularly noteworthy.

Another composer who made use of the E♭ and D in a number of his major compositions was Igor Stravinsky. It is often suggested that composers have used the E♭ and D as they use the B♭ and A, according to which will make the passage work easier. Rimsky-Korsakov in *Mlada* did use the E♭ and D in this way; others, like Strauss and Mahler, made their choice for musical reasons. Stravinsky uses both in the *Rite* and chose the D for the *L'Adoration de la Terre* section. In Example 3.7*a*, as originally written for the D, the triplets can only be played by sliding from d♯″ to c♯″, or from c♯″ to *c″*, and the solo passage after fig. 9 is not only difficult, but uses the two worst notes on the instrument, d♭‴ and e♭‴ (cf. Ex. 3.7*b*, transposed for E♭). Why did Stravinsky choose to write for the D? Did he want a certain sound, or did he make a mistake? Later he gives the E♭ a solo in its very best register (Ex. 3.8).

Ex. 3.7a from Igor Stravinsky, *The Rite of Spring*

Ex. 3.7b transposition of Ex. 3.7a for E♭ clarinet

Ex. 3.8 from Igor Stravinsky, *The Rite of Spring*

There is also an important part for the *petite clarinette* in the complete ballet *The Firebird* (though there is no part for it in the well-known orchestral suite), and in *Le Rossignol*, *Oedipus Rex*, and the delightful *Berceuses du chat* for soprano voice and three clarinets – B♭, E♭ and bass.

Schoenberg and Berg used the E♭ quite frequently. Berg's opera *Wozzeck* requires two and there are parts in the *Chamber Concerto*, and the *Three Orchestral Pieces*. Schoenberg, in particular, wrote music of great difficulty, involving a high tessitura to be played extremely softly. To play the E♭ or D quietly in the highest register is even more difficult than on the B♭. To do so, with good intonation and tone, requires considerable skill – and a very good reed. Amongst the many interesting parts he wrote for E♭ or D are the *Chamber Symphony No. 1* (for fifteen solo instruments) for D – though the orchestral version is for E♭ – *Gurrelieder* and *Ewartung* (D clarinet).

Shostakovich writes frequently for E♭ in his symphonies and in other works – The Age of Gold has some especially sparkling solos – and there are a number of solos in the symphonies. Example 3.9 from his Sixth Symphony gives a good idea of his style of writing for the E♭. In *tuttis* he often writes very fast technical passages using the whole compass of the instrument.

Ravel probably provides the E♭ clarinettist with more splendid opportunities to display a variety of styles than any other composer – jazzy, in the G major Piano Concerto, brilliant in *Daphnis et Chloé*, and in *Bolero* he has probably written the most rewarding of all orchestral solos for E♭.

Finally, to make the case for the E♭ as a charming melodist is Example 3.10 from Benjamin Britten's ballet *The Prince of the Pagodas*, in which the E♭ and B♭ play a sensuous melody in octaves.

From the days of Lanner and Johann and Josef Strauss, who all used the D and E♭ in their waltzes and polkas (seldom played in their original orchestrations nowadays), the high clarinets have been widely used outside the symphony orchestra, in music for films and TV and in musicals – by Leonard Bernstein, in particular, in *Candide*, *West Side Story* and *On the Town*. There is not a great deal of solo music for E♭. Ernesto Cavallini composed several works for E♭ and piano; the *Carnival of Venice* variations (now in print), a *Fantasia on a Theme from Ultimo Giorno Di Pompeii*, and, with Giacomo Panizza, *I figli di Eduardo 4th*. Panizza, conductor at La Scala in Milan when Cavallini was principal clarinet, inspired by Cavallini's prodigious technique, breath control and artistry, included a set of variations, *Il Ballabile con Variazioni*,[3] for part of the ballet in his opera *The Challenge of Barletta*. Another composer who wrote extensively for the E♭ was Giuseppe Cappelli.[4] Henri Benjamin Rabaud whilst Director of the Paris Con-servatoire wrote a *Solo de Concours* for E♭ clarinet, and Amicaro

Ex. 3.9 from Dmitri Shostakovich, Symphony No. 6, opening of second movement

Ex. 3.10 from Benjamin Britten, *The Prince of the Pagodas*, 'Pas de Trois'

Ponchielli has written a charming quintet for B♭ and E♭ clarinets, flute, oboe and piano. Contemporary composers are using the E♭ increasingly in chamber music and orchestral compositions, and two American composers, Jerome Neff and William Neil, have written concertos for E♭.[5]

When jazz made its appearance in the early 1900s the New Orleans marching bands were always led by a wailing 'keening' E♭ clarinet on their way to the cemetery. On the return, after the funeral ceremony, a very different kind of music was required. Upbeat music was then needed, that gave the 'second line' (those following the band to and from the funeral) the occasion for high jinks – strutting, dancing and prancing. Now the E♭ can be heard in wild ecstasies of exuberant embellishment. The famous Bunk Johnson Band, with the renowned George Lewis, who also had a band of his own, the Eureka Brass Band,[6] and John Casimir who leads his own Young Tuxedo Jazz Band,[7] can be heard on archive recordings.

Casimir lets fly with wonderful abandon; intonation and subtlety of tone may be missing in his playing, but this is the real thing – wild, raw and irresistible! George Lewis sounds more restrained than Casimir. It seems he was not playing the Eb regularly at the time the recordings were made. He is reported to have said that when he tried to use the Bb in the band the effort of trying to cut through the brass gave him a sore throat! His comment brings to mind a delightful anonymous poem:

> With the lovely sound of my bright clarinet,
> I cover noise however loud it becomes.
> Even the pleasant sound of the shrill Peace-trumpet,
> Must yield in beauty to my clarinet.

The Eb was also used at times in dance bands, but no doubt the dance hall was less suited to the excesses of the Eb, so it lost its place to the Bb, as the D clarinet had done a couple of centuries earlier.

The F clarinet

In the late eighteenth century, from about 1780 onwards, the F clarinet gradually replaced the D in most military bands. By around 1800 the F and C seem to have become the favoured clarinets in most European bands. The fact that Berlioz chose the Eb, rather than the F, for the *Symphonie fantastique* suggests that the Eb had by then supplanted the F clarinet. Beethoven, for his *Military Marches* in F, WoO 18 and 19 (1809) and in D, WoO 24 (1816, not published until 1827), and Mendelssohn for his Overture in C major for wind instruments, Op. 24 (1816), both chose the F clarinet.

Kroll, p. 96, writes: 'for many decades the Eb clarinet, together with the F clarinet, was the favourite conducting instrument of band masters in the German infantry, until in the 1860s it was replaced by the baton'. One does not like to contemplate the damage done at rehearsal, when, as is not uncommon, the band master struck the music stand in irritation at some poor musician's repeated mistake.

In Britain the Eb appears to have obtained a secure place by 1839. The band list for that year in *Memoirs of the Royal Artillery Band* by Henry George Farmer (London 1904), gives the complement of the band as: one piccolo, two flutes, four oboes, three Ebs, fourteen Bbs, and four bassoons. By 1857 the band had four Ebs, and four saxophones had been added, two in Eb and two in Bb.

There does not seem to be any evidence of the F clarinet having been employed other than in the military band or wind band.

The G clarinet

This very small clarinet does not seem to have obtained a foothold in any composer's affection, since, like the ghostly octave C and its companions, it has had no musical relevance in orchestral or military music.

Then in about 1879, a year after the Schrammel brothers, Johann and Josef, and bass guitarist Strohmayer had formed a trio to play popular Viennese music in the *Heurigen* around Vienna, they were joined by Georg Dänzer, playing G clarinet. Their fame spread and led to international tours. It is reported that the Schrammelquartett was much admired by Richard Strauss, Brahms and Hans Richter. What prompted Dänzer to make use of this tiny instrument remains a mystery. Did he find an instrument, or have one specially made? There was already a tradition of folk and popular music played by the Hungarian gypsy bands and it is possible that a small, high-pitched wind instrument had been included. After Dänzer's death the group continued, replacing the G clarinet with a harmonica.

In 1890 the quartet was disbanded and no more was heard of this music until in 1964 a new group was formed to perform the Schrammel brothers' music, following the discovery, in 1963, of the autograph parts of the original music, The new group, the Klassisches Wiener Schrammelquartett, was formed by two violinists in the Vienna Symphony Orchestra, a guitarist and Richard Schönhofer, the principal clarinettist of the Vienna Symphony, playing G clarinet. There is a delightful recording[8] of the latter-day quartet playing charming, slightly sub-Strauss waltzes and polkas in which the G clarinettist, in concert with this tiny band of three string players, plays with wonderful delicacy and instrumental control. Anyone who has attempted to play the similarly small A♭ clarinet will know the unbelievable problems of playing so quietly and having to match two violins. Played like this there could be a future for this otherwise unknown instrument.

In German the G clarinet was nicknamed 'picksüsses Hölzl'. The nearest translation of what may well be Viennese slang, is 'fabulous matchstick'. Perhaps, recalling the old army nickname for the clarinet, 'liquorice stick', and the charm of the sound of this little instrument, that might be nearer the mark.

The A♭ clarinet

The A♭ clarinet is the highest in pitch of the clarinets still extant. For a long time the A♭ was an essential member of many European wind bands, especially in Spain and Italy – the large Municipal Band in Venice which could be heard regularly in St Mark's Square until the early 1950s included A♭, E♭, B♭, alto and bass clarinets. There is no evidence so far of any bands in Britain including A♭ clarinets. The Italian band scores often include two A♭s, and Kroll (p. 96) writes: 'the great miners' band of Brussels, the Harmonie de la Bouverie had three'.

Ex. 3.11 from a free band transcription of Puccini's *Turandot* by Antonio d'Elia, *Direttore del Corpo musicale del Governatorato di Roma*

In example 3.11 the principal A♭ player is in unison with the piccolo, and an octave above the E♭.

The stage-band parts for some of the Verdi operas include parts for one or two A♭s. It seems that these have never been used (certainly within living memory) in British opera productions. Examination of the original parts shows that in two of his operas, *Un ballo in maschera* and *La traviata*, an A♭ is required for the stage band, and that two are called for in *Ernani*. Neither Donizetti nor Bellini used an A♭.[9] Donizetti did not use piccolo clarinets at all, and Bellini only asks for a D clarinet in *La sonnambula*.

The A♭ has rarely been used in the orchestra; Béla Bartók provides quite a large part for it in his Scherzo for Piano and Orchestra, Op. 2, mostly in unison with the E♭ or piccolo. More recently John Tavener used the A♭ in his *Celtic Requiem* (1969).

The lack of printed orchestral extracts for E♭ and D clarinets requires that those considering playing these instruments in the orchestra should obtain the scores of works with important and difficult passages and make copies for themselves. Beware! Catalogues and the list of instruments required printed in the score itself may only show: three clarinets, bass, when, in fact, it should be two clarinets, E♭, bass. The compositions referred to in the text and those listed below will repay study.

Orchestral music

BARTÓK: *The Miraculous Mandarin, The Wooden Prince, Kossuth*
BERG: *Lulu:* Symphonic Pieces, Three Orchestral Pieces
BERIO: *Epifanie, Sinfonia*
BIRTWISTLE: *Down by the Greenwood Side, Nomos,* Verses for Ensembles (thirteen players)
BOULEZ: *Pli selon pli, Rituel*
BRITTEN: *Our Hunting Fathers, Sinfonia da Requiem,* War Requiem
COPLAND: *The Red Pony, El Salón México,* Symphony No. 3
ELGAR: Symphony No. 2
FERNEYHOUGH: *Carceri D'Invenzione*
JANÁČEK: *Sinfonietta, Taras Bulba*
ORFF: *Carmina Burana*
RESPIGHI: *Feste romane* (D clarinet)
REVUELTAS: many works with E♭, sometimes without B♭/A clarinets
RIMSKY-KORSAKOV: *Mlada*
RUGGLES: *Sun-treader*
SCHOENBERG: *Die glückliche Hand* (D clarinet), Chamber Symphony No. 1 (D clarinet in the fifteen solo instrument version; E♭ in the orchestral version), *Moses und Aaron, Von heute auf morgen*
STRAUSS FAMILY: a number of the waltzes, polkas and marches
RICHARD STRAUSS: *Symphonia domestica,* An Alpine Symphony, *Salome, Elektra, Die Frau ohne Schatten, Josephs-Legende* (D clarinet)
STRAVINSKY: *Scherzo fantastique*
TIPPETT: Symphony No. 3
VAUGHAN WILLIAMS: *Norfolk Rhapsody,* Symphony No. 1
WALTON: *Belshazzar's Feast*
WEBERN: Five Pieces for Small Orchestra Op. 10, Six Pieces Op. 6 arr. for chamber ensemble
XENAKIS: *Akrata, Oresteia.*

Chamber music

ABSIL: *Quatuor* (cl qt)
ARRIEU: *Cinq Mouvements* (cl qt)
BARRETT (Richard): Trio (E♭/elec. guitar/double bass)
BERG: Chamber Concerto
HENZE: *Le Miracle de la Rose* (cl & ens)
HINDEMITH: Quintet for Clarinet and Strings (third movement for E♭)
JANÁČEK: Concertino (pn and ens)
PETRASSI: *Tre per sete*
RASMUSSEN: Italian Concerto (seven instruments)
RUNSWICK: *Main-Lining*
SCELSI: *Tre Studi* (solo E♭)
SCHOENBERG: Suite Op. 29
STRAVINSKY: *Berceuses du chat* (voice/E♭/B♭/bass cl)

This section on high clarinets was written with the assistance of colleagues and fellow clarinettists who responded so valuably to my questionnaire; I am also indebted to the staff at Boosey and Hawkes, Chester, Schott, Peters, June Emerson, the BBC, and in particular to Daniel Roberts at Ricordi. Amongst those whose help and advice has been of special assistance are Gordon Lewin, Keith Puddy, Michael Bryant, Anthony Baines and Chris Blount.

The basset horn

GEORGINA DOBRÉE

Introduction

The first reason for playing the basset horn may well arise from an opportunity to take part in some of the greatest of Mozart's works, such as the *Requiem* or the Serenade for thirteen instruments K361. An initial disappointment may well turn out to be that the basset horn available for use at the time, like all instruments relatively infrequently called for, may need immediate first aid before it can be used in performance. However, far outweighing any problems in coming to terms with the individual nature of the instrument is the ultimate fascination of an instrument with a four-octave range and distinctive tone-colourings, its strong bass notes contrasting with an almost veiled quality of sound in the upper part of the range. None the less, the basset horn is not an instrument that can ever simply be taken out of its case and played without a good deal of preparation. A cardinal rule is to obtain the instrument well before it is needed and to spend a great deal of time becoming acquainted with its character. It is the most temperamental of all the clarinets and will produce embarrassing squawks at the slightest excuse. (No wonder that Sir Thomas Beecham refused to use it at a time when no new instruments were being made and none could be relied upon!) One common mistake made by would-be players is to think that the basset horn can be played with a normal clarinet embouchure. It is an instrument that needs to be coaxed, not forced, so an open embouchure with a fairly soft reed is necessary to control it. This can, of course, make the task of doubling on other members of the clarinet family additionally hazardous.

Alto clarinet and basset horn

The alto clarinet in E♭ and the basset horn in F might be thought to have a relationship similar to soprano clarinets in B♭ and C. But this is not the case. In terms of usage they are both certainly considered the 'tenor' instruments of the clarinet family.[1] The crucial difference between the alto and the basset horn relates to the bore. The alto has a bore which begins to approach that of the bass clarinet, whereas the bore of the basset horn is closer to that of the clarinets in B♭ and A. The result is a very different tone-colour, whilst in addition to its extra low notes the basset horn is able quite comfortably to produce the upper part of its compass, giving us the marvel of its four-octave range.

The choice of tenor instrument in wind bands and clarinet choirs depends to some extent on national tradition. In the USA the basset horn is still fairly rare and almost unknown in ensembles of this kind, whereas in Europe it is the alto which is less common. This preference is also reflected in chamber music. To find a basset horn as part of the instrumentation of a clarinet quartet, quintet, etc., written by a European composer is quite usual, whilst in the USA today's composers rarely use it even in the orchestra.

Features of the basset horn

In addition to differences in bore between the E♭ alto and the basset horn, it must be noted that the bores of modern basset horns can vary more than with any other clarinet, not just between manufacturers in countries with different traditions but between different periods of manufacture by the same firm. The most fundamental of these variations may also reflect the demands of the different key/fingering systems associated with certain countries; French instruments are variously tapered in different parts of the bore, whereas German makers (of both Boehm and German system) usually favour a parallel bore down to the bell. In general, the principal French manufacturers build their basset horns with a relatively small bore – nominally *c.* 16 to 16.4 mm – while German models will range from *c.* 17 to 17.2 mm. There is, however, one French maker producing a basset horn with a nominal bore of *c.* 18 mm (which then corresponds to that of most E♭ altos). There are now also a number of independent makers experimenting with other ideas, and they will often undertake to build an instrument to the requirements of an individual player.

The wider-bore instruments are possibly easier to control, but some players contend that there is a noticeable loss of the distinctive, if somewhat lighter, tone-colour associated with the narrower bore. Furthermore, the wider-bore instrument requires a mouthpiece to match, whereas those with a smaller bore are often constructed so that a corresponding B♭ mouthpiece and reed can be used. However, even in this case it is still not advisable to use the mouthpiece from one's own soprano clarinet, since the lay may not suit the more open embouchure or the strength of reed needed for the larger instrument.

Another factor that can influence the sound of any basset horn is the shape and direction of the bell. Many manufacturers use an upturned metal bell, which is good for sound projection; however, a number of players have felt that the continuation of the bore into a flared wooden bell is more authentic and have had these especially made for their instruments. It is not unusual now to find makers producing such designs specifically for this market. Because of its length the basset horn requires a curved crook to replace the familiar barrel between the mouthpiece and the main body of the instrument. Sometimes crooks are made of wood, but more frequently they are of metal, thereby giving more scope for introducing a tuning slide – invaluable when playing with any fixed pitch instrument such as the piano.

Playing the basset horn

Notation

For a while it may be possible to confine oneself to reading music notated only in the treble clef, especially when playing works for wind band, clarinet choirs, etc. But inevitably the time will come when in an orchestral or solo context familiarity with bass clef notation is essential. Here it is necessary to understand the convention used when notating for the basset horn in the bass clef. Whereas in the treble clef the transposition is a fifth lower, in the bass clef the notes are written to sound a fourth higher. The main purpose of this is to avoid ledger lines below the staff. Unfortunately, some composers still do not understand this, and continue to write the part to sound a fifth lower, producing real mental difficulties for the player who has become accustomed to the traditional notation. Usually the bass clef is not used exclusively within a part. It appears most often in writing for the second or third instrument in a group or section, but is also commonly found whenever there are notes for the lower extension. It is not always possible to know in advance whether a part has been written entirely in the treble clef (often referred to as the French system), or in both treble and bass clefs (the German system). In the case of orchestral material in particular, this can depend on where the parts have been copied, or recopied (perhaps by a previous player). Even a study of the full score may not in the end be very helpful. The only advice is to be prepared, for example by practising bassoon parts such as arrangements of the J. S. Bach cello suites, whose expressive scope provides a real musical and technical challenge.

Basset notes

On the basset horn it is usual to find the key for e♭ (often suitable also for b♭′ as an alternative to the throat-note fingerings) beside the lower

Ex. 3.12 from Karel Janovický, Sonata for basset horn and piano (1991)

of one or other of the R4 keys, but there is no guarantee as to where the other basset notes, with their various duplicate fingerings, will be positioned. The different models opt for using L4, R4 or Rth, and the designs of additional coupling systems to stabilise the keywork are equally variable. All these coupling systems are very delicately balanced, and a lot of trouble can be caused for the player if they are not functioning efficiently; they should be checked regularly, or pad leakage may occur.

No fingering system will be found that is ideal, so it will be necessary to spend quite a lot of time practising various scales and intervals covering this lowest part of the instrument; a good deal of dexterity may be needed, especially in contemporary repertoire such as Example 3.12. Quick sliding or jumping of the fingers, as well as the use of two joints of the finger R4, will sooner or later be unavoidable; since what is practicable on one make of instrument may not be possible on another, even changing the composer's original articulation may sometimes have to be considered. Furthermore, with Rth probably no longer able fully to stabilise the movement of the instrument, the argument for using a spike rather than a sling becomes unassailable except where (as in some works written by Stockhausen for Suzanne Stephens) it is necessary to act a role while playing the instrument.

The extended downward range of the basset horn was at one time unique, but in recent years not only has the basset clarinet reappeared on the scene, but the bass clarinet is now almost universally built with the same additional range and consequent extra keywork. This unfortunately compounds a very real problem, and any player wishing to become proficient on both basset horn and bass clarinet should aim to purchase instruments whose fingerings are compatible.

The fourth octave

The basset horn speaks surprisingly easily in the top register *c*♯′′′ to *c*′′′′, especially the narrow-bore instruments. However, these notes can be difficult to pitch successfully, and choosing the best fingerings from what can be a bewildering number of possibilities may become a considerable task. Naturally, all the fingerings commonly available on B♭ and A clarinets may be used, but due to the extra length of the bore, it may be necessary to modify the choice of additional keys for fine tuning. For instance, instead of the *g♯/d♯″* key it may be advisable to use the *f/c″*. It may be better not to half-hole L1 for the extreme high notes, though as a result more breath support will be required to replace the usual additional venting. It is important to experiment, but also to remember the context. To pass smoothly from one note to the next may sometimes have to take precedence over intonation, and in this part of the range there are many register changes relating to the position of each note in the harmonic series – a problem all clarinettists have to contend with, but one which is especially critical to the basset horn player.

Repertoire

A cornerstone of the basset horn repertoire is the *Requiem* by Mozart, where his woodwind colours are confined to pairs of basset horns and bassoons. In subsequent completions of Mozart's manuscript (nowadays only the Introitus is recognised as entirely his own), this has offered scope for orchestrators to blend the unique tone of the basset horn with vocal resources. Mozart had previously combined basset horns with voices in his six Notturni for three solo voices and three instruments; K437 and K438 employ two clarinets and one basset horn, whilst K346, K436, K439 and K549 have three basset horns. Exceptionally, K437 is scored for basset horn in G, with two clarinets in A. Mozart's Concerto for clarinet K622 was originally begun in G for a basset horn pitched in that tonality, and the basset horn in G was not unknown to other composers of that time.[2] We may note in passing that the Czech composer Jiří Družecký wrote works scored for three basset horns in D, whilst there is documentation of at least one instrument in the key of E.[3]

The more usual basset horns in F are also to be found in three of Mozart's operas, most spectacularly in the obbligato to Vitellia's aria 'Non più di fiori' in *La clemenza di Tito*; there is also an aria for *Le nozze di Figaro*, 'Al desio di chi ch'adora' K577, believed to be the work about which Brahms wrote in a letter of 1855 to Clara Schumann 'to my great joy she [the singer Frau Guhrau] was accompanied by two basset horns which had been obtained with great difficulty. I do not think any instrument blends more perfectly with the human voice.'[4]

Mozart's instrumental works with basset horn are mostly found amongst his chamber music. One exception is the *Maurerische Trauermusik* K477, which originally included only one basset horn. Mozart later added a further two, thereby preserving the balance within the three wind groups: two oboes and clarinet; three basset horns; two

Ex. 3.13 from W. A. Mozart, Serenade K361, second movement

horns and contrabassoon. Amongst some recently completed fragments is the Quintet exposition K580b with basset horn already mentioned on page 39. It is now accepted that the Divertimenti K439b were originally written for three basset horns,[5] though for many years they achieved wide currency in the transcription for two clarinets and bassoon. Closely related to these are the two Adagios K410 and K411, again involving basset horns in ensemble. The celebrated Serenade K361 for thirteen instruments is of course one of the most glorious works of the entire repertoire, whose date of composition has been the subject of recent research.[6] The two basset horns play a pivotal role and are often paired with the two clarinets, nowhere more effectively than in Trio 1 of the second movement (Ex. 3.13).

The basset horn was not an instrument that every composer used as extensively as did Mozart. Beethoven included it only once, in his ballet music *Die Geschöpfe des Prometheus* Op. 43, which contains a delightful duet with oboe, lightly scored so as to expose its special qualities. It would appear from his sonata that Franz Danzi (1763–1826) had far less confidence in the instrument than either Mozart or Beethoven, since the title page of the early André edition announced a *Grande Sonate pour Piano-forte & Cor de Bassette (ou Violoncelle)*, and in the outer movements it is indeed the piano writing which is virtuosic, leaving the basset horn little to contribute. However, the slow movement is a touching Larghetto, well worth playing on its own.

While the clarinet player of today is likely to have been attracted to the basset horn through the music of Mozart, to have been invited to take part in a performance of the single number from Beethoven's *Prometheus* (there is even a printed arrangement for the two wind instruments with piano), or to have been tempted by the familiar name of Franz Danzi, he will soon realise that this is only the beginning. For the basset horn became a favourite instrument of the travelling clarinet virtuosi of the nineteenth century, and many of these players were themselves composers. Anton Stadler, to whom we owe so many of Mozart's works for both clarinet and basset horn, composed eighteen attractive single-movement terzetti for three basset horns. Other players who added to the repertoire were Heinrich Backofen (1768–1839), who wrote at least one concerto and a quintet with strings; Alois Beerhalter (1798–1858); Josef Küffner (1777–1856); Christian Rummel (1787–1849); and many more.

Curiously enough, Carl Baermann (1810–85) does not seem to have composed anything himself for the instrument for which he was most famous, but he can claim our profound gratitude for furnishing Mendelssohn with the inspirational scoring for the *Konzertstücke* Opp. 113 and 114, which he wrote for clarinet (father Heinrich) and basset horn (Carl himself), initially with piano. The subsequent orchestrations were by Mendelssohn (Op. 113) and Carl Baermann (Op. 114).[7] The opening flourishes by the two solo instruments in the Mendelssohn orchestration of Op. 113 illustrate just how well they complement each other (Ex. 3.14).

After Mozart the next most significant composer to write extensively for the basset horn was Richard Strauss. He used it first in his *Zwei Gesänge* Op. 51, where in No. 1, 'Das Thal' (1902), his scoring for the clarinet section alone fully illustrates his immense skill as an orchestrator: two clarinets in B♭/A, two basset horns and one bass clarinet in B♭/A. From then onwards, beginning with *Elektra* (including two basset horn parts) first performed in 1909, he was to include one or two basset horns in five further operas. *Der Rosenkavalier* has the basset horn doubling bass clarinet, and it is worth noting that the configuration of the mechanism on some basset horns makes certain of

Ex 3.14 from Felix Mendelssohn, Konzertstück No. 1 in F minor Op. 113 *(Die Schlacht bei Prag)*, solo parts at opening of the orchestrated version

its passages unplayable! As remarked upon on page 42, *Die Frau ohne Schatten* has the basset horn doubling C clarinet, another unkind – if not impossible – task for the player, since these two instruments are in reality totally incompatible. The large clarinet sections of *Daphne*, *Die Liebe der Danae* and *Capriccio* also include the basset horn. The late sonatinas for wind, already mentioned in relation to the C clarinet, contain virtuoso basset horn parts, in which the instrument is often entrusted with important solos. For example, the second movement of the Sonatina in E♭ contains a substantial duet for clarinet and basset horn, accompanied almost throughout by only the four horns (Ex. 3.15).

Essentially the basset horn is a chamber-music instrument. Although some players may prefer the more penetrating tone provided by a larger bore, especially in an operatic context, it is in more intimate surroundings that the basset horn excels. When treated with respect, it is incredibly flexible and can produce a wide spectrum of tonal colour and expression throughout its four-octave range.

The basset horn has not so far established itself firmly enough outside Europe to enjoy a reputation worldwide. Some of its music appears with alternative instrumentation, but there is nevertheless a considerable repertoire by composers such as Elisabeth Lutyens, David Gow and Richard Rodney Bennett in Britain, and Miroslav Krejčí, Jaroslav Maštalíř, Oldřich Flosman, Frank Martin, Petr Pokorny and Juraj Beneš in Central and Eastern Europe, besides a handful of American writers. We cannot list here all the works in which the basset horn appears, but John Newhill's excellent book *The Basset-Horn & Its Music* (Sale, 1983, revised 1986) is an invaluable source of information. His references range from anonymous eighteenth-century

Ex. 3.15 from Richard Strauss, Sonatina in E flat, second movement

trios for three basset horns to solos by Stockhausen, whilst calling attention to an important part for the instrument (perhaps unexpectedly) in the slow movement of the Violin Concerto by Roger Sessions. It is unfortunate that all too little of this repertoire is published or readily available, but its rediscovery and reinstatement is not an impossible task and can bring its own very special rewards.

The bass clarinet

MICHAEL HARRIS

Introduction

Like the basset horn, the bass clarinet was still regarded as rather a peripheral instrument even a generation ago; many musicians were genuinely surprised when a clarinettist appeared who could really play it well. However, the past thirty years or so have changed the situation so dramatically that professional players must really specialise in the instrument; it is no longer sufficient to pick it up casually for the occasional concert. To a certain extent, the amount of playing under-taken by an orchestral bass clarinettist during a given period depends on current repertoire. If an orchestra's principal conductor has a special interest in Mahler, Berg and Webern, the player may be on almost permanent duty, whereas if the German classics of Beethoven and Brahms form the staple diet he will be regularly excluded.

Playing the bass clarinet in a modern symphony orchestra provides a wonderfully varied musical lifestyle. On the one hand, you may be engaged merely to play the celebrated four notes following the clarinet solo in the first movement of Tchaikovsky's 'Pathétique' Symphony (originally intended by the composer for bassoon, but now almost always played by the bass clarinet). On the other hand, you may be required to play semi-jazz style in Bernstein's *West Side Story* suite, or to take responsibility for some of the most telling moments in Wagner's *Tristan und Isolde.* Whilst forming part of the teamwork of a clarinet section, one is also at times a soloist – ideal for someone who prefers to avoid the limelight all the time, but who can none the less make a significant musical contribution on this vitally important and expressive instrument.

Playing technique, instruments and equipment

Until the early 1960s, most manufacturers were building B♭ bass clarinets which descended only to written E♭, such as those illustrated

Figure 3.3   Henri and Alexandre Selmer testing clarinets at the Selmer (Paris) factory, *c.* 1932. From A. Selmer, *Instructive Talks to Clarinettists* (Elkhart, Indiana, 1932)

in Figure 3.3. This enabled the player to cope with a great deal of the standard repertoire, but made many significant works impossible to play, such as Stravinsky's *Petrushka* and Prokofiev's *Romeo and Juliet*, which require a range to low *c*. The shorter instruments were more portable and therefore ideal for use in military bands, and these were often furnished with an extension to provide the necessary three extra semitones. However, by around 1970 all the principal makers were building instruments to low *c*, and this type of bass clarinet has since become indispensable. Contemporary composers in all fields – including light music, film and television – now assume that this is the normal range available to them.

How then does one choose a bass clarinet? Due to the complexity of keywork and the acoustics of such a large instrument, one is faced with differing sets of compromises within each model. Mechanically superior instruments are not necessarily well in tune, whereas those with improved intonation may not necessarily have such a good basic sound. Among points to assess are the degree of clarity and stability in the very low register from *g* downwards, since some instruments are increasingly resistant in this area. The twelfth *b*/*f*#″ can be very stuffy in sound and a rather too narrow interval, which on some instruments is nicely corrected via an extra side venting hole. The throat *b*♭′ should be clear and not too flat, the latter problem sometimes occurring if the speaker tube has been altered to correct the tuning of notes immediately over the break. These notes – *b*′, *c*″ and *c*#″ – are very often quite sharp, a shortcoming difficult to correct and therefore one to be avoided in a prospective purchase! Of course, the main desirable quality is a fine sound, especially since so many bass clarinet solos are slow, expressive melodies, where the player must find his full individual expression in the sound being produced.

As any serious devotee of the clarinet will realise, choice of mouthpiece and reed is at least as important as the instrument itself. The characteristics of a good bass clarinet mouthpiece differ from its B♭ counterpart in several respects. Many inexperienced players find that the instrument squeaks very easily, especially in loud passages. This is often caused by the player, but can also be due to a fault in the lay of the mouthpiece. This should be the first area to be checked, if this most common of problems occurs. Whilst the usual qualities of fine sound, clarity and good intonation are essential, a bass clarinet mouthpiece needs to be even more flexible between registers than on the B♭ clarinet. Slurring over certain large downward intervals is a particularly difficult exercise on the bass clarinet, which a flexible mouthpiece can facilitate. Examples 3.16*a* and 3.16*b* from the opening of the finale of Mahler's Fourth Symphony are cases in point.

Curiously, the very high register (*c*‴– *c*⁗ and above) poses less of a problem than on the B♭ clarinet, (see fig. 10.8 on page 183) and therefore this is less of a factor in the choice of mouthpiece. However, it is also important to find a mouthpiece which allows freedom of articulation in all registers. Even when the lower register feels very free, the middle one – especially towards *g*″- *c*‴ – can feel highly resistant. Great patience is required to discover the technique of keeping the embouchure relaxed enough to articulate these notes, whilst at the same time controlling the sound and intonation. It remains common to choose one of the many fine commercially available mouthpieces and to have it finished by an expert, who will rectify any tiny imbalances in manufacture.

Playing in a modern symphony orchestra requires a huge range of dynamics to be produced, and this can often mislead the player into choosing reeds which are too hard. This may well produce a seemingly bigger sound, but it will probably be at the expense of flexibility and also intonation. Furthermore, the notes just over the break (*b*′, *c*″, *c*#″) may become uncontrollable and even sharper in pitch. Many players find that each of the registers of the bass clarinet responds so

Ex. 3.16*a*, 3.16*b* from Gustav Mahler, Symphony No. 4, fourth movement

distinctively that it is expedient to reserve different sorts of reed for different pieces. For instance, in Mahler's *Das Lied von der Erde* all the solo passages lie beautifully in the lower register and so a softer reed is more appropriate than in Strauss's *Don Quixote*, where most of the tricky solos lie within the range *c″ – c‴*. Ultimately, fine bass clarinet playing demands a mouthpiece that favours soft enough reeds to provide the necessary flexibility, whilst allowing a sufficiently wide dynamic range to be produced.

In terms of the sheer dexterity now required, bass clarinet and B♭ clarinet technique have become virtually indistinguishable. Composers write difficult passages in all registers, so that any study for the soprano clarinet may be usefully practised. The Bach solo cello suites (already mentioned in relation to the basset horn) also provide invaluable material for the bass clarinet, with an ideal range to low *c* and a largely melodic character. They are also a perfect introduction to the bass clef, which many new students find something of an obstacle. All studies must also be transposed as if originally written for A clarinet, as this situation is commonly encountered within the standard repertoire, and is an essential skill to acquire.

Repertoire

The list of late romantic composers who took the bass clarinet to heart is a long one. The works of just three of these – Wagner, Mahler and Richard Strauss – provide an irresistible incentive to take up the instrument. There were of course many important nineteenth-century solos (for example by Meyerbeer, Tchaikovsky and Verdi) but it was Wagner who really established it as an integral element within the orchestra.[1]

In many ways the symphonies of Gustav Mahler provide an excellent introduction to the sort of challenges and contexts that an orchestral bass clarinettist is likely to encounter, which are unlikely to be revealed within a book of orchestral excerpts. In Mahler's first five symphonies the player is variously required to double on A, B♭ and C clarinets, as well as to handle parts for bass clarinet in A. In the First and Fifth, E♭ and D parts are also included, prompting many clarinet

Ex. 3.17 from Gustav Mahler, Symphony No. 1, first movement

Ex. 3.18 from Gustav Mahler, Symphony No. 1, first movement

sections to reschedule the parts so that E♭ and bass players remain with their own specialist instruments. The First Symphony contains only fleeting moments for the bass, the majority of the part being for soprano clarinets; but the Introduction immediately establishes the instrument as an important colour within the piece. The little fanfare (bars 9–15) for two B♭ clarinets and bass (Ex. 3.17) is an admirable example of Mahler's instinctive writing, making use of the instruments' idiomatic *pianissimo*. The minim phrase at Example 3.18 looks easy, but it is a test of any woodwind section (and the bass clarinettist in particular) to play it in tune. The scoring is an unusual combination in octaves of piccolo, oboe, cor anglais and bass clarinet against a background of string harmonics, which usually sound flat. For the bass clarinettist this illustrates the flexibility required in a situation which on paper looks extremely straightforward.

The Second Symphony, 'The Resurrection', again contains very little for the bass, though its role is both telling and challenging. A short way into the long funeral march which is the first movement, Mahler writes an eerie chorale for the bass clarinet in unison with the cor anglais (Ex. 3.19). This is another exotic combination which creates problems of intonation and ensemble, especially since the two players sit at

Ex. 3.19 from Gustav Mahler, Symphony No. 2, first movement

opposite ends of the woodwind section! But it produces a wonderfully dark sound, with the strings providing a jumpy skeletal dotted-rhythm accompaniment. The Fourth Symphony is a piece where execution to the letter of Mahler's bass clarinet part demands a total of five instruments, including bass in B♭ and A. Furthermore, as with Bartók later on, many of the changes of instrument occur during very few bars' rest, which means that in practice the music is played on just three clarinets, in B♭, A and bass in B♭. The very end of the entire symphony is the most important moment, since Mahler again chooses two of his favourite woodwinds – bass clarinet and cor anglais – to wind down this beautiful and poignant music, to the accompaniment of a harp. It requires a calm nerve successfully to end this fifty-minute masterpiece. One may wonder why, if Mahler actually had at his disposal a bass clarinet in A, he opted here for the B♭, notated in F♯ major rather than G.

This seems an appropriate moment to discuss the question of parts for bass clarinet in A, written around the turn of the twentieth century. There seems no doubt that many major European symphony orchestras and opera houses must have possessed bass clarinets in both B♭ and A. So composers obviously expected to find the A instrument and wrote extensively for it, especially in Germany and Austria. The extent to which composers wrote for the sound of the A rather than for the convenience of key remains something of a mystery; perhaps the situation is variable, as with the soprano clarinets. The bass clarinet in A is now commercially available, although transposition of its parts for B♭ will always prove a popular option. The luxury of owning two separate instruments in effect creates more problems than it solves, given the sheer physical inconvenience of maintenance and transport.

Mahler's Sixth Symphony includes an important part for bass clarinet in B♭ and A, without doubling soprano clarinets. Here the sheer quantity of writing in A makes a transposed part advisable. During a peaceful, pastoral moment in the second subject of the first movement – a stormy and often brutal march – he writes a particularly evocative and haunting bass clarinet solo. This is an exciting but slightly anxious moment, since it needs to be played in a single breath and is often taken very slowly by the conductor! The scherzo similarly demands the ability to sustain a solo line, whilst in contrast it also

Ex. 3.20 from Gustav Mahler, Symphony No. 2

Bass clt in B♭

requires some very loud, confident playing in the low register. This symphony is unusual for the quantity of *tutti* bass clarinet writing, but it also features textures more characteristic of chamber music, which are a particular feature of the two *Nachtmusik* movements of the Seventh Symphony. Here the bass clarinet almost assumes the role of the cello in a string quartet. Sandwiched between these delicate and sensitive idioms are some really *fortissimo* effects in the scherzo.

The Ninth Symphony has a prominent solo role, which lies mostly in the rich low register, and is thus especially gratifying to play. The dark colour of the evocative first movement is emphasised by doubling of bassoon and cellos. In the Ländler which follows, Mahler reverts to chamber music, and towards the end writes a strange little solo (Ex. 3.20), whose *forte* in the third bar needs a great deal of confidence, since if this overblows, the result is catastrophic! In the final Adagio, the bass clarinet comes into its own as the *pianissimo* bass instrument of the wind section. This is a quality which Wagner and Puccini cultivated extensively, realising that in certain registers the bass clarinet is able to play much more quietly and with greater ease than the bassoon.

If Mahler's use of the bass clarinet is truly kaleidoscopic, a number of other composers wrote extensively and imaginatively for the instrument. Richard Strauss was an important devotee, nowhere more so than in his tone-poem *Don Quixote*, where the bass clarinet plays a characterful and major role in the drama, taking the part of Sancho Panza, Don Quixote's ridiculous side-kick, often in the company of solo viola or tenor tuba. The many unison passages with the tuba demand great care and attention, whilst amongst the solos is the especially awkward passage of Example 3.21, whose range nicely illustrates the necessity for keeping the embouchure relaxed and open, so that the sound is not choked out and the intonation remains stable. This is an area where the instrument can seem to want to retaliate and can feel reluctant to speak. The repeated staccato notes must be allowed to speak, but the embouchure must not be so slack that the pitch becomes flat.

The bass clarinet has held a particular attraction for operatic composers, its ability to play extremely quietly in the very low register being an obvious asset in creating dramatic effects in the theatre. Wagner wrote some of his most poignant instrumental music for the bass clarinet, and many of his operas contain beautiful, lyrical solos –

Ex. 3.21 from Richard Strauss, *Don Quixote*

Ex. 3.22 from Igor Stravinsky, *The Rite of Spring*

many of them in A – often with very little or absolutely no accompaniment. They illustrate the necessity for confidence in reading the bass clarinet (at pitch), whereas French composers have preferred to write the parts an octave higher in the treble clef, enabling one to read the music as if playing a standard soprano clarinet.

Of the great twentieth-century orchestrators, Ravel used the bass clarinet to particularly great effect. *La Valse* may be notated in the treble clef, but it is mainly for the A instrument, and is one of a handful of pieces for which most players will have a jealously guarded transposed part. Ravel's bass clarinet writing here is a *tour de force*, and illustrates the fact that by the 1920s the technical facility expected by some composers was virtually indistinguishable from that of the B♭ clarinet. Occasionally composers have used two bass clarinets to extend the tonal range at the bass end of the orchestra; Stravinsky did this in *The Rite of Spring*, using a rather confusing mixture of treble and bass clefs (Ex. 3.22). Russian composers have always been attracted by the dark, oily sounds of the very low register of the bass clarinet, and were among the first to incorporate the extended downward range to *c* and *d*. Shostakovich, for example, expected considerable dexterity in this register, as the scherzo of his Violin Concerto well illustrates.

The tradition and style of bass clarinet writing established in Vienna was continued and developed by the Second Viennese School of composers. Schoenberg in particular wrote not only some very difficult orchestral parts, but also included the bass clarinet in two of his major chamber pieces. His Serenade Op. 24 and especially the Suite Op. 29 find the instrument integrated in a real chamber setting. Exactly contemporary with the latter work is Janáček's wind sextet *Mládi*, with a prominent role for bass clarinet. During the first half of the twentieth century the combination of bass clarinet and piano found little favour with composers, although the Sonata by Othmar Schoeck Op. 41 is a serious attempt in this direction. This situation has since changed radically and (as Roger Heaton observes in Chapter 10) the bass clarinet has more recently become established as an important and prominent voice on the contemporary scene.

The contrabass

The bass clarinet's larger relative, the contrabass, is another fascinating option for the enterprising clarinettist. There is a small but interesting choice of instruments for the potential player. Whereas experiments to build the higher clarinets in metal have in general not been successful, the contrabass works pretty well and is available commercially. However, in the absence of financial constraints one might ideally opt for the rosewood model, shaped like a large bass clarinet, rather than bent double like the bassoon. The contrabass is built in B♭ descending to low *c*, and is especially popular in the USA, where large wind bands make use of it regularly. However, its most frequent use is in film scores, where its sinister low register has been heard to great effect in many horror movies. Its use orchestrally has been very limited, though there are parts in d'Indy's *Fervaal,* Strauss's *Josephs-legende*, Schoenberg's *Five Orchestral Pieces* and Ligeti's *Lontano.* In recent times more and more contemporary composers have been realising its true potential as a genuine colour rather than merely an effect, and it retains an important role in clarinet ensembles, especially the sextets still popular in France. Its roundness and softness of tone, especially in the low register, is unrivalled by its double-reed counterpart the contrabassoon. Wind bands sometimes include parts for the less common smaller E♭ contrabass, which also finds a very occasional place in film scores.

4 The development of the clarinet repertoire

JO REES-DAVIES

1750–1800

The clarinet's full and penetrating sound made it a popular choice for outdoor ensembles and bands; to realise just how popular, one need only glance at the Harmonie listings in the first edition of Whistling's *Handbuch der Musikalischen Literatur*,[1] which devotes several pages to works for wind band published before 1816. Its uniquely controllable volume made it equally useful for the chamber or concert hall. While the Mannheim court orchestra was not the first to adopt the clarinet as an essential instrument, the orchestra's high standard of performance and its resultant good reputation played a vital part in the adoption of the instrument elsewhere. The repertoire of the instrument's first century included many concertos designed to display its capabilities. In its early days, concertos and orchestral works mainly utilised the clarinet register and the notes immediately above it; the clarinet parts in Abel's Symphony Op. VII/6 (formerly attributed to Mozart as K18) are typical and seldom venture below the throat notes in either part.

Franz Anton Hoffmeister, Mozart's publisher and a popular composer in his own right, wrote concertos, sonatas and pieces for various wind ensembles. While (as is probably true of many composers whose lists of works number hundreds rather than dozens) he could not be accused of originality, his music is competently written, agreeable to play and comfortable for audiences. There are moments of genuine quality; one feels that he scarcely deserves Fétis's unkind comment 'O, sterile fécondité!'[2]

Others who composed concertos included Peter von Winter, who wrote a concertino and a variety of concertante works; Franz Tausch, himself a clarinettist, the range and brilliance of whose concertos give some idea of his quality as a performer though unhappily some of his other works are less satisfying musically; Johann Friedrich Grenser, whose concerto was performed on several occasions by Crusell. Philipp

Meissner is also known to have written variations and concertos for the clarinet, now lost. His surviving works include four quartets for clarinet and strings and a number of duos for two clarinets. Andreas Goepfert, who had studied with Mozart, was a very successful composer as well as an excellent clarinettist. In addition to a concertante for clarinet, bassoon and orchestra and several quartets, his compositions include many sets of duos for two clarinets which still make excellent study works.

The compositions of Carl Stamitz are far more substantial works, although sometimes uneven in quality. In particular, his concerto for two clarinets is an excellent early classical piece, well written and well balanced, and his quartets are also musically satisfying to play. Ignaz Pleyel composed a concerto for clarinet or flute or cello with orchestra; he also wrote a serenade, a nocturne, and trios for two clarinets with bassoon. The sonata by Franz Danzi is a fine work, neither dull nor difficult and useful for study.

But the clarinet's main glory was undoubtedly due to Mozart. His Concerto in A major K622 for clarinet and orchestra is arguably the greatest concerto written for the instrument, as the magnificent Quintet K581 for clarinet and string quartet is the most important of its kind. The slow movements of both concerto and quintet are as near perfection as can be found, while the delightful Trio K498 for clarinet, viola and piano (known as the *Kegelstatt* trio since it was reputedly written during a game of bowls or skittles) is a superbly constructed work which no student of the clarinet should ignore. Mozart's serenades and divertimenti are equally rewarding, both to play and to hear, and the clarinet is used to its best possible advantage in all of them. Choice is always difficult, but, asked to name the finest among these, a majority of players would probably award the crown to the Serenade K361 for thirteen instruments. Under Anton Stadler's influence, the chalumeau register is used to the fullest advantage.

Stadler left us three caprices for solo clarinet. Their novelty value and Stadler's undoubtedly brilliant playing must have made them excellent concert works in their day; consisting of popular melodies (folk tunes and operatic airs) interspersed with roulades and arpeggios, they seem a little disappointing now and in the present musical climate are mainly of historical interest, depending for their effect on the brilliance of the performer rather than on their musical content. His other surviving works also lack depth. From all accounts, Stadler was reputed to have a very good opinion of himself; one wonders whether he realised how much of his reputation he owed to Mozart.

In contrast to Mozart's quintet with its warm brilliance, the clarinet quintet by Andreas Romberg uses the darker-sounding string ensemble of one violin, two violas and cello. The German clarinettist Georg Fuchs studied composition with Christian Cannabich at Mannheim but spent most of his life in Paris as a working musician and, from 1793 onwards, as a teacher. To this end, many of his compositions are duos for clarinets and arrangements of airs from popular or fashionable operas (e.g. *Les Visitandines* and *The Magic Flute*). Like Goepfert, he wrote a number of duets, also several trios and quartets. Many of these were published during his lifetime.

In France, Mathias Blasius was highly respected as a conductor, but is now better remembered for his compositions. It is a measure of Blasius's quality that Bouffil, himself a superb performer and composer, dedicated his *Trois Grands Duos* Op. 3 to him. Charles Duvernoy worked as a clarinettist in various bands and orchestras, and was respected among his colleagues and by the public both as a teacher and as a performer. His works include three concertos for clarinet and orchestra (the first of which exists only in manuscript), a double concerto with violin, and various other sonatas and duos. Etienne Solère was also a fashionable and popular performer-composer.

The Swiss-born musician Jean Xavier Lefèvre was the most important figure in French clarinet history in the late eighteenth century. The excellently detailed clarinet method which he wrote for use at the newly founded Paris Conservatoire provided a model for future tutors (see figs. 3.2, 8.4). He also composed solos and duets, the sonatas being particularly attractive.

Amand Vanderhagen is best known now for his educational works; his tutor for the clarinet was, in both design and content, far in advance of other tutors current at the time for other instruments. A concerto by him was performed by the clarinettist Labatut in Charleston, South Carolina, on 14 December 1799, and may have been one of the first concertos to be performed in America.

Michel Yost, frequently known simply as Michel, was another public favourite. According to Fétis, Yost had a talent for melody but had not studied composition; he would make a rough sketch of the melody and its requisite decorations, and his friend Vogel would provide the harmonies and orchestration. Whoever was responsible, Yost's compositions, which include several concertos and a number of duos and other works for the instrument, were deservedly popular.

Outside Germany and Austria, Bohemia and its composers seemed to have a particular affinity with the clarinet; at least, many more documented clarinet works have survived there than elsewhere, notably due to the invaluable researches of Jiří Kratochvíl. The two concertos by František Xaver Pokórny are worthy of mention, as are those by Joachim Cron, Antonín Heller, Jan Kalous and the brothers Kozeluch. The horn player Anton Dimler, a member of the Mannheim court orchestra, left three clarinet concertos; these may have been intended for his son, who took up the clarinet at an early age and became a well-known performer. In addition to his concerto, Heller also wrote pieces for clarinet and featured the instrument in his wind partitas. František Xaver Dušek, Mozart's friend and colleague, composed several parthias, one of which was arranged for three clarinets. Both Johann Wendt and Wenzel Sedlak were also deservedly popular for their Harmonie works, though their skill lay in arrangement rather than in original composition.

Joseph Beer composed several concertos for the instrument and, if the note on the title page may be believed, collaborated with Carl Stamitz on the latter's Concerto No. 11. Beer's works include a concertino for clarinet and orchestra, an *air varié* for clarinet and piano, a number of duets for two clarinets, and a sonata for clarinet and bassoon. Johann Baptist Vanhal, a pupil of Dittersdorf, added two more concertos to the repertoire (one arranged from his flute concerto), a quartet, several trios and two sonatas; the last are his best-known works, and display his melodic talents to the full. The recently republished sonata by the Archduke Rudolph is also of interest.

Josef Fiala wrote a double concerto for clarinet, cor anglais and orchestra. Mozart, who rated Fiala very highly as a conductor, said that some of his works were 'very pretty, and he has some very good ideas'[3] – praise indeed! Wenzel Knežek, now almost forgotten, composed six concertos and also several partitas, one of them for the interesting combination of two clarinets in G, two violas and bass.

Franz Krommer (also found under the Czech spelling as František Kramář) was among the most important of the Bohemian musicians. His output included concertos for clarinet, a fine double concerto for two clarinets, and a number of excellent Harmonie works. Some of the better slow movements have been likened to 'good quality Mozart'. At one time the double concerto was attributed to the Finnish virtuoso and composer Crusell, who arranged it with band accompaniment.

While the clarinet became a popular instrument in England during the last years of the eighteenth century (mainly through its use in military bands), the standard of playing in the provinces was variable and in consequence the country produced few composers for the instrument. Many of the better professional musicians were German or French. Native players such as John Parry (who became solo clarinet in a military band in north Wales when young and went to London to make his fortune as a performer, only to give up the clarinet entirely in favour of playing the cello and composing operas) may not have been unusual. The real exceptions were people like James Hook, for many years musical director of London's Vauxhall Pleasure Gardens, who wrote a clarinet concerto which was probably intended for performance there. The solo part is brilliant, good both to play and to listen to. John Mahon (*c.* 1749–1834) and his brother William were both performing musicians, but only John composed. His works include concertos for clarinet, as well as marches for the Oxford Association Military Band, a set of duets incorporating popular airs, and a song, *Hope Thou Cheerful Ray of Light*, which was a great favourite with English audiences until well into the nineteenth century. However, much of the English repertoire of the period consists of popular and educational works or arrangements of church music.

As player and composer, Bernhard Hendrik Crusell overshadowed most of his Scandinavian contemporaries. His concertos are well-constructed works, full of musical feeling and intelligence, and his quartets and duets are also deservedly popular. Nevertheless, some other Scandinavian composers made their way into the public's affections, including the Swedish bassoonist Jean Martin de Ron, reported to be a student of Crusell, who paid implied tribute to the Finnish virtuoso with his *Thème finois avec variations* for clarinet and orchestra. In 1782 the Norwegian Lorents Nicolai Berg secured his place in clarinet history by writing one of the first tutors to recommend playing with the reed downward, which facilitates brilliant staccato playing.

c. 1800–1850

By the end of the eighteenth century the clarinet had spread across most of Europe, and a few had reached America; concertos and display pieces were still very popular. From the composers' point of view, the instrument had reached the musical limits of its current design and the time was ripe for a surge in technical developments to keep pace with composers' demands.

Many of the concertos and other works by Iwan Müller were intended to display the potential of his new thirteen-keyed clarinet. They are virtuoso pieces and almost all employ the full range of the instrument, from the lowest possible note up to, in several cases, *c''''*. The quality of these notes may have prompted Glinka's comment that Müller had a harsh tone, sounding like the screech of a goose. It would be interesting to know which piece prompted the criticism; making a beautiful sound in the altissimo register is not always easy and may have been even less so then. Glinka perhaps complained about the performer when his criticism might more justly have been levelled against the composer.

Ludwig van Beethoven composed a number of works which gave the clarinet more or less prominence. The Trio Op. 11, written just at the onset of his deafness, was the earliest. It needs superb playing to be fully effective. Beethoven did not seem totally at home with the clarinet, and, while not technically difficult, the work does not feel really comfortable. This may have been either the result of Beethoven's lack of detailed knowledge of the instrument or an expression of the composer's unwillingness to take advice; not without cause was he defined by at least one offended contemporary as 'an unlicked bear'. No such reservations haunt the magnificent Septet Op. 20, or the delightful Quintet Op. 16 for piano and winds, both deservedly known and loved, or the Trio Op. 38 (after the Septet).

Carl Maria von Weber's works, composed in the main for his close friend Heinrich Baermann, are among the best-known and loved works in the nineteenth-century clarinet repertoire, both for their musical content and for their understanding of the instrument. The two concertos are magnificent works, which may fairly be regarded as second only to Mozart's great concerto. The *Grand Duo Concertant* is superbly idiomatic writing, and while the Quintet for clarinet and strings is not quite on the same level as those of Mozart and Brahms, the world of the clarinet would be much poorer without it. The Concertino does suffer from a slight surfeit of E flat major; but there are worse musical sins, and it is never predictable enough to be tedious. These works are perfectly suited to the idiom of the clarinet then in use; indeed, some bars are more awkward to play on the Boehm clarinet.

The violinist Louis Spohr owed his understanding of the clarinet's possibilities to his association with the virtuoso player Simon Hermstedt. So much of the clarinet's repertoire seems to have depended on this type of partnership; whereas the world of the violinist-composer is that of the isolated performer and may be justly regarded as a history of individualists, the clarinet world seems to have recorded a history of friendships. This particular phenomenon is the subject of Pamela Weston's chapter. Spohr's four concertos bear witness to Hermstedt's abilities as a performer, and their idiom is mainly clarinet-based; but some of Spohr's studies for clarinet are, in their figuration, pure violin music. The *Sechs Deutsche Lieder* Op. 103 for soprano, clarinet and piano are excellent recital works. Spohr also wrote several sets of variations for clarinet and piano and a nonet, the latter being among the best of its kind.

Johann Georg Heinrich Backofen was a many-sided genius, known for his skills as a linguist and portrait painter as well as for his musical abilities. Well known as a performer in his native Germany, he was also a talented composer; among his surviving works is a quintet for clarinet and strings (violin, two violas and cello, as in the quintet by Romberg), as well as a number of concertos and several duos. The flautist Ferdinand Ries composed a trio for clarinet, cello and piano, also several larger ensembles. His slightly older contemporary, Joseph Hummel, a pupil and close friend of Mozart, composed a *Septet militaire*; larger ensembles seem to have been particularly favoured at this period.

Franz Schubert composed few works for clarinet, and one feels the lack of a concerto or a sonata from his hand. But the Octet D803 is a masterpiece by any standard, and *The Shepherd on the Rock* is possibly the finest work extant for voice with clarinet obbligato.

Peter von Lindpaintner studied with Peter von Winter in Munich, to whom he may have owed some of his knowledge of the clarinet. Admired by Mendelssohn as one of the best conductors in Germany, he produced music characterised principally by attractive melody and skilful dramatic effect rather than originality. Christian Rummel was a clarinettist and violinist as well as a composer, many of whose fantasies and concertos were published in the first half of the nineteenth century. The concerto by Bernard Molique has regained favour; Molique admired and was influenced by Mendelssohn and intensely disliked the 'modern' school of German composition. Ferdinand David, an extremely prolific composer, is now only remembered for his *Introduction and Variations on Schubert's Sehnsucht-Walzer*. A dotted rhythm combined with a descending scale is such a simple idea that its use can, in the context of a work such as Louis Schindelmeisser's concertante for four clarinets, scarcely count as quotation or plagiarism; but to the English ear this work conveys an irresistible suggestion of the morris tune *Country Gardens*!

The compositions of Heinrich Baermann, for whom Weber wrote his masterworks, include concertos, fantasias and *airs variés* with orchestra; among their number are several quartets and quintets, one of the latter containing the famous Adagio so long incorrectly attributed to Wagner.

Mendelssohn's sonata for clarinet and piano was written when the composer was only fifteen years old and, while well constructed, is predictably lacking in depth; of interest from the point of view of the composer's musical development, it makes no great technical or intellectual demands. As Georgina Dobrée has already implied in Chapter 3, Mendelssohn's *Konzertstücke* Op. 113 and Op. 114 for clarinet, basset horn and piano or orchestra are a different matter altogether; brilliant in the more familiar form with piano (as might be expected of anything written for the Baermann family), and superb when orchestrated. Among other works of value is the *Duo* for clarinet and piano by Norbert Burgmüller, unambitious but tremendously talented, who died tragically young.

The three *Phantasiestücke* Op. 73 by Robert Schumann were originally intended for clarinet; the *Romanzen* Op. 94, originally for oboe, are now frequently heard in transcriptions for clarinet. Modern editions for both specify the use of the A clarinet, though some older editions give alternative B♭ clarinet parts. Schumann also wrote a trio for clarinet, viola and piano, *Märchenerzählungen* (Fairy Tales); this is a light but interesting work.

France was richer in players than composers. Prominent among compositions of the period are the trios and duos by Jacques Bouffil, substantial works with valuable and interesting musical content; not for the beginner or the faint-hearted even now, they were almost certainly written for professional performance. François Devienne provided the repertoire with a number of symphonies concertantes, one for two clarinets and others for clarinet with other instruments. He also wrote a large number of trios which give prominence to the clarinet, and his influence did much to raise the musical standard of French woodwind writing. The two volumes of Sonatas Op. 3 by François Baissière are comfortable rather than impressive; one or two of them have been thought worthy of reprinting in modern editions.

Hyacinthe Klosé may well be regarded as the father of the modern clarinet, being responsible for the invention of the Boehm clarinet (see page 28). He also composed; his studies and larger concert works are good, but some of the fantasies on operatic airs are rather disappointing. His tutor remained in favour until fairly recently; a very thorough work, it contains useful basic material on points of technique which have not always been dealt with as thoroughly elsewhere.

In England, Cipriani Potter, then principal of the Royal Academy in London, arranged one of his three *Grand Trios* for clarinet, bassoon and piano *c*. 1824. Among player-composers, Joseph Williams of Hereford wrote some attractive studies which stand on their own as solo works, though there have been plans to provide them with a piano accompaniment. Henry Lazarus, whose life and career covered almost the whole of the nineteenth century, wrote a clarinet method (now a little dated, but still very good for sight-reading material). He also composed, his works being mainly sets of variations on folk tunes and operatic airs. They were very popular on both sides of the Atlantic, appearing towards the end of the century in American editions as standard repertoire pieces.

František Tadeáš Blatt, professor of the clarinet at the Prague Conservatoire, composed a quintet for clarinet and strings, in addition to a number of interesting sets of exercises. The blind clarinettist Joseph Procksch wrote a concerto and a concertino, in addition to fantasies and variations for two clarinets, while Antonín Reicha wrote a number of wind quintets which give the clarinet prominence.

Further south, works by the Swiss composer Xaver Schnyder von Wartensee include a concerto for two clarinets. The nineteenth-century Italian clarinet world was largely dominated by the compositions of Rossini and by the compositions and playing of Ernesto Cavallini, described as the 'Paganini of the clarinet.' An admirer of Rossini, Cavallini acknowledged the older composer's influence in his *Fiori Rossiniana* and *Una Lagrima sulla Tomba dell'Immortale Rossini* – the latter a sensitive and moving tribute to Cavallini's friend and master. Felix Alessandro Radicati, an Italian violinist and composer, who wrote a concerto for clarinet, was a pupil of Pugnani and an admirer of Boccherini, whose influence permeates his work .

Spain's first important clarinettist, José Avelino Canongia, composed three concertos, a *thème varié* and other items. His works, mainly large and with orchestral accompaniment, are brilliant rather than original; in the rather derogatory words of a younger contemporary – 'like José Avelino – new music, old notes'.

While the clarinet was a popular instrument in Eastern Europe, as in England and Spain, there were few fine players and few native composers for the instrument. Karel Kasimierz Kurpiński was one of the most important Polish composers before Chopin and his concerto is a rewarding and well-written work. His later contemporary, Ignacy Feliks Dobrzynski, was firmly entrenched in the Viennese classical tradition though there is some trace of folk influence in parts of his Duo Op. 47. In Russia, Glinka composed a *Trio pathétique* for clarinet, cello and piano; this is a relatively insignificant work, but is of interest to the clarinettist for the instruction to use vibrato in the slow movement – an unusual feature for the date (1832).

1850–1900

The eighteenth century and the early decades of the nineteenth century might be viewed as the age of the showy *air varié*, the virtuoso work with orchestra. This image gradually changed as the nineteenth century wore on, and by the end of the 1840s the earlier flood of wind concertos was slowing down to a trickle. Politically, many of the small courts were being absorbed into larger duchies or kingdoms, with a consequent loss in the number of orchestras available. Socially, the clarinet was becoming more accessible to a wider cross-section of the general public, more an instrument of the drawing room or small concert hall; the improvements in piano manufacture and the instrument's increasing popularity (and accessibility) also had their influence on composers. Fashionably, the musical world was by now in need of a change of colour; Hanslick (himself too bored or too busy to attend the young virtuoso's concert) may have spoken for a large part of the public when he advised Romeo Orsi to '... join an orchestra – that is the place where we know the value of clarinettists, flautists, oboists and bassoonists; the times are past when crowds of these wandering musicians came to give recitals on their boring little pipes'.[4] In the orchestra, repertoire was expanding in the hands of such composers as Mendelssohn, whose clarinet parts are far more demanding technically than those of Mozart.

Old soldiers returning after the Napoleonic and other wars took the instrument from the band to the church and the small concert. While the mid to late nineteenth century still had its full share of large-scale compositions, it could equally be regarded as the age of the suite of fantasy or characteristic pieces, short pieces in contrasting styles or moods which could be used either as a set or individually according to the requirements of the occasion. From the clarinettist's point of view, Schumann's *Phantasiestücke* are the earliest examples to retain their popularity. His later Danish friend and contemporary, Niels Vilhelm Gade, also wrote a set of four *Fantasiestücke* Op. 43; technically, these are simpler than Schumann's pieces, and the first was frequently used as an encore or short recital piece in its own right. Carl Reinecke wrote his *Fantasiestücke* Op. 22 in 1865, the year after Gade. The genre is represented in Holland by the *Vier Character-stücke* of Theodor H. H. Verhey, and in England by those written by William Yeats Hurlstone; the latter's violin pieces *Romance* and *Revery* [*sic*] have been transcribed for clarinet and are slowly making a place for themselves in the repertoire. Verhey's *Characterstücke* were indeed originally written for clarinet; however, they were also available for cello, and were evidently more popular in that form; by 1911 they had disappeared from catalogues of wind music and even their composer seemed to have forgotten that they had been for clarinet. Verhey also wrote a concerto for clarinet, the nocturne from which makes occasional (and welcome) appearances in anthologies. The serenade for winds by the Dutch composer Julius Röntgen shows Schumann's influence. Max Bruch's *Acht Stücke* for clarinet, viola and piano were written for a domestic group and were designed to suit the skills of the performers; three of them have traces of Hungarian gypsy influence.

If the instrument had to be defined by a colour or a season, the words which occur repeatedly throughout the clarinet's history are: warm, rich, dark, brown and autumnal. And in some respects the clarinet is the instrument of experience, the colour of mature thought for those not actually brought up with it in childhood. The infant prodigy has tended to write for the violin or piano. Clarinet works listed in this chapter are mainly by composers aged at least 25–30+ (quite a mature age in the days of bad hygiene and high mortality), not student works, and they tend, as Brahms's compositions bear witness, to improve with the composer's age. Johannes Brahms wrote his clarinet works near the end of his life; their dedicatee Richard Mühlfeld was loved by audiences for his beautiful tone, and Brahms's two Sonatas Op. 120, Trio Op. 114 for clarinet, cello and piano, and Quintet Op. 115 for clarinet and strings displayed this to its best advantage. Not that there is any lack of technical difficulties; but these works are among the most perfect of their kind, and generously repay the practice necessary to reveal them as such.

Nothing has surpassed the Brahms's sonatas. But Reger's two Sonatas Op. 49, written while under the inspiration of a good performance of

Brahms's works, in many ways equal them. They are finely crafted pieces, attractive and intelligent, which (like his quintet for clarinet and strings) have never had the popularity they deserve. Felix Draeseke also wrote a sonata for clarinet.

The clarinet quintet was a popular late romantic form, but few composers of that time reached the artistic heights of Brahms or Reger; many of those extant tend to be agreeable but conventional, like that by Volbach.

One usually thinks of Richard Strauss as a twentieth-century composer, but he was born in 1864, and composed his *Romanze* for clarinet and orchestra in 1879 while still at school. It is an attractive piece, and has recently been published in a piano reduction.

A short correspondence in *Musical Opinion & Music Trade Review* (March 1893) discussing 'recommendation of good concerted music ... worthy of being listed with Weber's Grand Duo Op. 48 and Schumann's Fantasiestücke Op. 73', gives a clear picture of the public taste of the time. Among the pieces recommended by contributors were, predictably, the works of Mozart, Weber and Beethoven. English composers included in the list were Henry Lazarus, Ebenezer Prout and Charles Swinnerton Heap. The latter studied in Leipzig with Moscheles and Reinecke, and was well known as a conductor and organist as well as a composer. His sonata for clarinet and piano is a substantial work, more satisfying today than that by Prout which sounds somewhat academic and dated. The works of Charles Lethière were also recommended; they are mainly light and showy, and his name is now almost forgotten outside military-band circles. Sonatas listed also included those by Gouvy and Seiffert – and Vanhal, who had apparently never been out of favour. Demersseman's Serenade and *airs variés* by Bauderuc, Berr and Mohr were also mentioned, as was the pastorale *Selanka* by Zdeněk Fibich. Charles Villiers Stanford's *Three Intermezzi* appeared on the list. Stanford composed other works for the clarinet; his concerto and sonata both show distinct traces of Irish folk melody, and his nonet was for many years unjustly neglected.

Swiss composers of this period seemed to favour large-scale works; August Walter composed an octet, and Joachim Raff's *Sinfonietta* Op. 188 for double wind quintet is well known.

Italian music of the period abounds in smaller works, some extremely demanding technically but less interesting musically. However, the concerto by Saverio Mercadante and Domenico Liverani's *Chants réligieux* on airs from Rossini's *Stabat Mater* both have musical quality. Ponchielli's quartet for flute, oboe, E♭ and B♭ clarinets is overshadowed by his accompanied duet for two clarinets, *Il Convegno*, one of the great works for that ensemble.

Mabellini's compositions treat the clarinet as a contrasting voice against a brass group. Flugelhorn and baritone saxhorn are featured in the *Fantasia a terzetto* and in the *Concerto per quartettino*, the trumpet making the fourth partner in the latter.

The clarinet was gradually attracting more attention from native Russian composers. An attractively melancholy work, Sergei Ivanovich Taneiev's *Canzona* for clarinet and orchestra clearly reflects the lyricism of his teacher, Tchaikovsky. The *Konzertstück* with military band by Nicolai Rimsky-Korsakov is disappointingly trite; his quintet for piano and winds is much more imaginative and rewarding, both to play and to listen to. Anatoli Liadov's Prelude for clarinet and piano has undeniable charm.

1900–1950 and beyond

By now the clarinet was a familiar sound all over Europe and, in the military band, was used in the east from Egypt to Japan. The twentieth century saw the return of the concerto as a popular form, and with it the re-emergence of the solo wind player. The concerto is frequently as much a vehicle for subtlety as for display, many being accompanied by strings only, or strings with harp and/or percussion. (Iain Hamilton's concerto, scored for full orchestra and consequently posing severe balance problems, is a notable exception to this.) At the beginning of the nineteenth century, performers' demands led to mechanical improvements; at the beginning of the twentieth, the demands of composers similarly forced advances in playing technique.

The *Vier Stücke* Op. 5 by Alban Berg, for clarinet and piano, must take pride of place in any listing of clarinet repertoire. While they are not easy, they are extremely rewarding; works of deep feeling as well as intellectual content, they never demand more of the performer than they offer in satisfaction. An ability to flutter-tongue is essential.

The sonata by Paul Juon is rather short, but makes up in quality what it lacks in size. Siegfried Karg-Elert wrote three sonatas, one being for solo clarinet. Viktor Ullmann, like Alois Hába in Czechoslovakia, composed quarter-tone works which included a sonata. The Sonata (1939) by Paul Hindemith is a great work which requires more musical intelligence than technique, and is consequently not as popular as it deserves. His concerto is good, but less memorable; the quartets and duos are also very worthwhile, musically intelligent and rhythmically interesting.

Heinrich Kaminski's quartet for clarinet, violin, cello and piano shows traces of Brahmsian influence, and lacks the austerity so noticeable in his later works. Clarinet quintets were composed by Franz Schmidt, Günther Raphael and Josef Schelb; Schelb and Raphael also wrote other chamber works involving the clarinet. The *Duett-Concertino* for clarinet and bassoon by Richard Strauss is typically florid. Ernst Krenek is probably best known for his jazz-influenced opera *Jonny spielt auf*; the

Marches Op. 44 and *Intrada for Winds* Op. 51a were composed during the mid-1920s, when he was working in the opera houses of Kassel and Wiesbaden. His early Serenade Op. 4 for clarinet and string trio is less dissonant, but his style (whether in the short pieces from Op. 85 for four clarinets and for clarinet and piano published under the pseudonym Thornton Winsloe, or in more serious works such as the Trio for clarinet, violin and piano) is very individual and finely crafted.

Alfred Uhl wrote a number of works for clarinet. Difficult, frequently exuberant and always rewarding, they include a *Konzertante sinfonie* with orchestra and *Kleines Konzert* for clarinet, viola and piano, as well as a *Divertimento* for three clarinets and bass clarinet and some extremely worthwhile studies.

The French repertoire was enriched by the Paris Conservatoire's habit of commissioning *morceaux de concert* for its annual competitions. Not all of the composers involved were as colourful as Augusta Holmès; greatly admired by her contemporaries, history has sadly confirmed that her musical talents, though of undoubted quality, were less striking than her personality. Nevertheless, the *Fantaisie* for clarinet and piano, written as a *solo de concours* for the Conservatoire, is an attractive work and, since she had been a pupil of Klosé, is based on a sound knowledge of the instrument's capabilities. Notable among other *solos de concours* are those by André Messager and Henri Tomasi, the latter contributing a concertino. Tomasi also wrote a number of extremely useful smaller works for clarinet and piano.

The *Première rapsodie* by Claude Debussy is probably the best-known clarinet *pièce de concours*; subtly lyrical, it requires very sensitive playing and total command of *pianissimo.*

A late developer musically, Charles Koechlin's almost total lack of self-criticism meant that he seldom revised works with a view to reducing them to the bare essentials. The results are sometimes rather self-indulgent; he was at his most successful as a miniaturist, and his *Idyll* for two clarinets and the *Pastorale* for flute and clarinet are works of undeniable charm. Among other worthwhile small pieces in the French repertoire are the *Aria* by Albert Roussel and the *Andantino* Op. 30 by Florent Schmitt.

The influence of jazz swept across the Atlantic at the end of the First World War, and was quickly adopted by many composers, particularly in France. Arthur Honegger's *Sonatine* is a lively and interesting piece – a little dated by now, but with a jazzy finale which works extremely well. His *Rapsodie* for flutes, clarinets and piano is an oddly melancholy work. The *Sonatine* by Darius Milhaud is characterised by spiky wit and quirky rhythms, as is his later *Duo Concertant*. His Suite for clarinet, violin and piano is in similar vein. More demanding than the Honegger works, they are as satisfying to play. Jacques Ibert composed two entertaining and useful reed trios, as well as a variety of smaller pieces.

Francis Poulenc left the clarinet world richer by several sonatas. The Sonata for clarinet and piano is one of the great works in the repertoire, while the shorter and technically simpler sonatas for clarinet and bassoon and for two clarinets scarcely lag behind in terms of musical content and entertainment value.

The *Quatuor pour la Fin du Temps*, written by Olivier Messiaen in a prison camp during the Second World War, ranks as a contemporary classic, and in spite of its difficulties is an indispensable work for any serious clarinettist.

On the other side of the Alps, the Swiss composer Edward Staempfli wrote a concertino for clarinet and strings, as well as works for wind quintet, and Paul Müller-Zurich composed a *Petite sonate* Op. 37. Constantin Regamey's quintet for clarinet, bassoon, violin, cello and piano, and works by the Russian-born Wladímir Vogel are likewise of interest. However, the best-known and respected work in the Swiss clarinet repertoire is the lively and effective *Capriccio* for solo clarinet by Heinrich Sutermeister.

Among English solo works, Arnold Bax's Sonata is firmly established in the concert repertoire. John Ireland's *Fantasy Sonata* is difficult, especially the opening and the sweeping arabesque figures, and presents a number of ensemble problems. The sonatas by Donald Tovey and York Bowen, while not so well known, are worthy of attention. The sonata for clarinet and piano by Herbert Howells is an excellent work, full of depth, and should not be neglected. The *Pocket-sized Sonatas* Nos. 1 and 2 by the Cardiff-born blind composer and pianist Alec Templeton are lighter, but justly popular. Both are strongly jazz-influenced; the first is possibly the more attractive of the two, and the *ad lib* side drum in the last movement should never be omitted!

Gordon Jacob's works including clarinet are all well constructed, imaginative and satisfying for both players and audiences; among them are a sonatine, a trio, and works for larger ensembles.

The Edwardian composer Richard Walthew wrote a concerto for clarinet and orchestra which has recently been revived and republished, also a trio for clarinet or violin, cello and piano, and a set of four *Bagatelles* for clarinet and piano. The concerto by Gerald Finzi, who died young, is a thoughtful work, while his *Five Bagatelles* for clarinet and piano are among the most popular of English compositions for that ensemble; others which are of interest are Thomas F. Dunhill's lighter *Phantasy Suite* and the *Four Pieces* by Howard Ferguson.

Some of Joseph Holbrooke's works for clarinet are, in terms of dates and numbers, rather puzzling. For the benefit of future generations of scholars who may find conflicting opus numbers and nomenclature confusing, one can only recommend Lowe's small (though not very slim) volume on Holbrooke's life and works; it gives a very clear listing for its period.[5] At the present time, the official canon of Holbrooke's works includes only *one* clarinet quintet (a synthesis of the stronger movements from the original two quintets). Among his other works, the double concerto *Tamerlane* for clarinet and bassoon is worthy of attention.

Phyllis Tate was at her finest in chamber works, many of which use clarinets to great advantage; among the best of these is the sonata for clarinet and cello (unfortunately seldom heard, although its musical quality merits more frequent performance). Alan Rawsthorne composed a concerto and a clarinet quartet which are unjustly neglected.

The concerto for clarinet and orchestra by Carl Nielsen is one of the twentieth century's classics: brilliant, witty and difficult, it has moments of extraordinary beauty. Other Danish composers to have favoured the clarinet during the first half of this century include Hermann Koppel, who wrote a concerto, variations for clarinet and piano, and also featured the instrument in his Sextet Op. 36; Finn Høffding, whose *Dialoger* for oboe and clarinet is a very useful work; Fleming Weis, with a concertino for clarinet and strings and a clarinet sonata; and Vagn Holmboe, a pupil of Høffding and the most important Danish composer after Nielsen, whose *Chamber Concertino No. 3* Op. 21 is scored for clarinet, two trumpets, two horns and strings. Holmboe also wrote a *Serenade* Op. 3 for clarinet with piano quartet and *Rapsodisk Interludium* Op. 8 for clarinet, violin and piano.

The clarinet was not quite so popular in Norway, though Edvard Hagerup Bull's earlier works included a sonata and Karl Andersen's trio for flute, clarinet and cello. The Swedish composer Edvin Kallstenius composed a clarinet quintet, and a number of his compatriots have written wind quintets. In Finland, Aare Merikanto has featured the clarinet prominently in his works for larger ensembles. Iceland has provided sonatas by Gunnar Reynis and Jon Thorarinson, and a variety of chamber works.

In Belgium and the Netherlands, the clarinet has remained a constant favourite, mainly used for its colour and flexibility in large instrumental groups. Works written by the Dutch composer Jan Ingenhoven during the First World War and the decade following include a clarinet sonata and a *Sonatine* for clarinet and violin. Interesting clarinet concertos were composed by the Belgian composers Joseph Jongen and Georges Lonque (*Idoles* Op. 41), the former a brilliantly extrovert work.

Italian composers have mainly concentrated on vocal works, exceptions being Ferruccio Busoni who wrote an unusual and brilliant Concertino and a gentle *Elégie* for clarinet and piano. Also for clarinet and piano is Scontrino's *Bozzeto*. Alfred Casella's quartet is characterised by crisp diatonic dissonances and clear lines.

In the Spanish-speaking world, Amedeo Roldán, a Cuban composer born in Paris who studied in Madrid, is known for the intellectual content of his works, among which is *Danza Negre* for voice, two clarinets, two violas and percussion. The Argentinian Juan Carlos Paz composed a sonatina for clarinet and piano, also *4 Piezas* for clarinet. *Chôros No. 2* by the Brazilian composer Heitor Villa-Lobos is for flute and clarinet; his trio for reed instruments is difficult but interesting, and well worth the battle with printing errors. Claudio Santoro, also Brazilian, wrote pieces for clarinet and miniature variations for clarinet and strings; he also composed a number of trios including clarinets, which were withdrawn.

Béla Bartók's *Contrasts* for clarinet, violin and piano (for Benny Goodman) was originally projected as a double concerto for clarinet and violin. However, it was never orchestrated and it is difficult to see how any tonal expansion would have improved the work's intensity. Other interesting Hungarian works include a quartet, *Michaelangelo*, for clarinet, horn, bassoon and piano by Albert Siklós and the Sonata Op. 5 by Hans Kornauth, who also wrote a quintet and a nonet.

The sonatina for clarinet and piano by the Polish composer Anton Szalowski is a brilliant and rewarding work, easy to listen to, yet not as difficult as it sounds in places. His duo for flute and clarinet is equally graceful. Kasimierz Sikorski and Michal Spisak both composed concertos for the instrument.

Chronologically, Leoš Janáček belongs mainly to the nineteenth century; musically, he is very much of the twentieth century, and his most important clarinet works belong to its first two decades. The sextet *Mládi*, for wind quintet with the addition of a bass clarinet, ranks as a major work by any standards; *Říkadla* (Nursery Rhymes) was originally written for women's voices with accompaniment of clarinet and piano but later enlarged to include more songs and more instruments.

Concertos were written by Miroslav Krejčí, Rudolf Kubín and Václav Vačkář; the latter's son, Dalibor Vačkář, composed a *Scherzo & cantabile* for clarinet and piano, also a quartet for reed instruments and piano.

Alois Hába (see fig. 5.2) is probably best known for his experimental compositions, and his sonata for quarter-tone clarinet and piano is an unexpectedly attractive work. Other important or interesting sonatas were composed by Jaromir Weinberger (*Sonatina*), Viktor Kalabis and Iša Krejčí, who also wrote a clarinet quintet and various trios. Jaroslav Ježek composed a quartet for the interesting combination of flute, two clarinets and tuba.

Igor Stravinsky's *Three Pieces for Clarinet*, idiomatic but difficult and first published in 1919, are deservedly well known. The last of these, while reputedly jazz-influenced, owes more to the popular music of its period. Among his other compositions, the *Berceuses du chat* and *Histoire du soldat* are both difficult, but very effective.

Nicolai Berezowsky and Vladímir Kryukov composed concertos (the former dedicated to Cahuzac), as did the Latvian Jěkabs Medinš. The trio for clarinet, violin and piano by Aram Khachaturian is oriental and exotic in mood. Sergei Prokofiev's *Overture on Hebrew Themes*, for clarinet, string quartet and piano has a similarly florid clarinet part and is worth attention.

In Greece and the eastern Mediterranean countries, the clarinet is still mainly known as a folk instrument; but a number of composers have made interesting additions to its repertoire, notably the Greek composer Manolis Kalomiris (songs with clarinet obbligato), the Yugoslav composers Slavko Osterc (a sonatine for two clarinets), Lucijan Marija Škerjanc (a concerto for clarinet, strings, percussion and harp) and Josip Slavenski, and the Bulgarians Konstantin Iliev and Simeon Pironkov (quintets and trios including clarinets).

In the New World, Aaron Copland's concerto for clarinet, strings and harp is an established favourite among players and audiences. The first part is lyrical, the second part, from the cadenza onwards, jazzy, and all of it good. Sonatas for clarinet were composed by, among others, Leo Sowerby, Bernard Heiden, the conductor and composer Leonard Bernstein, and the musicologist, collector and composer Burnet Corwin Tuthill; the last-named also wrote a clarinet concerto and an intermezzo for three clarinets. Virgil Thomson's *Five Portraits* is scored for four clarinets.

The *Hillandale Waltzes* for clarinet and piano by the pianist and composer Victor Babin are excellent recital pieces for almost any audience, and deserve to be far better known. Other Americans who have composed for the instrument include Hunter Johnson who wrote a serenade for flute and clarinet, also a wind quintet (*Elegy for Hart Crane*). His compatriot, Robert Levine Sanders, wrote a *Rhapsody* for flute, clarinet and bassoon. Elliott Carter's *Pastorale* for clarinet and piano is simple but very pleasant.

The Australian clarinet repertoire is not large, and what exists is in the main too recent to be within the scope of this chapter; but the sonata for clarinet and piano by Margaret Sutherland is worth looking at. The clarinet has also become more popular in the Far East during the last fifty years; the Chinese and Japanese repertoire is expanding steadily, though most of the composers are as yet little known in Europe.

Finally, no listing of this kind can hope to be more than selective; in all periods, for every work mentioned in this essay another score exists, many just as worthy of attention. Much research has been done, and many interesting compositions have been rediscovered during the last twenty or thirty years. But there are still tantalising mentions of works which have not yet come to light; there is still much to explore.

5   Players and composers

PAMELA WESTON

Introduction

When an overall view is taken of those who have influenced composition for any instrument, a number of specific types may be observed. The most obvious type is the professional virtuoso who provides direct inspiration; outstanding clarinettists who have done this are Karl Stamitz's Joseph Beer, Mozart's Anton Stadler, Spohr's Simon Hermstedt, Weber's Heinrich Baermann and Brahms's Richard Mühlfeld. Where, as in the case of the clarinet, the instrument is mechanically operated there is also the player-inventor who gives the spark to fire a composition; the most notable of these is Iwan Müller. Thirdly, there are those who give commissions which result in significant additions to the repertoire; amongst these are Benny Goodman, 'King of Swing', and the amateur player-philanthropists Werner Reinhart, the Duke of Sondershausen and Count Troyer.

The rise of the virtuoso

Connecting specific players with the very first works for the clarinet is not easy, though we can be fairly certain that it was Johann Reusch (c. 1710–1787) who inspired Durlach's Kapellmeister Johann Melchior Molter to compose his six concertos in the late 1740s. At that time Reusch was Durlach's flautist, merely doubling on oboe and clarinet. Significantly, he later moved to Karlsruhe as a bona fide clarinettist.

In 1748 the tax-farmer Jean le Riche de la Pouplinière engaged Gaspard Procksch and Simon Flieger as clarinettists for his private orchestra in Paris; his music director was Rameau and it was undoubtedly these two players who influenced the composer's early use of the instrument in *Zoroastre* (1749) and *Acante et Céphise* (1751). Mannheim's Kapellmeister Johann Stamitz was in residence at La Pouplinière's palace during 1754–5, and it is thought that he may have written his concerto at this time for Procksch, as Mannheim had no clarinets in its orchestra until after Stamitz died.

During the 1770s Stamitz's son Carl formed a close relationship with Joseph Beer (1744–1812), the first great clarinet soloist. Of Carl's eleven concertos, six – possibly all – were for Beer. So much significance was attached to these, thanks to Beer's performances in Paris, that Carl was listed in *Almanach Dauphin* as 'compositeur pour clarinette'. Beer is credited with founding the French style of playing; he left Paris in 1780 and, after spending twelve successful years at St Petersburg, found employment at the Berlin court for the last twenty years of his life.

Mozart scorned Beer as 'a dissolute sort of fellow' when he was in Paris during 1778. The previous year he had visited Mannheim, which by now had clarinets, and been entranced with the beauty of their sound. The players he heard were Johannes Hampel, Michael Quallenberg, Jacob Tausch and his son Franz. Franz Tausch (1762–1817), credited with establishing the German style of playing, achieved distinction as a member of the Berlin court orchestra from 1789 until his death. Whilst no important compositions were written for him, his own works posed a degree of technical difficulty that led to a greater understanding of the instrument's potential.

The celebrated association between Mozart and Anton Stadler began at least as early as 1784. Anton (1753–1812) and his brother Johann (1755–1804) were the first clarinet and basset horn players to be employed on a regular basis at the Viennese court. Anton's newly invented clarinet with an extended lower range inspired Mozart's Quintet K581 (1789) and Concerto K622 (1791), as well as the clarinet and basset horn obbligatos in *La clemenza di Tito* (1791). Other composers were charmed by the low notes on Stadler's instrument, and amongst music written specifically for it were obbligato arias and a concerto movement (1792) by Süssmayr and an obbligato aria in Paer's *Sargino* (1801).

At the première of Beethoven's *Prometheus* ballet in 1801, the important basset horn part was played by Johann Stadler. Joseph Bähr (1770–1819) was the earliest clarinettist to influence Beethoven. He was first employed at the Wallerstein court where Friedrich Witt wrote several chamber works and a concerto (1794) for him. By 1796 he had arrived in Vienna and the following year took part in the first performance of Beethoven's Quintet Op. 16 for piano and winds, with the composer playing the piano. At his suggestion Beethoven took the aria 'Pria ch'io impegno' from Weigl's popular opera *L'amor marinaro* as the theme for the last movement of his Trio Op. 11 (1797) and they gave the first performance of this together in 1800. Bähr also took part in premières of the Sextet Op. 71 (1796) and Septet Op. 20 (1799–1800).

After Bähr died, Beethoven turned to Joseph Friedlowsky (1777–1859) for advice on his clarinet parts. Spohr was also influenced by Friedlowsky and wrote for him the clarinet part in the Octet Op. 32 (1814), which they premièred together. Friedlowsky taught Count Ferdinand Troyer (1780–1851), chief steward to Beethoven's patron and pupil, the Archduke Rudolph of Austria. The count was the dedicatee of a sonata (*c.* 1820) by the archduke and *Variationen über der beliebte Abschiedslied* Op. 19 (1815) by Johann Peter Pixis. Troyer's most important influence came with his commissioning of Schubert's Octet D803 in 1824. Schubert had written the C clarinet part in his *Offertorium* D136 (*c.* 1815) for Josef Doppler, an amateur player who became manager of Diabelli, the composer's principal publisher.

Before Spohr met Friedlowsky or Hermstedt he had written a *Recitativo ed Adagio* (1804–5) for the Brunswick clarinettist Tretbach; the piece was not published in this form but Spohr used it again in his Violin Concerto No. 6, Op. 28 (1809). Simon Hermstedt (1778–1846) was employed at the court of Duke Günther I of Sondershausen. The duke became a keen clarinettist under Hermstedt's tuition and in 1808 sent him to Spohr with a commission to write a concerto. This was the beginning of a long and fruitful relationship which produced the following works, all dedicated to and premièred by Hermstedt: Concerto No. 1, Op. 26 (1808); *Alruna* Variations (1809); Concerto No. 2, Op. 57 (1810); *Potpourri* Op. 80 (1811); *Fantasie und Variationen* Op. 81 (1814); Concerto No. 3, WoO 19 (1821); Concerto No. 4, WoO 20 (1828). Works were also written for him by Max Eberwein, Albert Methfessel and André Spaeth.

Hermstedt had one serious rival: Heinrich Baermann (1784–1847), who was employed from 1807 until his death in the court orchestra at Munich. The court's Kapellmeister, Peter von Winter, wrote a concertino and a rondo (both 1808) for Baermann and the cellist Legrand; earlier he had written a concerto and a quartet for Franz Tausch. Peter von Lindpaintner, music director of Munich's Isartor Theatre, wrote a concerto as well as an obbligato to an aria in *Der Vampyr* for Baermann. His Concertino Op. 41 is for Tausch's son Friedrich Wilhelm (1799–1845) who, like his father, played in the Berlin court orchestra. It is said that Danzi derived his liking for the clarinet through his friendship with Weber and thus with Baermann. He did indeed compose the third *Potpourri* (1822) for Baermann; the second *Potpourri* (1819) is for D. W. Kleine (1778–1837), his principal clarinet at Karlsruhe.

The most important composers to write for Baermann were Weber, Meyerbeer and Mendelssohn. He met the first two in 1811 and during that year Weber wrote for him the following works: Concertino Op. 26; Concertos Op. 73 and Op. 74; *Sylvana* Variations Op. 33. The Quintet

Op. 34, also for Baermann, was begun in 1811 and completed in 1815. Meyerbeer likewise wrote a quintet (1812) for Baermann, as well as the cantata *Gli amori di Teolinda* (1816) for him and his wife. As we have noted in previous chapters, Mendelssohn, who was but one year older than Baermann's son Carl (1810–85), wrote the *Konzertstücke* Op. 113 and Op. 114 (1833) for father and son to play together.

Two spurious works have connections with Baermann: the *Introduction, Theme and Variations*, published as a work by Weber written for Baermann in 1815, and the famous Adagio already mentioned on page 81, published as an early work of Wagner. It is now known that the first of these is by the clarinettist Josef Küffner (1776–1856) who dedicated it, as well as the Serenade Op. 21 (*c.* 1814) to Baermann's pupil Adam Schott (1794–1864). Schott was also the dedicatee of the Concertino Op. 58 (1829) and the *Introduction and Variations* Op. 67 (*c.* 1830) by the clarinettist Christian Rummel (1787–1849). Rummel was the person responsible for the other spurious work's attribution to Wagner; it is in fact the second movement of Baermann's Quintet Op. 23 (1821).

Weber inscribed Baermann's name on all his clarinet works except the *Grand Duo Concertant* Op. 48 (1815–16). There are two possible contenders for its dedication: Hermstedt, who is known to have offered Weber a commission, and Johann Kotte (1797–1857), Weber's principal clarinet in the Dresden orchestra, who gave the first known performance of the completed work. There is no doubt that Kotte influenced both Weber and Wagner in their orchestral writing for the clarinet during their respective tenures as Kapellmeister in Dresden. He also inspired a number of solo works from Karl Reissiger, another incumbent of the post. Schumann composed *Phantasiestücke* Op. 73 (1849) in the same city; *Märchenerzählungen* Op. 132 (1853) was written at Düsseldorf. Although neither work is dedicated to a clarinettist – Op. 73 is for the cellist Andreas Grabau and Op. 132 for music director Albert Dietrich – it is significant that, in each case, Schumann invited a clarinettist to perform the work with his wife Clara within a few days of composition: at Dresden it was a certain Herr Kroth and at Düsseldorf Herr Kochner.

Player-inventors

Throughout the nineteenth century runs a thread of player-inventors, the most important being Iwan Müller (1786–1854) and Hyancinthe Klosé (1808–80). Klosé's application of the Boehm system to the clarinet, although of paramount importance, did not directly inspire compositions, unlike Müller's thirteen-keyed *clarinette omnitonique*, which we have already encountered in Chapters 2 and 3. In 1810 Müller found a sponsor for his invention in Paris – the stockbroker Marie-Pierre Petit. Petit had been one of the first clarinet students at the Conservatoire and began a promising career in music, receiving the dedication of duets by both Aléxis de Garaudé and Etienne Gebauer, before going into business. In 1812 Müller submitted his clarinet for review by a jury of Conservatoire professors (see pages 26 and 34). It was rejected, the verdict undoubtedly swayed by Xavier Lefèvre (1763–1829) who, having added a sixth key to the then standard five-keyed clarinet, had a vested interest; thus Petit's generosity went for nought.

In spite of the Conservatoire's decision, there were those who saw a future in Müller's instrument, and concertos were written specifically for it by Riotte (1809), Abraham Schneider (1809) and Reicha (1815). Schneider also wrote two concertos for Müller's 'improved' basset horn. Reicha had already dedicated the Clarinet Quintet Op. 89 (*c.* 1809) to Jacques-Jules Bouffil (1783–1868), who studied composition with him. Bouffil was the clarinettist in all first performances of Reicha's twenty-four wind quintets (1810–20). When Müller's pupils, Conrad and Ludwig Bänder, were playing in Paris during 1818–19, Reicha wrote a *Grand Duo Concertant* (now lost) for them.

Müller's system formed the basis of early experiments (see pages 26–27) by Adolphe Sax (1814–94), and his application of it to the bass clarinet attracted the attention of Berlioz, Donizetti and Meyerbeer. Donizetti had shown interest in Müller's basset horn and in 1843 wrote for two of Sax's bass clarinets in *Dom Sébastien*. At this time England had a noted exponent on both instruments in John Maycock (1817–1907), for whom Balfe wrote the obbligato basset horn part in *The Bohemian Girl* (1843) and the famous bass clarinet solo in *The Daughter of St Mark* (1844). Verdi was intrigued by some of the unusual instruments invented by the clarinettist-manufacturer Romeo Orsi (1843–1918) and used them in his scores. Orsi's *clarinetto a doppia tonalità* inspired a solo *Improviso* (*c.* 1880) by Cesare Dominiceti.

Further developments

Italy's nineteenth-century clarinettists, whilst lagging behind their northern counterparts in the adoption of mechanical and technical developments, were none the less capable of a surprising agility, and were given a role by their composers complementary to that of the prima donna. Alessandro Abate was the dedicatee of Rossini's early student work, the *Introduction, Theme and Variations* (1809); his *Fantasie* (*c.* 1826) was written in Paris for an amateur player, Valentin de Lapelouze. Like Rossini, Donizetti essayed a student work, *Studio primo* (1821) for solo clarinet, which he dedicated to his fellow student Benigni. Both composers used the clarinet extensively in their operas, writing for such players as Cavallini, Labanchi, Liverani and Sebastiani. The greatest of these, Ernesto Cavallini (1807–74), inspired Verdi to write the magnificent solo and cadenza in *La forza del destino* (1862).

Glinka was much influenced by Donizetti when he was in Italy during the 1830s. It was at this time that he wrote the *Trio pathétique*, choosing the clarinettist Mossitro and bassoonist Conti to première it with him at Milan's La Scala. His initiation into music had been dramatic and occurred when, at the age of ten, he heard the Quartet Op. 2 (1812) by the Finnish clarinettist Bernhard Crusell (1775–1838). He wrote of the occasion: 'This music produced an incomprehensible, new, and delightful impression on me. Thereafter I remained for the whole day in a sort of feverish condition ... indeed, from that time I passionately loved music.'

Niels Gade had a particular liking for the clarinet, playing often with his compatriots Mozart Petersen (1817–74) and Carl Skjerne (1854–1927). His *Fantasiestücke* Op. 43 (1864) are dedicated to Petersen, as are *Drei Phantasiestücke* Op. 19 by Gade's pupil, August Winding. The *Fantasistykke* (*c*. 1885) by Carl Nielsen was written for Hans Marius Hansen. Nielsen created the clarinet part of his wind quintet (1922) specially for Aage Oxenvad (1884–1944) and went on to dedicate his formidable Concerto Op. 57 (1928) to him. Oxenvad was also dedicatee of *Tema med Variationer* Op. 14 by Nielsen's pupil, Jørgen Bentzon.

Brahms first heard Richard Mühlfeld (1856–1907) as a member of the orchestra at the ducal court of Meiningen in the spring of 1891. He had composed nothing for almost a year but was so stimulated by Mühlfeld's playing that he began again and during the summer months, in quick succession, wrote the Trio Op. 114 and the Quintet Op. 115. An extraordinarily close relationship developed between the two musicians and after Brahms composed the two Sonatas Op. 120 in 1894 they undertook a number of concert tours together (Fig. 5.1).

Mühlfeld inspired other composers besides Brahms, and the following were also written for him: Waldemar von Baussnern's *Serenade* (1898); Gustav Jenner's Sonata Op. 5 (1899); Theodor Verhey's Concerto Op. 47 (1900); Carl Reinecke's *Introduzione ed Allegro appasionata* Op. 256 (1901). Verhey also wrote *Vier Charakterstücke* Op. 3 (1880) for W. A. van Erp. Reinecke, as conductor of the Leipzig Gewandhaus Orchestra, had a number of fine players on his doorstep and one of these, Edmund Heyneck, gave the first performance of his Trio Op. 264 (1903). Almost simultaneous first performances of the Trio Op. 274 (1906) were given by Oskar Schubert (1849–1933) in Leipzig and Herman Lange in Dresden.

With the beginning of the twentieth century came important works from three more of Germany's major composers – Bruch, Reger and Hindemith. It was Max Bruch's clarinettist son Felix (named after Mendelssohn) who prompted him to write the *Acht Stücke* Op. 83 (1908–9) and the Concerto for clarinet and viola Op. 88 (1911). The Double Concerto was lost, then found again after the composer's death,

Figure 5.1   Richard Mühlfeld with Johannes Brahms, Berchtesgaden, 1894

and given its first performance in 1940 by Alfred Burkner with Reinhard Wolf (viola) and the Berlin Philharmonic Orchestra.

Reger wrote his two Sonatas Op. 49 (1900) after hearing his teacher in Weiden, Adalbert Lindner, and the local clarinettist, Johann Kürmeyer, perform Brahms's F minor Sonata. He dedicated the first sonata and a trio (now lost) to Kürmeyer; the second is for Karl Wagner, with whom he premièred both sonatas in 1902. Reger premièred his Sonata Op. 107 (1908) with Julius Winkler of Darmstadt in 1909. The Quintet Op. 146 (1915) is dedicated to Karl Wendling, leader of the string quartet bearing his name. The Wendling Quartet had played often with Mühlfeld and after the latter's death searched long for a worthy successor; they found him in the Stuttgart clarinettist Philipp Dreisbach (1891–1980), who gave the first performance of Reger's Quintet with them in 1916.

It was a performance of Brahms's Quintet by Dreisbach with the Amar Quartet that inspired its viola player Hindemith to write his Quintet Op. 30 in 1923. He dedicated it to Dreisbach, who premièred it with the Amars in the same year. Composer and clarinettist became close friends, calling each other 'Paulamit' and 'Kreizbach'. It is probable that Hindemith also had Dreisbach in mind for the Quartet (1930) and Sonata (1939). Franz Schmidt's quintets of 1932 and 1938 show the marked influence of Reger, performances by the Viennese clarinettist Leopold Wlach (1902–56) still being especially remembered. Wlach inspired Schmidt's pupil Alfred Uhl to write the following for him: *Kleines Konzert* (1937); 48 *Etüden* (1938); *Divertimento* (1942); *Konzertante Sinfonie* (1943).

The clarinet in England

Whilst Reger's works became popular in Germany, it was those of Brahms that took hold in England. Brahms refused to cross the English Channel, but Mühlfeld came many times, giving thirty-two concerts in London besides many in the provinces. On his first appearance, at the Monday Pops of 28 March 1892, a covey of important musicians including Grove, Parry and Stanford went to hear him perform the Brahms Quintet. Grove proclaimed the work 'a beauty', but Bernard Shaw poured scorn on it. Stanford, after a performance of the Quintet early in 1895 at the Royal College of Music, challenged the students in his composition class to write a similar work. Coleridge-Taylor rose to the occasion with his Quintet Op. 10 and this was performed later that year by none other than Mühlfeld. Stanford's disappointment can be imagined when his Concerto Op. 80 of 1902 was never played by Mühlfeld, its dedicatee; in a rage he scratched out his name from the manuscript. The earliest of Stanford's works for the clarinet, the three *Intermezzi* Op. 13 (*c.* 1880), were written for Canon Francis Galpin, a keen amateur clarinettist and founder of the Society which bears his name.

Two years before writing his quintet, Coleridge-Taylor had composed the first movement of a sonata (unpublished), which he performed with fellow student Charles Draper (1869–1952). Draper was taught by Henry Lazarus (1815–95), to whom in the 1860s George Macfarren dedicated his obbligato songs 'A Widow Bird' and 'Pack Clouds Away'. It was Draper who gave the first performance of Stanford's concerto in 1903. Stanford then dedicated his Sonata Op. 129 (1912) jointly to Draper and to the amateur clarinettist Oscar Street. Elgar had a great admiration for Draper's playing and inscribed his name beside all major solos in his scores. Arthur Bliss too was an admirer and dedicated the *Two Nursery Rhymes* Op. 20 (1921) to him.

In his youth John Ireland heard Mühlfeld play the Brahms sonatas and loved them. He was horrified at Joachim's adaptations for the viola and when he came to write his *Fantasy-Sonata* (1943), made sure that it was unplayable on that instrument. *Fantasy-Sonata* is dedicated to Frederick Thurston (1901–53), who gave many early performances of the work with the composer. Thurston's influence on English composers was considerable, as will be seen from the following dedications: Alan Rawsthorne's Concerto (1936); Elisabeth Lutyens's *Five Little Pieces* Op. 14 (1945); Elizabeth Maconchy's Concertino No. 1 (1945); Malcolm Arnold's Concerto No. 1, Op. 80 (1948); Herbert Howells's Sonata (1949). He gave the first performance of Bliss's Quintet Op. 50 (1931) and also of Gerald Finzi's Concerto Op. 31 (1949), which is dedicated to his pupil Pauline Juler.

In 1956 Benjamin Frankel composed his Quintet Op. 28 in memory of Thurston, dedicating it to Thurston's wife and pupil Thea King. She is also the dedicatee of Arnold Cooke's Sonata (1959) and Maconchy's *Fantasia* (1980). Cooke dedicated his Quintet (1962) to Gervase de Peyer, for whom the following were also written: Alun Hoddinott's Concerto Op. 3 (1950) and Sonata Op. 50 (1967); Maconchy's Quintet (1963); Thea Musgrave's Concerto (1967). Thea Musgrave has also written an *Autumn Sonata* (1993) for bass clarinet (for Victoria Soames), as well as *Pierrot* (1986) for the American Verdehr Trio, who have commissioned more than fifty works for clarinet, violin and piano.

Other areas of influence

Smetana had the playing of Julius Písařovic (1811–81) in mind when writing for the clarinet, especially the important part in *Má vlast* (1880). Písařovic, dedicatee of obbligato songs 'Nevesta Predouci' and 'Salasnice' by his countryman František Škroup, was one of a long line of fine teachers beginning with Václav Farník (1765–1838) and descending through to Milan Kostohryz (*b*. 1911) and Jiří Kratochvíl (*b*. 1924) of today. Both the latter have exerted a strong influence on contemporary Czech composition, as players of the basset horn and of the quarter-tone clarinet. Kostohryz is dedicatee of Miroslav Krejčí's Concerto Op. 76 (1949) as well as the following by Josef Páleníček: Sonata, Op. 1 (1936); *Little Suite* (1943); Concertino (1957). Kratochvíl is dedicatee of Oldřich Flosman's popular *Brigands' Sonatina* Op. 16 (1952).

It was through his teacher Artur Holás (1886–1945), who was the first to play a quarter-tone clarinet, that Kostohryz took up the instrument. His playing on it inspired Alois Hába, director of a department of microtonal music at the Prague Conservatoire, to write the following for him: *Phantasy* Op. 22 (1943); *Suite* Op. 55 (1944); Sonata Op. 78 (1952). Hába later formed a close friendship with the bass clarinettist Josef Horák (*b*. 1931), writing for him the Suites Op. 96 (1964) and Op. 69a (1966). When Horák teamed up with Emma Kovárnová to form the *Due Boemi di Praga*, Hába wrote *Fantazie* Op. 34a (1967) and *Suite* Op. 100 (1969) for them (Fig. 5.2). Horák has had a very considerable impact on bass clarinet composition and is responsible for adding some 600 works to the repertoire.

5.2   Alois Hába with Josef Horák and Emma Kovárnová, Prague, 1971

In Chapter 4 we noted the practice of the Paris Conservatoire (since 1897) of commissioning a work for the annual contests. These pieces are conditionally dedicated to the serving professor, whose style undoubtedly influences the composer. The most significant work, Debussy's *Première rapsodie* (1910), is dedicated to Prospère Mimart (1859–1928), together with the accompanying sight-reading test, *Petite pièce*. Mimart's predecessors in the professorship were his own teacher Cyrille Rose (1830–1902) and Charles Turban (1845–1905), who both studied with Klosé. Amongst test pieces dedicated to Rose are Widor's *Introduction et Rondo* Op. 72 (1898) and Augusta Holmès's *Fantaisie* (1900). Turban is dedicatee of Reynaldo Hahn's *Sarabande et Thème varié* (1903) and Arthur Coquard's *Mélodie et Scherzetto* Op. 68 (1904). He is also dedicatee of Théodore Gouvy's Sonata Op. 67 (1880) and Gabriel Pierné's *Canzonetta* Op. 19, which were not written for the Conservatoire.

In 1887 Turban was taken by Saint-Saëns to St Petersburg, where he gave the first performance of the composer's *Caprice* Op. 79, along with Taffanel (flute) and Gillet (oboe). Saint-Saëns had written *Tarantelle* Op. 6 as early as 1851 for the flautist Vincent Dorus and the clarinettist Adolphe Leroy (1827–1880), Rose's predecessor at the Conservatoire. Towards the very end of his life, in 1921, he wrote the Sonata Op. 167 for Auguste Périer (1883–1947), a pupil of Turban. Périer, who was professor from 1919 until his death, had no fewer than fifteen test pieces dedicated to him.

An amateur clarinettist-philanthropist who has never been given his due is Werner Reinhart (1884–1931) of Winterthur. The following works were written for him: Honegger's *Sonatine* (1921–2); Krenek's *Kleine Suite* Op. 28 (1924); Schoeck's Sonata Op. 41 (1927–8) for bass clarinet and piano; Adolf Busch's Suite for solo bass clarinet. But most importantly, Reinhart gave financial backing to the original production of the seven-instrument version of Stravinsky's *Histoire du soldat* (1918). In return for this generosity, Stravinsky dedicated the *Three Pieces* (1919) to him. When writing the latter, Stravinsky is said to have been influenced by jazz improvisations of Sidney Bechet, whom he had heard in Lausanne and London the previous year. In 1945 he wrote *Ebony Concerto* for band-leader Woody Herman (1913–87). It was the Italian clarinettist Edmondo Allegra who, at Lausanne in 1919, gave the first performance of *Three Pieces*, as well as the three-instrument version of *L'histoire du soldat*. Allegra is the dedicatee of Busoni's Concertino Op. 48 (1918) and also the *Elégie* (1920), which was written in London and bears the inscription 'Souvenir de Londres' on the manuscript.

The Benny Goodman phenomenon

One of the earliest works to combine jazz with the classical idiom was Gershwin's *Rhapsody in Blue* (1924). The opening glissando – not in Gershwin's original score but interpolated as a joke by Paul White-man's clarinettist Ross Gorman – made the composer famous overnight. This glissando is not every classical player's cup of tea, and indeed proved fatal to Baltimore's principal clarinet, Georges Grisez (1884–1946), who died on stage after performing it. To jazzman Benny Goodman (1909–86) it held no terrors and the story goes that, on walking into NBC studios one day in 1942 to record with his group and finding the stage set for a rehearsal of *Rhapsody*, he demanded of the doorman: 'How can they possibly do that without me?' Word spread and he was engaged by Toscanini. Goodman has had a profound influence on twentieth-century classical music for the clarinet through commissions offered to leading composers of the day. He had had a classical training himself before entering the world of jazz and when, having sat atop that world for some time, he gave his first commission, he was already a millionaire.

That first commission was to Bartók and resulted in *Contrasts* (1938) which Goodman premièred with Szigeti and Egon Petri at Carnegie Hall in 1939. Early in 1941 he decided he wanted a concerto and approached Britten, Hindemith (Fig. 5.3) and Milhaud, all then living in America. Britten made sketches for a first movement but then returned to England; his manuscripts were impounded at the time by US Customs and even when they were returned to him he did not

5.3 Benny Goodman with Paul Hindemith, 1947

complete the work. Hindemith accepted a commission, but during the summer months Goodman became alarmed at Germany's increasing involvement in war and backed off. In desperation, Goodman requested a concerto from Milhaud in the autumn of 1941, to be written quickly for a tour he was to undertake in the New Year. Milhaud disliked the rush and became disgusted with Goodman's haggling over the fee;

although he did produce the concerto on time, the exercise went sour and Goodman never played it. Milhaud had better luck with his *Sonatine* Op. 100 (1927), which he wrote for Louis Cahuzac (1880–1960) and the Paris Conservatoire test piece *Duo Concertant* Op. 351 (1956), which is for Ulysse Delécluse. Hindemith's concerto was eventually written in 1947.

In 1946 both Benny Goodman and Woody Herman requested a concerto from Copland. The composer jibbed at two, opted for Goodman and completed his concerto the following year. Malcolm Arnold wrote his Concerto No. 2, Op. 115, for Goodman in 1974 and the clarinettist came to England two years later to perform it under the composer's baton. Goodman's friend Morton Gould wrote *Derivations* (1954) and *Benny's Gig* (1979) for him. Benny died at home, clarinet in hand, a Brahms sonata on the music stand before him.

Contemporary influences

Works for solo clarinet have fared well in the twentieth century, with Stravinsky's *Three Pieces* of 1919 leading the way. Germaine Taille-ferre wrote her serialist Sonata for Henri Dionet of the Paris Opéra in 1958. Then came Boulez's monumental *Domaines* (1968) for Hans Deinzer (*b.* 1934), a pupil of Dreisbach; this work, requiring the performer to perambulate between music stands (see further, page 167), was one of the earliest to use harmonics on the clarinet, a technique first demonstrated by Hans-Rudolf Stalder (*b.* 1930) in compositions by Hans-Ulrich Lehmann. A further dedication to Deinzer is Isang Yun's *Riul* (1968) for clarinet and piano.

Yun wrote a concerto (1981) for Eduard Brunner (*b.* 1939) and a solo bass clarinet *Monolog* (1983) for Harry Sparnaay (*b.* 1944). Sparnaay has had nearly 300 bass clarinet works written for him (see also page 168), one of the most important of which is Berio's *Chemins IIc* (1972). England's Peter Maxwell Davies wrote *The Seven Brightnesses* (1975) for solo clarinet for Alan Hacker (*b.* 1938), a pioneer in multiple sounds during the 1960s and 1970s. Other works for Hacker are Maxwell Davies's *Hymnos* (1967) and *Stedman Doubles* (1968), Harrison Birtwistle's *Ring a Dumb Carillon* (1965), *Verses* (1965), *Four Interludes from a Tragedy* (1969), *Linoi* (1969) and *Melancolia I* (1976).

New York's Stanley Drucker (*b.* 1929) has inspired an innovative concerto (1977) from John Corigliano, and Mitchell Lurie (*b.* 1922) commissioned *Time Pieces* (1984) from Robert Muczynski, which has proved exceptionally popular. Two American players to have a significant impact overseas are Richard Stoltzman (*b.* 1942) and Suzanne Stephens (*b.* 1946). Stoltzman inspired Japan's foremost composer Toru Takemitsu to write *Waves* (1976) and a concerto (1991–2) for him. Suzanne Stephens's collaboration with Karlheinz

5.4   Suzanne Stephens with Karlheinz Stockhausen, London, 1985

Stockhausen is one of the most fruitful of all time between a particular clarinettist and composer (Fig. 5.4). Stockhausen has written the following for her: *Herbstmusik* (1974); *Harlekin* (1975); *Der kleine Harlekin* (1975), *Amour* (1976); *In Freundschaft* (1977); the bass clarinet part in *Sirius* (1977); the monumental basset horn part in *Licht: die sieben Tage der Woche* (1977–); *Traumformel* (1981); *Tierkreis* (1981). Their collaboration continues today.

Suggested further reading

Andersson, O., 'Bernhard Henrik Crusell', *Finsk Tidskrift* (Helsinki, 1926)

Baron, S., *Benny: King of Swing* (New York, 1979)

'Bernhard Crusell: Tonsättare Klarinettvirtuos', *Kungl. Musikaliska Akademiens* (Stockholm, 1977)

Dahlström, F., *Bernhard Henrik Crusell* (Helsinki, 1976)

Dazeley, G., 'De clarinettist van Mozart', *Symphonia* No. 17 (Hilversum, 1934)

Draper, A., 'A musical family: the Welsh connection', *The Guild for the Promotion of Welsh Music* , 7 (Cardiff, 1985)

Eborhardt, II., 'Johann Simon Hermstedt', *Mitteilungen des Vereins für deutsche Geschichte und Altertumskunde in Sondershausen*, vol. 10 (Sondershausen, 1940)

Hess, E., 'Anton Stadler's "Musik Plan"', *Mozart-Jahrbuch* (1962), pp. 37–54

Kroll, O., 'H. J. Baermann', *Musik im Zeit bewusstsein*, 7 (Berlin, 1934)

Lewald, A., 'Heinrich Baermann', *Der Freimüthige*, No. 162 (Berlin, 1834); *Panorama von München* (Stuttgart, 1840)

Mühlfeld, C., *Die herzogliche Hofkapelle in Meiningen* (Meiningen, 1910)

Pisarowitz, K. M., ' "Müasst ma nix in übel aufnehma ..."', Beitragsversuche zu einer Gebrüder-Stadler-Biographie', *Mitteilungen der Internationalen Stiftung Mozarteum*, 19 (1971), pp. 29–33

Poulin, P. L., 'A report on new information regarding Stadler's concert tour of Europe and two early examples of the basset clarinet', *Mozart-Jahrbuch* (1991), pp. 946–55

Snavely, J., 'The Goodman commissions', *Clarinet & Saxophone*, 19/3, (1994), pp. 19–22; 19/4 (1994), pp. 12–13

Weston, P., *Clarinet Virtuosi of the Past* (London, 1971)
   Clarinet Virtuosi of Today (Baldock, 1989)
   More Clarinet Virtuosi of the Past (London, 1977)

Youngs, L., *Jean Xavier Lefèvre* (Ann Arbor, 1970)

6 The mechanics of playing the clarinet

ANTONY PAY

Introduction

I was given my first clarinet by my parents as a Christmas present, when I was nine years old. I remember taking it out of its case, and putting it together for the first time. The smell of the second-hand instrument was a particular delight – a sort of musty, oiled-wood smell, which went well with the sound I imagined it should have. We passed it around the family, everyone taking turns to try to get a tune out of it, and I was soon pleased to be able to do better than the others. It was mine, and I fell in love with it.

When I went to my very first teacher, Wilfred Kealey, he started to talk to me about music, and suggested ways of thinking which weren't directly related to the instrument, or even to the details of what I myself did. One thing which stuck in my mind was that I should imagine the clarinet sound as a smooth, round tube, which should begin deep inside me and stretch out through, and beyond, the bell of the instrument. It was my first encounter with a playing metaphor.

When we begin to play, we do think of the clarinet very much as an object – a very special object, perhaps, but nevertheless an object. It is an object that we must try to persuade to do what we want it to, and which often seems to resist us. So we are in the business of *doing* the right *something* to it in order to play well.

As we progress as players, though, our relationship with this object changes. We are more aware of the results we obtain than we are of the instrument itself. Our teachers, if they are as wise as mine was, will encourage us to start to think beyond the clarinet, and beyond ourselves, too, as we overcome the problems. They will try to have us be musicians who happen also to be clarinet players, perhaps by giving us metaphors like the one for clarinet sound I just described. In general, books about the clarinet do not talk about such metaphors a great deal, though presenting them is, I think, one of the major contributions that teachers make to their students. In a way, these metaphors are the best we can do in the direction of describing the mechanics of that complicated system, clarinet plus player. I intend to explore them more fully in a later publication.

In this chapter I will use the 'tube of sound' as a sort of reference. It divides up naturally into a number of bits, beginning with the abdomen–diaphragm system, proceeding to the space inside the mouth and throat, then the embouchure and finally the physical instrument itself. I want to look at some aspects of each of these bits in turn. Because anything like a complete treatment would take up far too much space, I have tried to choose whenever possible a point of view a little out of the ordinary, in order not to duplicate the standard wisdom.

Although there seems to be a sequence, in the sense that the later bits wouldn't work without the earlier ones, it is a mistake to think that it is a sequence like an assembly line, in which some product undergoes independent processes at a number of different points and emerges complete at the end. When we play a note, all the bits are interacting with each other in a complicated way, so we shall need to remember that simply considering them in order may be misleading. This is particularly true when we talk about the sound of the clarinet.

Abdomen and diaphragm: support

We do not have direct physical experience of our diaphragm, the muscle particularly involved in respiration. Anatomists tell us this is because no sensory nerves run from the diaphragm to the brain, so we do not know when we are using it except by the things it does; the muscle itself cannot feel tired to us, for example. This fact can be a source of confusion to a player.

Some teachers add to this confusion by how they talk about the diaphragm. The central fact is that the diaphragm is a muscle that can only exert force downwards, to draw air into the lungs. It is of course pushed up by the abdominal muscles when we blow the instrument, and perhaps this is what teachers mean when they speak of 'playing from the diaphragm'. But this is not the same as using your diaphragm as a muscle in order to blow, which is a physical impossibility.

Because we cannot feel our diaphragm, there is an unexpected aspect of breathing and blowing that many players do not notice. A little thought is required to understand it fully, but it is so fundamental to excellent and flexible playing that the effort is worthwhile.

If I bend my arm, and then flex it like a body-builder showing off his muscles, I am flexing both of the opposing pair of muscles called the biceps and triceps. If I check that my arm is motionless, and I can feel that my biceps are flexed, I know that my triceps must be too. (The triceps are the ones on the back of the upper arm.) I would know this even if I couldn't feel or see my triceps. But this is exactly the situation with the opposition abdomen–diaphragm. If my airway is open and no air is going in or out, and my abdominal muscles are flexed, I know that my diaphragm must also be flexed. Indeed, this is the only way I can know it! After all, the diaphragm is inside, so I can't see it, and I can't feel it directly, as we have said.

To play on top of this opposition is like bending and unbending my arm with both muscles flexed. Clearly we can do this, if the muscles are not unduly flexed. In other parts of our lives, too, we often find it an advantage to have both parts of a muscular opposition operating together – waiting for the serve at tennis or carefully colouring in a picture are contrasted examples.

The unusual part of the experience of playing on top of the abdomen–diaphragm opposition, and the one that I want to bring out, is that when you play in this way you can make a crescendo, and perhaps even more clearly, a diminuendo, without anything else at all happening in your experience. You imagine a diminuendo – hey presto, a diminuendo. You want a slower diminuendo? – no problem. I don't just mean that the process of doing it has become subconscious. When we drive a car, say, our actions are mostly automatic, though we can become aware of them by paying attention. No, here I mean that you can't call up *any* physical experience corresponding to the change in dynamic. It all stays the same. Perhaps your mouth shape or your embouchure may alter subtly to control the intonation. But the effort of the abdominal muscles remains constant, even as we reach the silence at the end of a long diminuendo. (If you find this difficult to achieve, try blowing more strongly as you get quieter.)

The explanation, of course, is that the diaphragm is resisting the abdominal muscles (which remain at constant tension) to a varying degree. But that is inaccessible to experience. So our only feedback is to listen to the result, and thus we establish a direct link with our own sound.

This explains how passage-work becomes even by itself, if we listen to it, how we can show shorter phrases without interfering with the longer lines, or interject a sudden *sforzando*, and why we can play fast dotted rhythms seemingly without effort. Our diaphragm learns what it needs to do by itself, if we *support* – and here's the magic word! People use this word differently. Doesn't it help to know it means the exact opposite of blowing? Or rather that it is an opposition or complement to blowing – part of a magic technique that works without conscious intervention? Isn't that wonderful?

It is important not to overdo support – it can lead to tense playing. (Imagine going through daily life with your muscles flexed like a body-builder!) Sometimes we play almost entirely without support. This often has a light quality in low dynamics, suitable for short, floaty phrases, and a grand, gestural quality when loud. We have to do what is appropriate to the music.

Something to try: in medium-speed articulation (like Beethoven's Fifth Symphony: repeated *pianissimo* A's in the clarinet register) – where it is often difficult to guarantee an even response – support, and then ask your diaphragm to help! The quality of this 'request' is important. I don't mean you actually do anything – in fact, the opposite. Imagine writing your request on a small piece of paper and swallowing it! The idea is to give up trying to control it, and simply to listen.

Mouth and tongue – sound and nuance

One of the consequences of thinking of the sound of the clarinet as a smooth tube passing down the instrument may be that we are led always to associate a strong sound with a strong flow of air. This association, whilst useful in some ways, can create problems. We can begin to want the experience of pushing lots of air through the instrument in loud passages, and perhaps start to use reeds that are too stiff. A more useful metaphor is to think of the tube of air vibrating rather like the string on a cello.

The fact is that the sound of the instrument is made by the vibrations of the air column; and the air is already inside the instrument – we don't have to put it there. Some extra air obviously does pass down the instrument, but this is incidental. If the reed's motion were to be driven by some other means than blowing, we would still obtain a sound from the tube.

If we think about the matter in this way, we can see that we may indeed on some occasions be putting more air down the instrument than we need. It is not always the case that a large quantity of air is necessary to produce the most powerful, effective or resonant sound. It *is* required to have the most efficient coupling possible between the reed and the air-tube, and to allow the instrument and the reed to vibrate together. To succeed in this requires that there is sufficient air pressure to set the reed vibrating, and will also certainly have to do with precise details of the embouchure. The idea of the delicate control of a freely vibrating object (the reed), already co-operating with the resonance of the vibrating air inside the instrument, is a pleasing one, and it is also a mental image almost guaranteed to have the effect of avoiding an unduly tight or restrictive embouchure.

The shape of the inside of our mouth is not often thought of as having a strong effect on the sound of the clarinet. But though pressure waves inside the mouth are not audible in themselves, they clearly have some effect on how the reed behaves, just like the waves in the instrument, and therefore they indirectly make a contribution to the sound of the clarinet. Strong evidence in this direction is that in special circumstances we can completely change the 'normal' behaviour of the clarinet: simply by altering the position of the tongue we can glissando down from the one-thumb plus register key c''' through a sixth or more. Mouth shapes control intonation in other parts of the instrument too, provided the reed is sufficiently responsive.

We have available already a highly developed vocabulary for characterising different mouth shapes: the vowels we use in speech, and the different tones of voice, including whispering, with which we habitually characterise it. Experimenting with these different vowels, it will be found, actually does yield a subtle variation in sound quality on the instrument. Looked at in this way, the 'traditional' instruction to open the throat may add up to nothing more than the instruction not to whisper. This is of course fine unless 'whispering' is what is musically called for; which, one has to say, it quite often is. (Try it!)

Consider further the analogy with speech. We habitually place a tremendous variety of delicate emphases on the syllables of the words we utter. On the other hand, much of the traditional study of an instrument is devoted to the discipline of producing a consistently even sound in all registers, and between notes. Now, whilst it is true that a variation in something can be meaningful only in the context of it being possible for that something to remain unchanged, we seldom need to play passages completely evenly, just as we very seldom speak completely evenly. One of the characteristics of excellent playing is that the player has control of the microstructure of the variation in timbre or dynamic between notes. This control is what makes evident the organisation of the notes into groups. It may not be perceived directly by the listener, who may simply think of it as 'good rhythm', 'brilliance' or 'eloquence' even in a running passage that seems even.

For example, a part of what is required to play the second movement of Stravinsky's *Three Pieces for Clarinet* is to make the first semiquaver passage both phrased as marked (by the slurs) and grouped as marked (by the beaming, in threes). To do this naturally is made a little awkward by the leaps involved, but even in the easy bits it can be elusive to show the threes without labouring the point. It is clear that we must show them, too, because a little later some of the notes recur in a different grouping, and an audible difference between the two structures must therefore be intended.

But almost any semiquaver passage needs to be structured in some way. Notes are not all of equal importance, and although it is a matter for a performer to determine on any particular occasion exactly where what we might call the resonances of the passage need to fall, some such hierarchy is always established. When we have established it, we might say that we understand the passage better.

What we want is the general ability to group the notes in the same natural way that we group syllables into words in speech; which is to say, not obviously but nevertheless intelligibly. A good move may well be to think of some words that we can imagine go with the passage, and check that our playing has the same character. This trick has a long pedigree, and I for one would like to see and hear it more used. When it is successful, it puts us in a much better position to articulate whatever understanding of a passage we may possess.

Of course, the clarinet differs from the spoken voice: it may 'fight back' when we want it to do something. A note that we want to be resonant for musical reasons may, on the instrument, be one of the weakest; and the opposite also occurs, perhaps to our even greater discomfiture. But as I said earlier, we are not dealing just with a clarinet. We ourselves are a part of the system, clarinet plus player, and we can learn to overcome the difficulty – even when we play on period instruments, which have more uneven scales. Sometimes, of course, we are fortunate here, and can use the 'deficiency' of the instrument to expressive effect.

The following simple exercise (Fig. 6.1) helps us in the direction of being able to emulate on the instrument the ability we have, when we speak, unconsciously to control dynamic and timbral variation. The idea is that the exercise is a sort of template that we use to create our own studies from the piece of music we are playing. There are actually two exercises of which I have shown only one, but how to construct the other will become obvious, and doing so is left to the reader. There is no conventional staff, because the three notes are intended to be *any* three notes, in ascending order. Neither is there a tempo indication, because we want to be able to use it in an intelligent way, at varying tempi according to our needs. Semiquaver equals semiquaver throughout.

To apply the exercise, we choose three consecutive notes of the passage and put them in ascending order. We may choose these three notes because they have different responses, or because one or more of them needs to be stressed, or simply because they feel or sound awkward as we play them.

As we perform the exercise, we listen with the intention of having the result be both even and modulated. (If we use the trick of using words to help us imagine this, we may come up with something rather like *millimetre–millimetre–millimetre–millimetre–metronome–metronome–metronome–micro–* repeated over and over again. You are encouraged to write your own libretto!) The important point is to achieve an equilibrium between the long legato and the substructure, a relationship rather like that of waves to a calmish sea. Notice that in the passage the first and third notes each get their turn to be the most

Figure 6.1   Exercise for the control of dynamic and timbral variation

resonant or loudest, so we will need, as I said, to invent an analogous exercise that gives a chance to the second note.

Usually the complete passage we are studying will require only one of the various organisations of the three notes that these exercises create. In my view, though, it is almost always a good principle to study, in addition to what we ultimately want to achieve, the alternatives that lie close by. In this way the exercise has its own life, and the original passage does not seem stale when we return to it.

As we experiment, it should become apparent that there are at least two things that can change to show the substructure, these being timbre and dynamic.

The control of the first is best thought of as done by a change of resonance – I often like to imagine that prominent notes have the quality of being played on a marimbaphone, and the others on a xylophone. Doubtless we obtain such effects by making almost imperceptible movements of the mouth and tongue. The details of this are best left to be trained by our ear as in speech, especially since we want the process ultimately to be subconscious; though it is worth experimenting with the effect of making mouth shapes corresponding to different vowels to begin with. Sometimes strange vowels have strange effects (like multiphonics) – but trying new things out always tends to expand our range of possibilities.

The control of dynamic occurs via the technique of support we mentioned earlier. As before, this works best when allowed to occur.

What we are learning is to play unevenly, but in the way we want. The slightly tricky rhythm of the exercise is intentional; while what Timothy Gallwey calls 'Self One' is coping with this, we can learn the really complicated stuff despite ourselves. (See *The Inner Game of Tennis* (New York, 1974), which one top-flight violin soloist calls 'the best book about violin playing I know'. It's pretty good for clarinet players too!) There is also an important effect when we return to the passage itself. We experience a release into a less demanding environment. Exercises we create for ourselves should always have this quality of being both simpler and more complex than the passage they are designed to improve.

It is worth adding that as we play the exercise (or the passage) faster, we will do better if we are modulating a brighter basic timbre. This is because faster music needs a sound with more higher frequencies in it to sound as clear as slower music, for a given acoustic. Lower frequencies persist longer, and muddy the change from one note to the next unless the higher partials, which die faster, form a non-overlapping sequence. This is also why we find we need softer reeds in a very resonant acoustic.

Tongue – articulation

The most obvious use of the tongue is for articulation. Many players find this a difficulty and for a few it is a major obstacle. For some players at least, the problem lies in how they think about the actual physical technique of playing staccato. I want to investigate briefly the idea that by thinking about staccato in a different way we may begin to resolve the problem.

The verb 'to tongue' is a stumbling-block. This is because in common usage it can be applied to a single note (as in, 'that note is tongued'), and it carries the implication that it is something that we *do* with the tongue to begin that note. Moreover, it is sometimes suggested that the harder we tongue, the louder will be the beginning. In fact, the tongue begins the note only in the same sense that the light-switch lights the room. We do not get more light if we push it harder! Many people, though, start off by making this sort of mistake on the clarinet.

A better English word for our purposes is 'articulation'. This word is suggestive of both separating and joining. For example, we speak of the elbow as an 'articulated' joint, and use the phrase 'articulated lorry'. The word also applies naturally to a group of notes, indicating that those notes are to be separated to a greater or lesser degree whilst nevertheless remaining a group. We can say, 'this group of semiquavers is to be articulated', meaning, 'what we have to do is separate these joined-up notes'. If we imagine a series of notes that we want to be staccato, or articulated, we may think of them as represented in the diagram (Fig. 6.2).

This is a very schematic representation. The idea is that the shaded rectangles represent the sound of the semiquavers above them. The letters underneath are the usual vocalisations, with the letter *d* occurring where the tongue is on the reed and the letter *u* where it comes off, allowing the reed to vibrate.

In the conventional vocal representation of staccato, we are often asked to say the syllables *du-du-du-du-du* etc. Looking at the middle of

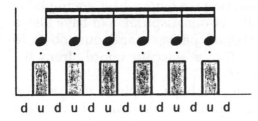

dudududududd

Figure 6.2   Schematic representation of articulation

the passage, though, there is no particular reason to group the *d* and the *u* in this way. We can just as well say the syllables *ud-ud-ud-ud-ud*, or, as I would suggest, creating a real English word, *mud-ud-ud-ud-ud* etc. We can imagine ourselves continually interrupting the word 'mud'.

The advantage of this move is twofold. Firstly, it has the effect of emphasising the unity of the passage – there is just one word 'mud' to be interrupted. Secondly, it makes clear that each individual note begins with a pure sound, created by the air pressure. There is no percussive 'clonk' made by the tongue! We do not begin each note with the tongue – the note begins when we stop stopping it.

Now, the question immediately arises: how much force does it require to stop it? Taking this question as a sort of research project, we can begin to experience the process of articulation from a diametrically opposed viewpoint to that suggested by the word 'tonguing'. You do have to experience it though – thinking about it isn't enough! (Get your clarinet out!)

First we must be sure that we really are producing a good firm sound before proceeding. Then, if we play a low E, say, it is possible to place the tongue gently on the reed without stopping the sound. The pitch of the note becomes flatter, but the reed is able to continue to vibrate even though it has a 'passenger' to carry.

It is essential to continue blowing strongly throughout the process. Some people find this difficult to do, because their tongue action is already bound up with their blowing. For them, breaking this connection is perhaps the most powerful move they can make to improve their playing, quite apart from their staccato.

By contrast, and quite strikingly, in the upper register it is impossible to touch the reed at all without immediately stopping the note. The action of the tongue in the upper register needs to be extremely light to release the note cleanly, but our experiment shows that we definitely need not worry about it being too light.

Notice that this discovery, of a difference between low and high registers, is the result of an experiment that we could not have thought of making had we not been open to the idea that the job of the tongue in 'tonguing' may not be to start the note.

Now, to reinforce this approach, imagine we have a hi-fi gramophone with a powerful amplifier and speaker at our disposal. We have also a recording that includes a loud sustained passage, and our job is to produce a loud, clear, short sound (i.e. a staccato chord) from the equipment. How would we go about it?

For my younger readers, I should perhaps explain that a hi-fi gramophone is a device for playing music encoded on a black-vinyl disc. A spiral track runs from the circumference of the disc to near the centre. Superimposed on the track are tiny wiggles which are transmitted to a diamond stylus on a pickup arm, which follows the spiral slowly from the circumference to the centre as the disc revolves; the resultant wiggles of the stylus are translated by the pickup arm into a varying electric current. This varying current is then amplified and used to drive a loudspeaker, yielding a close approximation of the music which was used to create the wiggly spiral in the first place.

If we turn up the volume control on the amplifier we can lower the stylus of the pickup arm until it is just above the part of the rotating record that contains the loud passage. At this point we can delicately lower the stylus on to the record for an instant, thereby producing the loud, abrupt chord.

Notice that there is nothing in our action that corresponds to the abruptness or the energy of the result. The powerful component of the system is the amplifier, which is operating constantly at the same level. If we were to match the intended loudness with a similarly violent action with the pickup arm, we would most likely negate the result!

The same situation obtains when we play a loud short note on the clarinet. The power comes from the pressure of our air-column, which is what causes the note to begin as the tongue stops stopping it. Admittedly it does also seem that a violent action of the tongue is being performed when we hear a *fortissimo* staccato note on the clarinet. But as we have seen from our experiment, it takes very little contact with the tongue to stop the reed, even when it is vibrating strongly. So the helpful analogy is with a control system, rather than with a power system. You can play a very loud short note with a very delicate and precise tongue action, just as, in principle, you could turn on and off even an atomic power station with your little finger.

This order of discrepancy between input and output can profitably be imagined as we play. We really need practically no contact between tongue and reed in the high register. The area of contact can be reduced almost to nothing and the effect still achieved, even in *fortissimo*. Nor is it necessary to specify exactly how the tongue moves. I find that in the higher register I tend to touch the reed with the underside of the tip of my tongue, which seems to alter shape rather than move bodily, especially in fast passages, whilst lower down the action is larger. (A student once said to me, 'But, my teacher says that's *wrong!*') Also the degree of tension in the tongue can vary. Perhaps those with a very fast staccato have succeeded in controlling the sort of oscillations that we sometimes get in flexed groups of muscles, though in general, in my experience, less rather than more tension is to be encouraged.

To conclude this very brief investigation of staccato, the following exercise may be useful. I said before that it is often advantageous to get one's attention out of the way to allow one's body to learn more fluently and naturally. If we concentrate on a difficulty other than that of articulating, our conscious minds cannot interfere.

One of the abilities we sometimes need when we play music is the ability to change between semiquavers and triplets, say, or between straight quavers and quintuplets, whilst the beat itself remains constant. This can be made into an exercise in staccato, using a metronome. We switch at random between groupings of two, three, four, five and even six to a beat, against a constant pulse. The mental difficulty of imagining the shift accurately and adjusting when we prove mistaken I have found to be an excellent context in which to develop basic articulation skills.

Embouchure

The famous French oboist Maurice Bourgue once said in a class, 'The real embouchure is in the stomach. The other is only a connection. You should take the reed as you take a forkful of food: simply.'

This is a wise remark, even on the clarinet. One of the reasons why the embouchure becomes so important to us is that we tend to give too much psychological weight to the idea of controlling the reed directly in order to produce a good basic sound. Notice that the behaviour of the reed is much less critical when we are playing what we might call 'good' notes. Here the external clarinet tube is a strong resonator, and the reed co-operates with it. So on any other notes we may well do better to try a simple embouchure to begin with and concentrate on giving the sound its warmth by choosing an appropriate mouth-resonance, opening the throat and so on. In my experience variations in the embouchure are mostly a contributory effect to nuances in the sound quality.

There are many different types of basic embouchure because there are many different types of mouthpiece, and it is evident that the strength of the reed also makes a difference. I think it is most useful to imagine the embouchure as controlling the reed by touching it almost exactly over the point where it leaves the mouthpiece facing. As we play louder or softer, the length of the part of the reed that moves away from the mouthpiece tends to change. We must compensate with our embouchure if the pitch is not to be affected. (One of the advantages of practising long notes is to render this type of compensation automatic.) Moreover, the lower lip is capable of varying degrees of firmness in itself, as well as being able to exert pressure against the reed. This is important because although the primary function of the lip is to stabilise the position of the fixed point of the reed-pendulum for a given note, there is also a damping of the reed's vibration.

The effect of such damping is to remove the very high-frequency partials in the sound. We need to do this to a certain degree because above a certain frequency, called the cutoff frequency, the vibration of the reed is not coupled to the tube. (The high frequencies are not reflected at the open holes.) The presence of too much of the resulting high-frequency 'noise' gives rise to a harsh and unpleasant sound. An important function of the embouchure is to control this harshness. However, if the area over which the lip touches the reed extends substantially beyond the fixed point, then the frequency above which the partials are removed is lower; so we get a duller sound, and actually also a slightly lower pitch. Obviously, if the lower lip muscle is flexed, it has a smaller 'footprint' on the reed (compare the area of ground contact of a fully blown-up bicycle tyre with that of a 'flat'), and so the resultant sound is richer in upper partials. We also want to be able to allow the embouchure to vary slightly, so that the sound alters moment by moment to modulate a phrase. This is another reason for the lower lip to be flexed – in this state it is capable of changing subtly. (For very special effects, of course, the lower lip can be as relaxed as required.)

By the way, a particularly good way of ensuring that the lower lip is alive (by this I mean flexed, as opposed to behaving like a bit of dead meat covering the teeth) is to think of pushing down with the top lip on the top of the mouthpiece. The desired effect is instantly achieved. Perhaps this is why double lip embouchures are reputed to produce a better clarinet sound.

The fingers

It is often said that we should try to minimise finger movements. Having seen players failing to play accurately whilst moving their fingers a lot, most of us would tend to agree. I remember designing and making a gadget out of a coathanger to encourage myself to play with my fingers closer to the keys. A length of wire ran from the barrel of the instrument to the bell, about an inch-and-a-half above the holes. Whenever my fingers moved further than this distance from the keys, they struck the wire and brought the matter to my attention. I recommended the system to my students, but found that I used it little myself.

I have since come to think that the instruction to minimise finger movement can be misguided. It is true that there are clarinettists of great ability who move their fingers only a small distance, but equally there are others just as fluent who use larger movements. Sometimes it seems as though the concentration on small finger actions in some way inhibits the expressivity of yet a third group – they may be able to play the passages, but somehow they seem to lack character, as though they are too distanced from what they are playing.

The problem is that the instruction is a negative one. Clearly, we want to avoid the desperate thrashing of fingers that we sometimes observe with inexpert players, but perhaps we can do better than the usual approach. I would like to recommend an alternative way of thinking about the situation that leads to our playing with small movements when it is really necessary, but allows us to use larger movements without deleterious effect when it is not.

If we play a one-octave ascending F major scale in the chalumeau register of the clarinet, first slowly and then quite substantially faster, a question we can ask, either of a student or of ourselves, is: supposing the second version of the scale to be, say, three times faster than the first, how many times faster do we have to move our fingers in order to play it?

Reflection shows that clearly nothing physical need move fast. All that is required is that each successive finger begin to move away from the corresponding key or hole sufficiently soon after its predecessor. In this situation, therefore, neither fast nor small finger movements are demanded. To put it technically, the high speed of the run is guaranteed if there is a high phase velocity associated with the finger movements. What is required is precision of movement. The movements themselves can be slow and large.

Of course, I have chosen an extreme case. Here, once a finger has moved it does not participate further in the run. Not all fast passages are like this, though I suspect that most players will be surprised by how large a proportion of any particular passage does turn out to be of this type. A trill is an example of the opposite extreme.

For me the important part of this is that it leads to a natural classification of the various parts of a passage of fast music as either requiring fast finger movements, or not. In general it is best to begin by regarding all of a passage as a candidate for slow finger movement, as it seems that faster movements occur more naturally in the context of slow movements than slow movements in the context of fast movements; and anyway we are likely to be erring in the opposite direction out of our natural response to the speed of the passage. We need not experience slow movement as a negative instruction if we think of it as a 'relaxing' one. Perhaps the advantage of the instruction to move slowly over the instruction to move less is that the latter can result in greater tension. Also slower movements take longer to execute, even if the run itself is still fast. One of the noticeable characteristics of expert playing is the elegance of it; there seems to be more time available to a master player than we experience. To engage with our own mastery, we mostly need to create for ourselves the illusion that we have more time.

We should always try to isolate the parts of a passage that give us difficulty. One of the traps into which we can fall is that of general-isation; as when we say, 'this passage is difficult' when it would be more accurate to say, 'I find these three notes awkward', or even better, 'I tend to play an extra note between these two', or, finally, '*that* time, I played a rather flat G natural between the A and the F'. If we know the moments that require fast finger movement, we can practise them intelligently.

It is amusing and instructive to try playing the ascending F major scale, always with slower and slower fingers, faster and faster until the notes fly out at a dizzying speed! The experience is exhilarating. Be careful to keep the dynamic strong and the sound bright even though the fingers are much more relaxed. Try following it up with selected passages from Weber, who nearly always writes so that we can play, if we wish, really fast without major difficulty (except that of being heard clearly). The result is hardly musical, but it is an indication of how easy it can feel if we let it.

As always, we need to make some remarks about the subtleties that should still be available after we have made the initial move towards slow fingers. There are some circumstances where it is advantageous to move our fingers almost fast enough for the actual closing of a hole to be audible as a sound in its own right. 'Brilliant' passage-work sometimes has this quality. It can be helpful to regard a passage as having a structure consisting of smaller movements as sub-movements of larger ones, with the larger ones slower than the smaller. (Some passages around the break, as well as those using the thumb keys in the extreme low register of the larger clarinets, respond well to this approach.) Also, although we will mostly find ourselves making the most economical movement consistent with the execution of a passage, sometimes we will also find ourselves wanting to add further move-ment, even of the fingers, in order to be congruent with the other expressive characteristics of the music. Sometimes this sort of physical expression can become exaggerated, but it is unwise to react by reducing it to an absolute minimum. Almost all expressive players indulge in some degree of movement, though with the best this stops short of being a distraction to the audience and does not interfere with their ability to play.

The instrument – sound and intonation

The clarinet as an isolated instrument is theoretically deficient from an acoustical point of view. This came as a surprise to me when I found out about it, although perhaps I should have known from experience! The matter is a bit technical, but essentially it turns out that there is a trade-off between excellence of sound and excellence of intonation. If you design a clarinet to be well in tune between the registers, by fiddling with the bore, you necessarily make the instrument less resonant and responsive. Fiddling with the bore is necessary to make the instrument in tune partly because the clarinet overblows at the twelfth, and an equal-tempered twelfth is slightly different from a natural twelfth; but mostly because the register key or speaker key alters the pitches of the notes of the upper register to a varying degree, since it cannot be in the correct position for all of them simultaneously. On most clarinets it also has to double as a tonehole for the throat B♭. When the bore is altered the instrument is less a 'clarinet' (a cylindrical tube closed at one end). The sound is correspondingly less rich. Those who want a fuller story should read *Fundamentals of Musical Acoustics* by Arthur Benade (Dover Publications, 1990, revised and corrected edition). See also Chapter 2, pages 27–30.

The lesson to be learnt here is perhaps that we are wise not to be too demanding of the instrument itself in terms of its intonation. An instrument with a good sound is more flexible with regard to intonation anyway – we may need to bend notes, but they bend more easily and the sound remains acceptable.

One small technical fact about intonation that is not widely known is that we play sharper just after we have taken a breath than we do a few seconds later. This is because the air in our lungs becomes denser as the oxygen in it is replaced by carbon dioxide. The process happens quite quickly, but it is worth waiting a second or two after breathing in at the start of the slow movement of the Schubert Octet, for example. It doesn't feel natural, but then a sharp C doesn't sound natural either. For the same reason, it's best in a long passage to avoid breathing just before a sharpish note. (Breathe before a flat one!)

It would be nice to give some survey of the various solutions to the problem of making a good clarinet, but the subject is very large and a cursory treatment would be useless. It's worth saying that the advantages and disadvantages of the French clarinet compared to the German clarinet (both in their different ways excellent) are bound to become more central to performers' choices as orchestras become more European. The current interest in playing on period instruments has also given clarinettists more courage to experiment, and anyone who has played Brahms or Wagner on a German clarinet is not going to forget the experience even if mostly his or her work is on a French instrument.

But whatever instrument we play on, it will remain true that we as players are the most powerful influence on the results we obtain. I have tried to make it clear throughout this chapter that we do best to think beyond the technicalities and towards the music. In the end we as musicians are an inextricable part, and the most important part, of anything we might want to call the 'mechanics' of playing.

7 Teaching the clarinet

PAUL HARRIS

Introduction

Today's young musician is growing up in a social and musical world considerably different from even the recent past. The methods and theories of such music educators as Carl Orff, R. Murray Schafer, John Paynter and Keith Swanwick have become widely known and assimilated (if, perhaps, unconsciously) and the more recent emergence of examinations which engage the student in original composition (as well as performing and 'listening') has produced a new generation of young musicians more creative in their thought, more emotionally mature and more vividly aware of their surroundings – they are, to use the contemporary term, more 'street-wise'. Our pupils are no longer to be seen as receptacles into which we 'drop' information – and thus we must acknowledge that the role of the teacher 'is transformed from that of musical "director" to that of pupil facilitator: stimulating, questioning, advising and helping, rather than showing or telling'.[1] We live in times of change and development, *fin-du-siècle* is a period of rethinking and innovation. It is in this spirit that we consider the various facets of clarinet teaching in the following pages.

The teacher

As instrumental teachers we are concerned with two distinct but interrelated disciplines. On the one hand, we must teach our pupils the skills necessary to play their instruments to the best of their abilities, and on the other, we must help them to develop their sense of artistry and musicianship. Drawing from students that subtle ability to communicate something of their innermost self through the medium of musical performance is simultaneously a most demanding and stimulating challenge. Without musical 'personality' performances will remain uninspired and the central message which music communicates is lost.

Learning to play a musical instrument and to perform music *at all levels* is both exacting and complex, requiring an approach that is methodical, imaginative, inspired, demanding, patient and sensitive. Such are the necessary prerequisites of the teacher. Rarely might you find *all* these attributes in one person, but a simple awareness of them is more than sufficient as a point of departure.

The lesson

The lesson constitutes the main, and often the only, point of contact with the pupil. Much care, thought and planning must therefore go into both its content and presentation. Ideally our pupils should leave their lessons feeling positive about themselves, about what they have achieved and about what they are to practise. This will arise from an approach that is challenging, absorbing, rewarding and stimulating. Anyone entering the teaching profession believing it to be an easy or second-rate option would be well advised to consider a different career! How then does one set about cultivating the ideal lesson?

The three principles: expectation – guidance – motivation

The key to presenting a successful lesson and indeed to cultivating a responsive and hard-working pupil is finding the appropriate balance between *expectation*, *guidance* and *motivation*, whilst all the time understanding the overriding necessity for communication. This balance will inevitably be different for every pupil; there is little doubt that the teacher who is sensitive to this can reasonably expect their pupils to try and give of their best. On entering the teaching room, the pupil should be greeted in a friendly and warm manner. Some discussion (whilst the pupil is putting the instrument together), be it topical, musical or perhaps connected with the pupil's academic, family or indeed social life, will serve to set up a good working rapport. Something remembered – a birthday, a recent exam taken, a visit to the dentist – will serve to indicate that you are taking an interest in them as a person. Use your own notes to remind yourself of such facts. The positive effect of taking such an interest cannot be over-emphasised. Try to establish and maintain an atmosphere of vigour; each teacher–pupil team will inevitably move at a different pace, but ensure that the forward impetus of the lesson is never lost. Once the lesson 'proper' has begun always *expect* the best. This will vary dramatically from one pupil to another, but the principle must always stand. In the first place you should expect work set for practice to have been well prepared (it's a very good idea to note in your notes, as well as the pupil's, what was set); during the lesson concentration should be maintained (though there must also be carefully timed periods of relaxation). Encourage dialogue; pupils should be made to feel that you would welcome the asking of intelligent questions or discussion of some technical or musical point. Try to get your pupil to solve musical and technical problems by steering their thoughts in the right direction rather than simply telling them what to do.

The second element of our three principles is concerned with the *guiding* of our pupils through the learning processes. In other words, what and how we actually teach. It is essential to teach methodically, moving from one point to another only when the first is fully understood. Watch carefully for a glazed look in the eye or the lapsing of concentration. Often this is not the result of boredom or lack of interest, but of a lack of understanding. Allow the mastering of, or at least the knowledge of how to master, each technical hurdle before introducing the next. As for the actual content and balance of a lesson, each teacher will have their own recipes based on experience and experimentation, individually tailored to fit the requirements of each student. Suffice to say, variety is the spice of a good lesson and there should be both consolidation of what has been recently learnt together with the introduction of new material. Bear in mind also that some pupils need a lot of teaching, whilst others need comparatively little; don't feel you have to dot all the i's and cross every t – it is important to allow your pupils a certain degree of freedom!

We can only hope that all our pupils are enthusiastic, practise efficiently and display a receptive and positive disposition throughout lessons. Only rarely is this the case on all counts. The pupil's level of *motivation*, particularly when affected by the moods of adolescence, will have its ups and downs. So can motivation be monitored and increased? There are certainly a number of factors that can be kept under careful scrutiny. Is your pupil practising regularly, efficiently and effectively? Are they showing enthusiasm for taking part in associated activities? Do they behave positively at lessons: listening and responding thoughtfully to your comments, adopting a good posture and remembering to bring their notebook and all their music? Are they undertaking any 'extra-curricular' work that you may not have set them? If the answer to the majority of these points is affirmative, then you have a well-motivated pupil. What can be done for those who are less well motivated? You, the teacher, must be enthusiastic and encouraging (though you must have it in you to put your foot down if the need arises; your pupil must sense that this is the case even if you never do!). Never underestimate the power of praise. Praise your pupils often – we all acknowledge the importance of praising the beginner every step of the way, but praise, when it is appropriate, should be no less forthcoming for the more advanced student. New material is best introduced imaginatively. The negative approach is less successful: 'You've got to learn these scales or you won't pass your exam' is not likely to inspire. There must always be variety in the work set and you should never set too much or make unrealistic technical demands.

Most students will benefit from regular musical activities – these are ideal ways of focusing and directing work and will, in most cases, act as powerful sources of motivation – concerts, examinations, festivals, participating in ensembles, wind bands, orchestras, clarinet choirs and attending music courses. Some pupils respond well to regular assess-ment – at the end of lessons you may like to give each pupil a grade (e.g. A–C) for practice (how well they have prepared set work), performance (the way they played during the lesson) and progress (since the last lesson).

Occasionally a pupil may become poorly motivated for practical or personal reasons. An instrument that is not functioning properly may well be a source of frustration – instruments should be checked and overhauled by an experienced technician on a regular basis. Your pupil may be suffering from over-zealous parents or they may be intimidated by their peers who tease them for practising rather than socialising. The best way to deal with such problems is probably to confront and discuss them – this may well provide a solution.

Towards a course of study

Unlike 'academic' subjects there is no prescribed national syllabus for the learning of musical instruments; this may be one reason why instrumental teaching often lacks structure and direction. It is so often a case of trial and error because instrumental teachers are left to create their own courses. As the new teacher sets off certain questions must be fully thought through. For example: do you base your teaching on a particular tutor or method? Should you evolve your own method? Do you structure your teaching around grade examina-tions? Whichever avenue you choose, and it will probably be a combination of these, always bear in mind the short-term objectives and the longer-term aims of your 'syllabus', and always explain them to your pupils rigorously. Young pupils need direction – aimless teaching (even if it is technically correct) will not bring forth particularly good results. So evolve your own 'syllabus' (at least in general terms) – this will develop as you experiment, experience, explore and discover and will almost certainly ensure a greater degree of success.

The pupil

In an ideal world we should always be able to choose our pupils; in reality, more often than not, we have little or no choice. It is important however to feel able to redirect unsuitable pupils to other instruments to avoid frustration and a negative experience for all concerned.

Assessing a potential pupil

There are certain fundamental questions to be answered before taking up the instrument. Are there sufficient finances? Instruments, their up-keep, reeds, music, lessons, exam and festival fees, and travelling all add up to make learning an instrument an expensive business. With the advent of the plastic C clarinet it is now possible to begin lessons at quite a tender age, but it is still important to take build, physical stamina, hand size and dental situation into account. Does the child demonstrate a sense of determination, tenacity, enthusiasm and a personality tending to the extrovert? Some gentle aural tests will indicate whether the child has a 'musical bent'. Can they sing back a note in tune? Maintain a steady pulse and clap back a simple rhythmic pattern? Having established the above it is also important to ascertain *why* the child wishes to learn. Beware if the idea is entirely parent centred.

Technique

The actual art of how you play the instrument has been analysed and written about by many great players and teachers. There are a number of different approaches to each aspect of technique, therefore the intention here is to set in motion a train of thought designed to clarify the central concepts of each of the main technical areas. These should be instilled in your pupils from the outset.

Sometimes the practice of technique needs to be almost purely mechanical, but always remember that even if you are, for example, working on a series of finger exercises or a scale pattern, they are still music, and should be treated as such.

Tone

Tone, the sound you actually make, is perhaps most fundamental to playing an instrument. No one will really want to hear a player, however fast the fingers move, if the sound is unpleasant. It is essential therefore to encourage care and attention to tone-quality from the very first lesson. As the young player develops it is important that they have a clear mental conception of a 'good' sound. This can be achieved by frequent demonstration at lessons. In addition pupils should be encouraged to purchase recordings of great players, play to each other in group lessons and attend concerts featuring the best players of the day.

The correct control of breathing and embouchure is paramount to the development of a fine tone. In terms of breathing it is clearly essential to teach the concept of support via the appropriate use of the abdominal, intercostal and diaphragmatic musculature. The use of analogy and imagery is always helpful when putting across new technical concepts to the young player. For deep inspiration, 'Suck air in slowly as though you were sucking a thick milk-shake through a straw' or 'Think what it feels like when you're really out of breath and gasping for air'. For producing the correct abdominal tension 'Hold your abdominal wall as though someone is about to punch you in the stomach'; 'Feel as though you are having to hold your trousers up without a belt'. Many of these are tried and tested, but the imaginative teacher will always be able to think of a 'fun' way of describing the necessary technical task. Ask your pupil what the perfect sound might look like – a densely filled-in shape with very clean edges would be a perceptive answer.

The embouchure is the word used to describe the formation of the lips and associated facial muscles around the mouthpiece. Its main functions are to provide an air-tight seal between the player and the instrument and form a platform for the reed. Again an analogy, this time that of an elastic band, surrounding and exerting equal pressure all round, will serve well.

Different kinds of breathing exercises and of course the playing of long notes are fundamental to developing tone. Constant reminders to avoid tension in the embouchure ('don't "bite" on the mouthpiece') and the maintenance of supported breath pressure will always be necessary.

The clarinet is a notoriously difficult instrument to play really well in tune. Careful and critical listening to foster awareness of intonation should be insisted upon from the first lesson – only in this way will the young student become sensitive to this important area. Some experimentation with different vowel shapes in the oral cavity may be useful in influencing fine tuning. An 'eee' shape will usually produce a sharper pitch than an 'aw'.[2] The use of the oral cavity may also improve the tone of the problematic throat notes by increasing resonance.

Articulation

Articulation refers to starting or separating notes. The four elements involved – breath, embouchure, fingers and tongue – are co-ordinated to control the attack, 'weight' and dynamic levels of notes. Again analogy can be useful: consider watering the garden with a hose pipe, the breath equals the water and the tongue is your thumb over the pipe. This analogy also instils the importance of maintaining continuous breath pressure throughout a tongued passage. In teaching articulation you will have to repeat time and time again that it is the air that actually produces the sound – your pupils must blow when tonguing: a lack of air pressure during the tonguing process is often the reason for an inferior tone-quality. The function of the tongue itself is to open and shut the air-stream and thus allow the breath, under pressure, into the instrument. Preparation, before the note begins, is crucial: breathing muscles and embouchure must be ready for the moment the tongue releases the air. Though there is a certain difference of opinion over the way to end a note, it is recommended that breath decay should account for most note endings except where a really short *staccatissimo* is required. Here the tongue is returned to the reed to finish the note abruptly. It is generally considered that the tip of the tongue on the tip of the reed is the most appropriate position. An alternative position may be necessary owing to the particular dental structure, and the size and shape of the player's tongue.

Different forms of articulation

The developing clarinet player has a vast number of 'colours' available to give variety and interest in performance. These are related to dynamic levels and different forms of articulation within those levels. As well as experimenting with different tongue syllables ('du', for example, instead of the more usual 'tu' will produce a more gentle attack) the player should study the style and character of the music to establish the most appropriate weight of attack and dynamic level. It is also recommended that you study books on violin technique, with special reference to bowing and articulation styles, these may well stimulate ideas for thought and experimentation.[3]

The importance of articulation in giving life to musical phrasing must also be understood. Often the 'meaning' of a phrase or 'sentence' is dependent on the way in which notes are related in patterns of separation – the matching of tonal levels and articulation styles must be a prime consideration here.

Finger technique

All clarinet players want to move their fingers with precision and velocity. If your pupils obey certain rules and practise diligently they should, in time, develop control, fluency and dexterity. The fingers should be held directly above the appropriate toneholes; finger movement should be precise, firm and economical. Fingers should be lifted and replaced with a crisp, mechanical action; in operating the various keys, economy of movement is always the essential factor. A tension-free posture is essential. Carefully devised exercises should be practised to facilitate this development. Scales and other related patterns are of course invaluable, but don't simply suggest to your pupils that the playing of scales will, *per se*, improve their technique. They must identify the technical problems, isolate particular patterns and then practise *them* carefully before working at the scale as a whole.

Musicianship

Playing musically

Learning to play a piece technically is of course only part of the learning process. Performing musically is much more difficult to define and certainly challenging to teach. Some of our pupils will probably have innate musicianship – but even if they display only very occasional glimpses of this there are many ways we can help them develop this side of their personality. In the first place we can pose questions and lines of thought for pupils to ponder: What is the piece about? When was it written? Who composed it? What do they know about the composer? What is the character of the music? What range of dynamic levels and articulations would be appropriate? Then, perhaps more important, the pupil who is involved culturally will inevitably produce more artistic results; therefore encourage your pupils to read, visit art galleries and attend concerts. Above all we must try to instil the idea that you must 'speak' through your performance – 'narrating' as if telling a story and always retaining a continual sense of direction. A truly musical performance is something very special and intimate – it must 'touch' or move the listener.

Aural training

Aural training is the basis for critical and active listening – it develops the musical ear to produce sensitivity to intonation, tone-quality and quantity and a heightened awareness of other parts when playing ensemble music. By helping pupils to spot their own mistakes it is the key to good practice.

Sight reading

The entire process of teaching would be so much easier if our pupils could read music as fluently as they do words. The major problem here is that they don't have to read music nearly as often as they do words. Additionally, you don't have to read words in time! If you can inspire your pupils to sight read every day, preferably using a metronome, considerable improvement will inevitably ensue.

Don't relegate sight reading to the last two minutes of a lesson – you might even begin lessons with it.

The beginner

The content of the first lessons is of paramount importance – if you plan nothing else, you must plan these! You must clearly set out all the fundamentals of playing, thus ensuring the development of good habits from the start. Correct posture – an upright position to allow maximum use of the lung capacity – and a lack of tension should be emphasised.

Correct embouchure, breathing and tonguing should be explained simply but accurately; after each new step ensure that your pupil fully understands what is required before proceeding to the next. By the end of the first lesson your pupil should be able to produce a neatly articulated and clear-sounding supported note. You may like to use a tutor or invent exercises and tunes of your own. If you opt for a tutor choose wisely; find one that is stimulating and challenging, avoiding those that leave little room for imagination.[4] Teach your pupil music from the earliest moment and instil a desire for perfection.

Practising

The young student needs very clear guidance on this topic otherwise practice will be nothing more than wasted time. Two fundamental rules always apply: the pupil should know exactly *what* to do and *how* to do it. A basic formula (in the absence of any other) is perhaps to use a 'reconstruction' of the lesson. Good practice, however, will result from thorough planning. The notebook is essential here – set out each week's practice details carefully. You may even suggest a way that practice might 'develop' throughout a week[5] – the importance of daily practice must always be stressed (Fig. 7.1).

Advise your pupils to practise in a relaxed, unrushed and methodical manner – total concentration is required if the session is to be of real value. It is the time for solving problems, making technical progress and *thinking* about the music. A lot of slow playing should take place with the pupil encouraged to listen critically to themselves, correcting their mistakes as they go along, just as the teacher would at a lesson. Suggest time to be taken on each topic. Ask your pupil to keep a practice diary noting aims, achievements, problems and time taken.

Repertoire

There is a vast quantity of music available – looking through any comprehensive catalogue can be a bewildering experience. Efficient teachers should visit a good music shop regularly and, by looking

Figure 7.1   Weekly practice schedule

	FIRST HALF	SECOND HALF
Technique	Long notes	Add dynamic variations
Scales	Slow practice – ensure patterns are known	Add variations of articulation, dynamics and develop fluency
Study	Isolate problem areas and practise slowly	Work at fluency
Pieces	Think about style; deal with technical problems	Develop your 'performance'

through the shelves, will gradually become familiar with and discriminate in their choice of materials. A well-balanced diet is fundamental: the tutor (see above) may be sufficient at the earliest stages. You can either opt for one of the classic methods written by the great player-teachers of the past; among these you might consider the tutors of Carl Baermann, Hyacinthe Klosé and Henry Lazarus.[6] It should be borne in mind that these were written for beginners more advanced in years than the average beginner of today. Alternatively there are a number of more modern tutors written especially for the young beginner. Soon you will need a book of studies and varied pieces encompassing different styles and periods of music. The lists are so long that it would be inappropriate to pick out particular titles – each teacher will form their own preferences. Beware though of employing a limited repertoire - this will inevitably lead to staleness and unimaginative teaching.

Performing

The intention of most young players, their teachers and parents, is to take part in various forms of music-making. There are, for example, the didactic occasions – examinations, festivals and competitions – with many coherent arguments both for and against. Of course music is not a sport, but if treated in the right spirit, with the emphasis on the preparation rather than the result, then these can be positive, stimulating and rewarding experiences.

The young player should be encouraged to perform at concerts as often as possible; it is here that all the technical 'ifs' and 'buts' must be subordinated to the communication of the music. Remember especially the importance of the composer over and above the performer. It is a regrettable characteristic of our 'street-wise' younger generation that they are often very self-orientated and liable to think of the projection of their own image rather than Mozart's!

In conclusion, the influence of the teacher is both broad and considerable:

Education is surely more than merely having 'experiences', or acquiring ... skills and facts. It has to do with developing understanding, insightfulness: qualities of mind.[7]

The importance of this profession must never be underestimated.

8 Playing historical clarinets

COLIN LAWSON

Background

Many different types of early clarinet have long been familiar from photographs in books and journals, but a number of these are now actually being used in historical performances world-wide, giving a quite new perspective to the art of clarinet playing. The expectations of the great composers in terms of sound and musical style ('performance practice') has become a lively subject for discussion, widely reflected within such periodicals as the *Galpin Society Journal* and *Early Music*. There has always been much detail which a composer did not trouble to write into his scores; he simply knew that certain conventions would be observed. Some of these conventions are no longer current, whereas others have undergone significant changes of meaning. Using a clarinet for which a particular repertoire was originally intended may well make the music sound more expressive and can make more sense of what the composer actually wrote. Is the kind of performance anticipated by Mozart in his own day valid for later generations of players? We can never really answer this question, if only because life has changed so much during the last couple of centuries. The importance of the microphone in our musical lives, coupled with the various implications of air travel, are two factors which have brought about such changes that we do not have the option to turn back the clock. Even if we could hear Anton Stadler's première of Mozart's Clarinet Concerto from 1791, we should not necessarily want to adopt all of its features, since to some degree twentieth-century taste would almost certainly continue to influence our interpretation.

As long ago as 1915 Arnold Dolmetsch remarked: 'We can no longer allow anyone to stand between us and the composer'.[1] The movement he helped to found has been well documented in Henry Haskell's *The Early Music Revival* (London, 1988), an account of the activities of various musicologists, editors, publishers, makers, collectors, curators, dealers, librarians, performers, teachers and record producers. For many years there remained a general feeling that there was no benefit in performing classical and romantic (as opposed to baroque) music on period instruments, a viewpoint expressed by Willi Apel as late as 1969 in the second edition of *The Harvard Dictionary of Music*. Some adventurous clarinettists of that time played a prominent part in disproving such a theory, notably Hans Deinzer, Alan Hacker, Piet Honingh and Hans-Rudolf Stalder. But even in 1980 the article 'Performing practice' in *The New Grove* claimed that in contrast to music written before 1750, '... there has been no severance of contact with post-Baroque music as a whole, nor with the instruments used in performing it'. Subsequent musical revelations have proved this argument untenable, as period interpretations of Mozart and Beethoven symphonies have been followed by cycles of Haydn, Mendelssohn, Schumann and even Brahms, all of which have incidentally served to fuel a growing interest in early clarinets. Furthermore, it is no accident that players of the Boehm system have tended to ignore much of the small-scale classical repertoire, whose character is arguably better suited to the lighter and less cumbersome tone of earlier clarinets. This music includes sonatas by Devienne, Lefèvre, Vanhal, Mendelssohn and Danzi, as well as solo pieces such as Stadler's *Caprices* and Donizetti's Study.

The value of a wide range of musical knowledge to complement intuition and artistry has been recognised by generations of composers and performers. Those elements of style which a composer found it unnecessary to notate will always remain for us a foreign language, but eventually we may be able to converse freely within it as musicians, and so bring a greater range of expression to our playing, rather than merely pursuing some kind of unattainable 'authenticity'. There will always be circumstances in musical history which we may well not wish to emulate – the atrocious orchestral conditions of Beethoven's Vienna, for example. On the other hand, the mere fact that in Mozart's day, detached, articulate playing was the norm is a salutary reminder that playing styles have changed out of all recognition.

Classical equipment

Naturally, clarinettists of the past played new instruments, and this in itself might be thought sufficient justification for commissioning a modern copy, rather than looking for an original. We certainly need to remind ourselves that old clarinets survive in a variety of conditions; the finest are still eminently playable, but (as noted in Chapter 2) internal bore dimensions are especially susceptible to change, and there may also be evidence of attempts to alter the instrument's pitch. Antiques can be particularly prone to cracking when subjected to the changes in atmospheric conditions associated with central heating or air travel. English clarinets survive in by far the greatest numbers, and we should be aware that in some respects they are quite distinct from their continental counterparts, for example in their relatively high pitch, often around a'=440. In his survey of eighteenth-century clarinets in European collections, David Ross found many more English clarinets for examination than from all other European countries combined.[2] The five- (and six-) keyed clarinet had an extraordinarily long time-span of service; many English specimens are nineteenth-century instruments perhaps used by bandsmen and amateur players rather than in the concert hall. It seems that this was the market for which the many instruction books were published, and the relatively high pitch (together with the scarcity of A clarinets) might support the theory of military band usage. In 1752 Quantz noted the diversity of pitches then current, but today we have opted to standardise classical pitch at a'=430, making English clarinets a difficult proposition, except for use with a keyboard tuned to modern pitch. Other characteristic features are their long-tenon mouthpiece and a 'waisted' barrel shape, quite unlike continental models. Furthermore, when a sixth key is present, it is a long R1 trill key for a'-b', rather than the L4 $c\sharp'/g\sharp''$ usually found elsewhere. David Ross observed that the relatively small amount of undercutting contributed to the lighter timbre of English clarinets, and in *The New Grove* Nicholas Shackleton has remarked that English instruments of the late eighteenth century were probably tonally similar to continental instruments of two or more decades earlier.

The most likely sources for acquiring an original instrument tend to be auction houses and dealers. Some idea of auction prices can be gleaned from the pages of *Early Music*, whose columns report regularly on sales and their catalogues. Old instruments are sometimes not in playing condition for minor reasons (such as leaking pads), though even small structural damage may detract from an instrument's value. Furthermore, a clarinet's musical potential may be evident only after some months' playing. Dealers have the contacts to discover instruments which the individual might not otherwise encounter, though it is still true that interesting old clarinets continue to surface in some unlikely places. Antiques have a special value for the amount of historical information they can impart; whereas clarinets by the very best makers tend to inspire replicas, there are sometimes originals for sale by lesser-known manufacturers which turn out well. An original clarinet may also have an investment value with which a copy can never compete, simply because of the laws of supply and demand.

The opportunity to commission a modern replica of a specific historical clarinet is a relatively recent development, and nowadays some of the best but rare French, German and Austrian instruments are being copied by makers of various nationalities. Thus the player is in a position to choose both make and model. As John Solum has suggested

in relation to the flute, the greatest antiques may have tonal super-
iorities to the best modern replicas, but the degree of difference is not
as much as generally exists between old and new stringed instruments.[3] A greater aesthetic danger is rather that relatively few historical
clarinets are being copied in relation to the rapidly increasing number
of players, implying a standardisation which originally did not exist.
However, the opportunity to work with a maker on an instrument is
the kind of privilege which can rarely be obtained in other areas of life.
In this context, the design of the clarinet to be copied needs discussion
– in particular the relationship of the proposed copy to the original.

As the various designs of modern Boehm readily prove, the tuning of
any clarinet is something of a compromise, each of the twelfths having
its own special problems, with bore size and undercutting of holes
varying from one design to the next (see pages 28–30 and 121). Playing
early clarinets inevitably involves the performer more closely in
questions of tuning, and the extent to which the solutions of the original
maker are to be followed should be an important initial decision. Once a
clarinet has been made, individual notes may be flattened by filling the
next open hole, emphasising the lower (undercut) part of the hole to
affect the fundamental register. Wax was originally used, though for
slight adjustments opaque nail varnish is a useful (and easily removable)
modern alternative. As Backofen's tutor remarks, embouchure has an
important part to play (and this is especially true of boxwood
instruments), together with liberal use of alternative fingerings. It is
worth noting that he placed a very high priority on accurate intonation.

As Nicholas Shackleton remarked in Chapter 2, players in Mozart's
day tended to be suspicious of extra keywork, because it seemed to add
to technical difficulties, and it also carried an increased risk of leaking
pads. Backofen remarked that half-broken springs were all too
common. The configuration of the widely played five-keyed clarinet
will be instantly recognisable to players of the Boehm system, and may
usefully be recapitulated here – a', speaker, L4 e/b' and $f\sharp/c\sharp''$, and R4
$a\flat/e\flat''$. A sixth key was mentioned as early as 1768, and by 1802
Lefèvre's tutor enthusiastically recommended a key for $c\sharp'$ which he
said was otherwise indistinguishable from the semitone above! Though
this sixth key is absent from the clarinets illustrating both his diatonic
and chromatic fingering charts, it is present in his sketch of the
component parts of the clarinet (Fig. 8.1). In the same year as Lefèvre
was writing, the double-hole sometimes provided as an alternative was
regarded in Koch's *Lexicon* as essential to avoid a dull and poorly
tuned note. By 1808 an anonymous writer in the *Allgemeine musica-
lische Zeitung* was recommending at least nine keys to avoid scarcely
usable chalumeau notes, citing Mozart's Concerto as evidence and
addressing fears of malfunction by stating that his own new clarinet
had been played daily for nine months without needing a single repair.

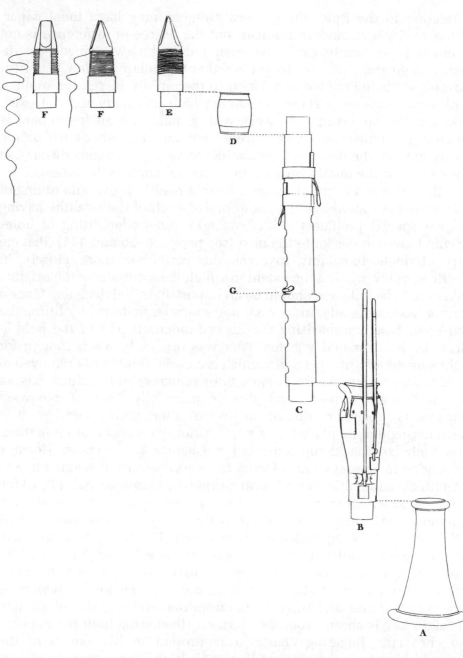

Figure 8.1   Diagram of the component parts of the clarinet, from Lefèvre's *Méthode de Clarinette*

Lefèvre specifically advises flexibility when playing in the chalumeau register, and gives the table of notes (Example 8.1) which on a five-keyed clarinet require sympathetic embouchure.

From the various evidence, it seems that a five- to eight-keyed clarinet might be suitable for Mozart (keys 7 and 8 being e♭/b♭″ and

Ex. 8.1 from J. X. Lefèvre, *Méthode de Clarinette*

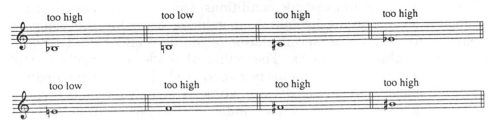

b/*f*♯′), whereas for Weber a Heinrich Grenser copy with at least ten keys could be appropriate. Most of the great makers (such as Simiot and the Grensers) manufactured clarinets with a wide variety of key configurations. The question of idiomatic tone-quality is if anything even more important; for example, a copy of a late eighteenth-century Viennese clarinet (e.g. by Tauber) might be ideal for Mozart, but by the second decade of the nineteenth century clarinet tone had rapidly acquired a power which such an instrument could not be expected to deliver.

Reeds and mouthpieces are other areas where historical awareness and practical convenience need to be delicately balanced. Relatively few original mouthpieces survive intact, but the wide variety of designs observed in Chapter 2 generally required a reed which is shorter and narrower at the base than its modern counterpart. Backofen's tutor paints a picture of considerable variety, some players shaving reeds down to a fine wedge, others giving them a parallel thinness. The reed was tied on to the mouthpiece with twine until Müller's invention of the metal ligature near the beginning of the nineteenth century. Mouthpieces of all types can now be copied with a considerable degree of accuracy, but opinions vary as to what material should be used; from a historical point of view it is generally true that once the idea of separating mouthpiece and barrel had been established, boxwood was replaced by harder materials. Ivory, glass and metal were alternatives to other woods, and ebonite was eventually introduced only at the end of the nineteenth century. A wooden mouthpiece always carries the risk of warping, and some of today's historical players have opted for ebonite, believing any change of tone-quality to be scarcely discernible and easily outweighed by its superior stability. There is a broader philosophical point here about the extent to which later developments in manufacture can reasonably be taken into account. Many of today's makers offer a compromise multi-purpose 'early' mouthpiece, whose superficial advantages can all too easily be allowed to preclude individual research and investigation. Copies are often furnished with a full-length table, which allows the use of a commercial (usually German-cut) reed as a basis.

Given that the keywork of an early clarinet is fully operational, with pads forming an effective seal, maintenance consists largely of taking

special care of the wood. Boxwood instruments are especially susceptible to changes in atmospheric conditions, and particular care needs to
be taken when playing in cold temperatures, since the difference in
temperature between a warm interior of the bore and a cold exterior
can cause splits and cracks. The oiling of modern clarinets is still
controversial, but is essential for boxwood. Ted Planas has pointed out
the difference between the dense texture of blackwood, the progres-
sively less dense woods of palisander, rosewood, tulip wood and
cocus, and the relatively light boxwood.[4] Entirely comprised of
sapwood, the fresh living part of the tree-trunk directly beneath the
bark, boxwood is capable of carrying moisture through its grain more
easily than the heartwoods at the centre of the trunk. Oiling with
boiled or raw linseed, or with Backofen's recommended almond oil
(better for the inside of the bore), produces a varnish and helps to
reduce the absorption of water when rubbed in well with the excess
shaken off. However, unlike the blackwoods, boxwood is very good at
absorbing water, and as the nineteenth-century maker Mahillon
remarked, is more suitable as a hygrometer than as a musical
instrument! Incidentally, leather pads soon harden and lose their
effectiveness if allowed to come into contact with the oil.

Technique

Tutors laid considerable emphasis on the correct way to hold the
instrument, Thomas Willman (*c.* 1825) proposing a distance of nine
and a half inches between the bell and the body of the player (Fig. 8.2
and Fig. 8.3). He warns that great care should be taken not to hold the
instrument too tightly, and adds: 'The beginner should avoid any
contortion of the Head or Features, a graceful attitude of Body and a
natural expression of the Countenance being essentially requisite to
constitute a good Performer'.

The history of clarinet embouchure is a complex affair. Most
clarinettists know that at first their instrument was played with reed
against the top lip, and some have been interested in reviving this
technique. A useful introduction to the subject is contained in Eric
Hoeprich's article 'Clarinet reed position in the eighteenth century' in
Early Music, 12 (1984). Many French tutors describe the reed-above
method, reed-below becoming official policy at the Paris Conservatoire
only in 1831; England and Italy also cultivated this technique well into
the nineteenth century (as in Fig. 8.2). However, in Austria and
Germany the change came much earlier, Backofen *c.* 1803 showing an
awareness of both methods, implying that reed-below had been in use
for some time; evidence of various kinds clearly suggests that this was
the technique adopted by Anton Stadler for performances of Mozart's
clarinet works. Overall, the sheer diversity of approaches to clarinet

Figure 8.2   The method of holding the clarinet; lithograph of Thomas Willman from his *A Complete Instruction Book for the Clarinet* (London, *c.* 1825)

playing was greater than we can imagine, and an invaluable guide here is David Charlton's article 'Classical clarinet technique; documentary approaches' in *Early Music*, 16 (1988). With reed-above method, there were at least three different types of articulation, involving respectively chest, throat and tongue. For today's player, investigation involves a great deal more than merely strengthening the top lip!

There are many descriptions of the tone-quality of past virtuosi, but especially significant is Anton Stadler's own recommendation that the

Figure 8.3   Willman's profile view of the clarinet; lithograph

essentials of music should be learned through singing, whatever the quality of one's voice. J. F. Schink's review of his playing in Mozart's Serenade K361 ought to prove inspirational to modern players of the boxwood clarinet: 'I have never heard the like of what you contrived with your instrument. Never should I have thought that a clarinet could be capable of imitating a human voice so deceptively as it was imitated by you. Indeed, your instrument has so soft and lovely a tone that no one with a heart can resist it.'[5] In more general terms, Daniel Schubart's *Ideen zu einer Ästhetik der Tonkunst* characterises the clarinet as overflowing with love, whilst praising its indescribable sweetness.[6] The importance of imitating the human voice is a theme which recurs persistently amongst writers.

The lack of standardised fingering for the classical clarinet is nicely confirmed in Joseph Fröhlich's *Vollständige theoretisch-praktische Musikschule* (Bonn 1810–11), p. 15:

Due to the different construction and various manners of blowing wind and reed instruments, there are no generally applicable rules of fingering. All one can do is give the usual fingerings and a critique on each tone, and, at the same time, to inform the student of the various manners in which the same tone can be fingered, in order to make the dark tones brighter and more sonorous, and to improve the bad ones. Consequently, one must really see to it that each player evolves the fingering for himself.

None the less, fingering charts can be consulted in modern facsimiles of the tutors by Lefèvre (Fig. 8.4) and Backofen, and these are among the twenty-eight discussed in Albert Rice's collation 'Clarinet fingering charts, 1732–1816' in the *Galpin Society Journal*, 37 (1984). In some important respects, fingering for all early clarinets resembles that of the recorder rather than the modern Boehm, notably in the cross-fingered *b♭/f″* (with R1 *and* R3), and the use of L2 + Lth for *f′/c‴*. The basic fingering for *e♭/b♭″* is L1, L3, Lth, with RH as necessary. *d‴* is also cross-fingered – Lth, L2, L3, R1, R3, + R4/key. Below the break, *f′* and *f♯′* are often unstable, requiring some experimentation. Exercises on the most obvious non-Boehm fingerings must be a priority, especially chromatic scales, which by Weber's time were a spectacular virtuoso effect. The difference in quality between adjacent notes was still to be prized rather than disguised. Besides studies across the break and the oscillation of cross-fingerings, Lefèvre's technical exercises contain transitions through *b′*, *c♯″* and *d♯″* in quick succession, for which of course no alternative keys were provided. He pays particular attention to the function of each of these keys, which were seen as a potential difficulty. Lefèvre himself changed from a six-keyed to a thirteen-keyed clarinet only at the age of sixty-one.

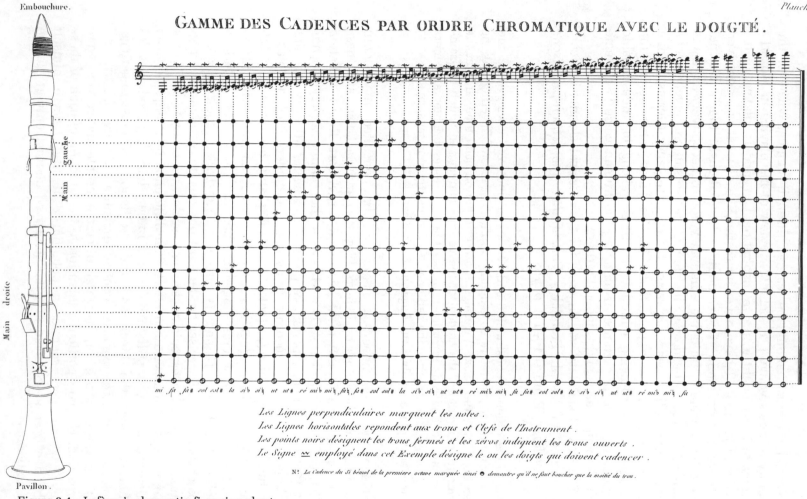

Figure 8.4 Lefèvre's chromatic fingering chart

Style

Lefèvre lays considerable emphasis on some areas which are scarcely mentioned in today's tutors. He warns that clarinet playing becomes monotonous without nuance of sound and articulation, and where there is neither expression nor panache. It is not enough to read the music and play the notes; one must supply those nuances which suit the character of the music and capture what the composer has not troubled to write down. Lefèvre makes the acute observation (which remains true today) that uniformity of execution and articulation means that a certain coldness has often been attributed to the nature of the instrument, whereas in fact this is the responsibility of the performer. The range, variety and quality of clarinet sound distinguishes it from all wind instruments; it can portray whatever character a composer assigns to it, whether a battle hymn or a shepherd's chant. Significantly, Lefèvre remarks that in order to nuance the sound, the clarinettist needs not only musical taste, but a true knowledge of harmony. He regards an Adagio as the most difficult movement to execute, its character quite distinct from that of an Allegro.

Although Lefèvre's observations offer some useful stylistic insights, it is beyond the clarinet literature that a comprehensive feeling for the classical language must be sought. We need at least to be aware of treatises for other instruments, such as those by Quantz (flute, 1752), Leopold Mozart (violin, 1756), C. P. E. Bach (keyboard, 1753 and 1762), Türk (keyboard, 1789) and Tromlitz (flute, 1791). These offer an astonishing range of discussion on various aspects of music as an art and a craft. Naturally, no single source can ever be regarded as definitive on any particular subject; these writers were individual musicians working in different parts of Europe, who often disagreed with one another in a quite stimulating way. Some musical matters, such as the interpretation of certain rhythms or how to play trills, were as controversial then as now; indeed, answers to many musical questions were in fact never as standardised as we might like to pretend nowadays.

The articulate style characteristic of Mozart's day is worth recapturing not merely for historical reasons but also for its aesthetic benefit, especially since in classical sources expressive performance was seen as the result of attention to detail. Quantz was forthright in his description of music as 'nothing but an artificial language, through which we seek to acquaint the listener with our musical ideas'. This analogy with oratory implies a range of articulation far removed from the goals of many clarinettists today, and it does seem in general that modern playing has moved further in the direction of a smooth, seamless approach than either the flute or oboe. To emulate this whilst playing a boxwood instrument is without question a wasted opportunity. Leopold Mozart lays particular emphasis on adherence to the written slurs, advising that the first note be strongly stressed, but the remainder slurred on to it quite smoothly and more and more quietly. As for notes without slurs, C. P. E. Bach offers the forthright (if rather extreme) comment that they should be played half-length as a matter of course, for which he was criticised by (amongst others) Türk. However, Bach qualified his statement by remarking that the briskness of Allegros was expressed in detached notes, and the tenderness of Adagios in broad, slurred notes – in other words, articulation must always serve the characterisation. In assuming a good knowledge of harmony and the art of singing, eighteenth-century writers were in fact expecting that the performer would glean a great deal of interpretative information from the rhythm, melodic intervals, phrasing and harmony notated in the score, and adapt his technique accordingly. In particular, it was expected that dissonances would be heavily stressed, with corresponding release at their resolution.

Quantz set out to train a skilled and intelligent musician, remarking that the majority of players have fingers and tongues, but that most are deficient in brains! Bach similarly warns that players whose chief asset is mere technique are clearly at a disadvantage. Both writers state that if a player is not himself moved by what he plays he will never move others, which should be his real aim. These days, it is easy for us to become embarrassed to read such sentiments, but in the eighteenth century, communication of emotion in music was an absolute priority, well before the enthusiasm for virtuosity as an end in itself during the nineteenth century, or the veneration of accuracy developed during the age of recording. Türk's *Klavierschule* offers an important stylistic viewpoint exactly contemporary with the composition of Mozart's Clarinet Quintet from an author who knew his music well. The chapter on execution contains remarks on melodic inflection which make essential reading for anyone embarking upon the classical repertoire.

Once we acknowledge the importance of slurs and other surface detail on a musical score, a good edition becomes essential (whether we are playing period or modern clarinets), in which the composer's original notation can be easily differentiated from later interpretative assistance.

Exploring other clarinets

Baroque

Of earlier single-reed instruments, the chalumeau has recently become a little more familiar through recordings. Re-creations of all four sizes have been made at the now standardised baroque pitch of $a'=415$, often based on the tenor chalumeau by J. C. Denner. As we noted in Chapter 1, the niceties of embouchure were scarcely discussed in the early eighteenth century, although we can be certain that the chalumeau was played reed-above. Choice of reeds and accuracy of tuning cross-fingerings is made easier by the necessity to focus only upon the fundamental register. The tiny proportion of repertoire in modern editions has been a serious barrier to promoting the instrument, despite the appearance in print of the works by Fasch, Graupner and Telemann mentioned in Chapter 1, and the availability of music for the instrument by Vivaldi and Handel.

For the baroque clarinet repertoire by these last two composers, two-keyed clarinets in C and in D by Jacob Denner have been widely copied, and their suitability has already been noted by Nicholas Shackleton. Eric Hoeprich's article 'Finding a clarinet for the three concertos by Vivaldi' in *Early Music* 11 (1983) offers some sound practical advice for the modern performer. Cross-fingered notes such as *b*, *c♯'* and *e♭'* need sympathetic and ingenious treatment, and must have been expected by composers to have their own special quality. Of the original fingering charts for the two-keyed instrument, Majer's appears to be a rather inaccurate attempt to tabulate a new instrument with registers an unfamiliar twelfth apart.[7] Eisel is more reliable, and in the light of the high tessitura of the Molter concertos his comment is significant that virtuosi could reach a fifth or sixth higher than the normal range up to *c'''*.[8]

Classical

An inevitable development of the period movement is that C clarinets are now regularly being copied, because where specified they are absolutely necessary for technical as well as aesthetic reasons.

The basset horn has also proved a tempting proposition, since of all the woodwinds its sound is particularly distinct from its modern counterpart. In the 1780s its bore was still relatively small, with finger-holes acoustically misplaced to accommodate the human hand. This results in a singular, unearthly quality, which proved particularly attractive to Mozart. An important Viennese source from 1796 noted the difficulty of playing the basset horn, but remarked that the Stadlers had mastered every aspect, including control of tone-production, nuance, expression and technical facility. Backofen commented that the instrument should be held to the right side of the player rather than between the knees, a posture which certainly helps the projection of sound.[9]

The general acceptance of the evidence that Mozart intended both his Quintet and Concerto for basset clarinet in A has meant that period players have wanted to revive Stadler's lost instrument, which also

Figure 8.5   Handbill for a Vienna concert by Anton Stadler, 20 February 1788, which included a Concerto on the Bass (i.e. Basset) Clarinet, and Variations on the same newly invented instrument, which had a range extended by two notes

included an extension accommodating all four semitones c, $c\sharp$, d and $e\flat$.[10] In re-creating the basset clarinet some players have preferred to transfer the *Buch* and metal bell from the basset horn, whilst others have simply extended the bore (as on the modern basset clarinet), there being some rare eighteenth-century antecedents for this design.[11] Backofen remarked that he knew of clarinets with the extra notes c and d, observing that the provision of the low tonic was especially useful; he expected to report further when they came into widespread circulation. The diatonically extended clarinet in B♭ is required for Mozart's (probably originally complete) Quintet movement K516c, and for the obbligato in 'Parto, parto!' from *La clemenza di Tito*; this may also have been the instrument played at its first documented appearance at a concert on 20 February 1788 (Fig. 8.5).

Romantic

Just as the historical performance movement has brought specialised investigation of the early period, so the later nineteenth century has become an area for study. For practical advice on playing thirteen-keyed derivatives of the Müller system, Baines offers an invaluable guide to the fingerings and technique of different models. French clarinets of this type are still in relatively wide circulation, and this must have been the instrument of which Berlioz wrote, 'it is an *epic* instrument ... whose voice is that of heroic love'. Baines (p. 332) describes such instruments as 'almost unbeatable for tone, so long as the correct mouthpiece and small, hard reed are used with them'. More generally available are the large-bore Albert- (simple-) system clarinets, whose development has been described in Chapter 2. Built at either the old high (*a*′=452) or low (modern) pitch, they were overtaken in England by the Boehm only in the 1930s, as greater technical fluency was increasingly demanded. Their relatively uncovered bore allows a superlative resonance which some believe has never been surpassed. On thirteen-keyed clarinets it is to be expected that each note should be available with near-perfect tuning, though not every interval may be easily negotiable,

Stylistic questions continue to be relevant in late nineteenth-century music. Despite a gradual move towards more legato playing (epitomised in Wagner), the rhetorical principle was still widely acknowledged, as shown in the violin tutor by Brahms's friend and colleague Joachim.[12] The care with which Brahms indicates the surface details through classical slurs within his clarinet works verifies the expected continued analogy with speech. Another element in the overall stylistic equation is the observation by Robert Philip throughout his *Early Recordings and Musical Style* (Cambridge, 1992) that a generally more spontaneous approach to performance was the norm before 1900. Indeed, even such a basic matter as tempo flexibility can scarcely be deduced from composers' own comments, which take for granted the musical taste of *their* times, not ours. Inevitably, earlier techniques and conventions can never be totally recaptured, but their very investigation has the capacity to enhance our lives both as musicians and clarinettists.

9 The professional clarinettist

NICHOLAS COX

Introduction

Whatever their preferred course at the outset, musicians these days are best equipped if they can apply themselves to several related trades. Playing a wind instrument can offer a most satisfying professional life combining orchestral work, solo playing, chamber music and teaching, but performers often end up diversifying in all sorts of directions. Examiners, lecturers, recording artists and producers, conductors, composers, businessmen, arrangers, authors, consultants, administrators in education or artistic managers – I can think of at least one clarinettist who has become each of these! Competition for rare orchestral vacancies is intense, whilst only one or two professional clarinettists in Britain can honestly say that they earn a living from playing solo and chamber music. There are, however, hundreds of players throughout the country who teach and many who play occasionally, if only in local amateur orchestras, bands or jazz groups. This has not always been the case. Between 1890 and 1900 the number of listed clarinettists in London increased tenfold, suggesting there was a time when the instrument was not as popular as it is today. Nowadays there is a flourishing market of freelance players supplying a large number of the capital's *ad hoc* orchestras and ensembles. Despite the risks of being a musician, it seems that playing the instrument for a living has never been so popular.

The demands and pressures of orchestral life

Life in an orchestral wind section has its fair share of pros and cons. Actually securing a job can take many years studying and patiently gaining experience, and during this time the individual should be prepared to do any number of different jobs, or at least to endure long periods of under-employment, before breaking into the profession. Clearly it is not a profession for the impatient. With such difficulties getting on the first rung of the ladder, it is hardly surprising that once they are in, most players are determined to stay, whatever they may have to put up with. The remuneration may be small, the hours anti-social and many conductors poor, but life as an orchestral musician, particularly as a member of a fine wind section, does have moments of enormous satisfaction and sheer joy in music-making – when getting paid for enjoying one's work does seem too good to be true. As in any other profession there may be moments of exasperation, boredom, exhaustion and disappointment, but most orchestral musicians count themselves fortunate just to play music for a living.

In an orchestra the pressures are very much those associated with being part of a team. Like goal scorers, the soloists (wind and string principals) are more noticeable, but the rank-and-file string players or third clarinettists are also important team players. At times various members of a section will be called upon to be a soloist, whether it be playing bass or E♭ clarinet or filling in for the regular principal; for the second clarinettist, blending with the tonal character of different players is a great art.

Playing up to five concerts a week with a considerable amount of travel involved can feel like hard work, particularly if the programme is a tricky one. Musicians have various ways of coping, but it is most important to have an understanding family and supportive colleagues. Jack Brymer's comments apply as much today as they did in 1979:

The only real privilege of musical success in Britain just now is overwork – quite serious overwork, the sort only possible with people who are sufficiently interested in their work to carry on long after the fatigue of sheer depression would have stopped others perhaps less fortunately identified with their profession. It may involve ten hours playing and three of rush-hour travel per day, a seven-day week and even a 350-day year. (*From Where I Sit*, (London, 1979) p. 6)

Some form of regular exercise is useful for remaining fit and alert as a performer. Some players resort to Alexander Technique, yoga or some other form of relaxation. Others find they deal with the pressure more by immersing themselves in interests outside music. Not surprisingly, alcohol and drug dependence can all too easily become for some the only way of dealing with the stress of performance.

Orchestral parts are normally available well in advance, so there is no excuse for being unprepared. For wind players, overdoing the practice on concert days is more of a problem than lack of preparation. This involves pacing your lip so that it is not worn out when it really matters. My own particular *bête noire* is poorly copied or notated music. If the eye begins to question what the brain thinks it has already learnt, the result can be total confusion. Short of recopying a part, the only way round this is assiduously to mark up the parts. If the publisher is letting you down, pairs of spectacles, breath marks, fingerings and marking the beats of the bar can all be helpful.

The musician's lot will certainly not be a happy one if he encounters problems with his instruments (breaking springs or leaky pads) or if the atmosphere ruins his best reeds. Should a pad drop out, the player must be able to effect a repair and regain his composure in seconds. Sometimes, however, there is no opportunity to replace a dying reed, and the player just has to continue as best he can. Avoiding such situations involves a dependable supply of good cane and a reliable system of seasoning (blowing in), adjusting and selecting reeds. Each player has his own method. Some make their own reeds from blanks, with a reed profiler. Others make do with the one or two playable reeds from a box of 'supermarket' reeds but never stop complaining. Happily there are now more types of reliable reed on the market. My own solution is to pay more for fewer reeds made to my specification. Reeds well fashioned from quality cane seem to last longer and give a higher percentage success rate.

Niggling health problems can increase the stress of playing. Almost all clarinettists and most wind players I have ever met suffer from some form of back or neck problem, normally the result of actually holding the instruments. Coping with this repetitive stress leads some to use slings and others to carry their own seats. Fortunately some orchestras and halls are now recognising the value of providing ergonomically designed seating. Since so much of what we do is affected by the position of teeth and the shape of the mouth, dental problems are also a potential hazard for wind and brass players. Losing teeth has finished many a career, and finding a dentist who understands the problems likely to be faced by players is essential. Most musicians will experience some deterioration in their hearing. Subjecting the ears to a prolonged battering by a loud brass or percussion section has been shown to damage hearing. Acoustic screens are partially effective at dealing with this, but the use of ear-plugs is indicated for Shostakovich's 'Leningrad' Symphony, although they significantly interfere with the player's perception of dynamics and tone-quality. Wearing headphones for clicktracks during recording sessions is another aural annoyance necessary in synchronising music to film.

Working in a wind section

Although playing an instrument might seem a comparatively simple process, orchestral musicians have to develop several complex skills which can only be learnt *in situ*. What sounds loud close to, may not project beyond the front of the stalls, and a sound which seems small may in fact sound louder than you think in the auditorium. Finding the right answer to this issue leads some players into experimentation with different 'set-ups' (instruments, mouthpieces and reeds). Others seem to hit on one set-up and stay with it for the rest of their lives. Some achieve this with a resistant set-up, others with a more free-blowing one. The best players aim for a set-up where the instrument sounds homogeneous and focused throughout its range and dynamic, without losing the vital elements of colour. Modern players may be less influenced by national schools than they used to be, but the music of different nationalities still demands to be played stylistically and with different sounds. A rich, warm legato Germanic sound may be fine for Brahms sonatas, but might possibly lack the brightness and incisiveness necessary for Bernstein's *Preludes, Fugues and Riffs*, or the lightness of articulation required in French repertoire.

In any discussion of balance, projection and acoustics, the importance of listening while you play is crucial. In his book *In the Orchestra* (London, 1987) Jack Brymer points out that this is now no longer a question of instinct for young players, but reliably taught in youth orchestras, such that 'by the time they start to study at our universities and colleges many of them have already absorbed these all-important skills' (p. 21). Projection is always relative to the acoustic of the hall, which naturally influences a player's interpretation of dynamics. In one hall a solo marked *piano* may have to be played closer to *mezzo forte* to be heard; in a better acoustic, it may be possible to play closer to *pianissimo*. In addition to projection, the player must be sympathetic to the relative balance between the instruments of the wind section. A clarinettist may discreetly have to adapt his *pianissimo c'* to allow for the problems an oboist may have just making this note sound soft rather than *forte*. Generally, both the style of music and the smaller string section in a chamber orchestra will enable the clarinettist to use a more intimate sound. Within the wind section, balance is a tightrope walked by at least eight players of different instruments. Often the biggest problem is starting together. This can depend as much on the distance from the conductor as his beat. Good conductors have a knack of conducting slightly ahead of the music without pushing the music forward, making it easier for those furthest away to play in time. For some conductors the music starts at the bottom of their down beat. With others the music could splutter into life anything up to half a second later, in which case the beginnings of chords will be led by the player with the most prominent part – often the first oboe or flute or, failing that, the leader.

To complicate matters, different instruments within a wind section 'speak' in entirely different ways, both in the amount of air necessary to start notes and the way in which the air is used. On the two double-reed instruments, the player has to generate a large amount of air pressure to get the reed vibrating and the note sounding. On the flute, the absence of resistance means that a large volume of air will be necessary to sustain phrases. The clarinet seems to be a combination of these two, with a larger single reed to vibrate and a larger aperture into the mouthpiece. Since it is easier to get the reed to sound on the clarinet, starting notes and breathing have been insufficiently emphasised in learning the instrument. This I find curious, because preparing for a note on the clarinet is essential for a good sound.

One needs only to mention tuning within the wind section, and at least someone's hackles are likely to rise. As pitch is relative to the temperature and wind instruments are the first to be affected by heat, playing with instruments of fixed pitches can be fraught with difficulties. In a fine orchestra, the winds and strings will normally be versatile enough to accommodate a piano on a warm summer's evening; however, really disciplined tuning can only be achieved by a joint effort between sections, not by the unilateral action of one. Whatever the pitch of the orchestra, the orchestral clarinettist must occasionally be prepared to transpose a passage on his warmer instrument to avoid sounding flat. Within any wind section, the second flute and second bassoon seem to be strangely crucial determinants of the general pitch. If they have the discipline to remain at a fixed pitch, the rest seem to follow suit. Chords in the wind section are easier to tune if only the upper voice uses vibrato. It is, however, a general problem with melody instruments that they become sharper towards the top and flatter towards the bottom, particularly as the ear naturally hears pitches further apart at both ends of the range.

Preparing for the profession

Most important here is a realistic evaluation of one's talent and chances of making it into the profession. Some of the most promising pupils rule themselves out of the chance of taking up music seriously, often for seemingly trivial reasons. Some possess the sound, the technical capability and the musical understanding, but lack a good enough rhythmic sense or the necessary discipline. Others seem to have everything, but their attitude lets them down – what Jack Brymer calls the bandroom approach (*Clarinet*, p. 190). All the essential characteristics have to come together in the same person at the same time.

Choosing where to study music will often depend on what you eventually want to do. Whether you are intent on becoming a teacher or a performer, an academic course and qualification could ultimately be more useful. Since only a minority of students will end up earning a living purely from performance, it would appear to make sense to equip yourself early on for some of the diversifications I mentioned earlier. The question of where to study is inevitably complicated by the diversity of courses and approaches to studying music in various countries. In Germany there is a marked difference between studying music as an academic subject at a university and training at a Musikhochschule to be a teacher or performer. These differences are now less obvious at British institutions. In general, conservatoires have had to become more academic in their courses, while university music departments have incorporated more performance options into their courses. In the USA, most universities consider study of the main instrument as important as any purely academic discipline. The most important decision is surely not 'where to study' or even 'what sort of course?', so much as 'with whom shall I have contact hours?' 'Is it someone from whom I can really learn something, whose playing and ideas I respect?' (Do they have a gift for teaching?) – in other words, 'are they relatively articulate?' and, increasingly, 'am I ever going to see them when I get there?'

To ensure that you make the right decision, it is quite usual to visit potential teachers in advance. The two gifts of performing and teaching are not often mutually inclusive. Those most naturally gifted as performers are often least able to communicate how they do it. Music is after all an abstract language of suggestion – for instrumentalists, literally a song without words. Explaining how this non-semantic art form is translated into performance – the medium through which music lives – presupposes a certain amount of articulateness and maturity on the part of the teacher. In addition to good communication skills, a good teacher should have the capacity to light the student's path towards music's power to evoke and suggest, and the ability to know when to allow the student to go his own way. In short the teacher-pupil relationship should be one of mutual respect and trust.

Examinations have for too long dictated the direction of traditional instrumental learning and teaching. The system has served teachers and the music profession well for many years, even if some teachers have relied too heavily on the syllabuses for their pupils' repertoire, but how well has it served the pupils? For some, the emphasis on competing and passing examinations has only succeeded in stifling creativity, and is partly responsible for perpetuating a stylistic rift which has tainted serious music with elitism. Music should strive to be seen as accessible, not merely the preserve of specialists or those who can do well in competitions and examinations, even if these remain essential challenges for the gifted, and a yardstick for evaluating progress.

Given a well-organised event, a fair jury and most of all a philosophical attitude, competitions can be fun and challenging. Learning from the melting pot of international styles and ideas at such events is the next best thing to actually studying abroad, and has much to recommend it.[1] Like sportsmen, musicians can learn to raise their game during competitions and they can then aspire to even greater

heights of technical excellence, tonal beauty and musical understanding. Ultimately, music should not be about competition but
communication.

The ability to audition is crucial for success in the orchestral world.
Thankfully, there are now fewer players who can boast that they have
never had to audition or that they were no good at them. Orchestras are
also beginning to adopt a more helpful attitude to the conduct and
outcome of these necessary, if daunting events. If the panel is prepared
to make its comments available, candidates can even come away in
some cases feeling that the experience was a positive one rather than a
complete waste of time. So how should you best prepare for an
audition? First of all, prepare well and allow sufficient time for practice.
There is really no point in attending for an audition if you have not had
the time to learn the set works or orchestral passages. Listen to
recordings, look at the scores and find out about the composer's style. It
is infuriating and disappointing for an audition panel which has just
read how gifted you are from your résumé to hear that you haven't a
clue about the speed or style of the passages. Secondly, don't produce a
wickedly difficult piano part or anything too modern as your chosen
piece, unless you are taking your own accompanist. The audition is not
a recital, it is simply a chance for you to demonstrate that you have a
good sound and intonation, a well-honed technique and articulation, an
acute rhythmic sense, musical understanding, and depending on the
job you are applying for, some personality and flair. If you can remain
composed and poised under audition conditions, you will be at an
enormous advantage. Deep breaths, taking your time (within reason)
and a good reed will also be a help!

Sight reading is a technique which can be improved with practice.
Most people feel intimidated by the sight of black rows of semiquavers,
rhythmic complexity or worse. The notation of music can be its own
worst enemy, frustrating its performance and communication. Learn to
look carefully along the ends of staves for changes of key, speed,
dynamics or clef. Look out for finger changes or tricky combinations of
fingerings. When you are ready, choose a speed you can keep up for
the whole passage. Try not to stop even for wrong notes, and above all
treat it not as an exercise but as music. Finally, if the audition is not
successful, learn to forgive yourself and accept the outcome. In most
countries successful auditions can lead directly to jobs. In Britain,
however, frequently lengthy trials ensure that both orchestra and
trialist get to know each other better.[2]

The challenges of the orchestral repertoire

This section is designed for clarinettists who are studying the
orchestral repertoire, probably by means of one of the volumes of

excerpts listed in the Appendix. It is not designed as an exhaustive list; the passages are intended rather to highlight particular difficulties.

Projecting the sound

- Weber, *Freischütz* Overture: here the clarinet soars over the horns' declamatory E♭ major chords – a most dramatic moment that marks the clarinet's arrival as a fully fledged romantic instrument. Make sure the top a'' is sharp enough for the volume of sound and use as much resonance on the throat notes as possible. When you join the strings' tune, listen and watch the conductor!
- Schumann, Piano Concerto, 1st movement: your solo is accompanied by the piano. Don't be too soft or you'll never be heard. Save your soft intimate sound for the central section on the B♭ clarinet. Try using the angle of the instrument to project.
- Tchaikovsky, Piano Concerto No. 1: solos at bar 186 and bar 494 of the first movement. Only the first of these is really a solo. During the second, watch the pianist's fingers closely.

Legato passages: using the clarinet's softness

- Tchaikovsky, Symphony No. 6: in the 1st movement's solos, putting the fingers down slowly on open holes can help the legato. Try to equalise the throat notes with sufficient resonance. Take the *ppp* and *pp* with a pinch of salt. Certainly, 5–7 bars after rehearsal letter T keep the tone up. Thereafter if you get too soft you will make life impossible for the bassoons!
- Schubert, 'Unfinished Symphony', 2nd movement: a larger breath after four bars and one before g''–e''–b'' (on the down beat of bar 79) will assist this most difficult of solos for breathing. Try to stay in tune on b'' whilst getting softer. Keep the air flowing and shade the g'' hole slightly.
- Brahms, Symphony No. 4, Andante Moderato: try to focus the *piano* b's, keeping the sound up below the break. Despite the marked diminuendo in the final solo, don't disappear!
- Prokofiev, Piano Concerto No. 3: a famous opening for two clarinets in thirds. Try to blend well together and avoid sharpness at the end.
- Rachmaninov, Symphony No. 2, slow movement: as this can be an exhausting solo, there is a good case to be made out for using a bumper (your second clarinettist) to cover where you take breaths.

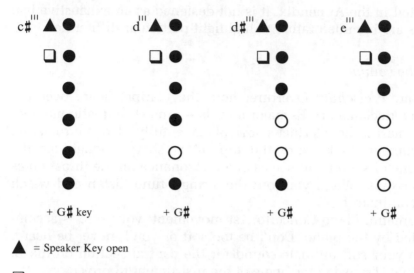

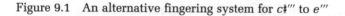

▲ = Speaker Key open

▢ = Thumb Hole open (or shaded)

Figure 9.1   An alternative fingering system for *c♯'''* to *e'''*

Alternative fingerings

It is always curious how many pupils have never been taught the correct use of the alternative fingerings for *f♯'* (side), *b/f♯''* fork fingerings. Apart from the more usual alternatives, there are many less well known for the altissimo. In fact one book on the subject lists twenty-five different fingerings for top *g''''*! For most students, having so many to choose from is more of a hindrance than a help, but there are several other fingerings which work well but do not appear in many text books. Among these is a system for *c♯'''* to *e'''* which works well on most Boehm clarinets (Fig. 9.1). It produces a softer, slightly flatter sound, closer in tone-colour to the clarino register, and can be used to great effect in high, soft passages, such as those in Berg's *Vier Stücke*. This is based on the equivalent German fingering system for these notes. In theory, the second speaker L1 used to obtain the notes from *c♯''* upwards is in the wrong place on the Boehm instrument. Keeping the Lth open or shaded with the speaker key open and closing L1 hole produces a flutey and disembodied sound. Arising out of this idea, try sliding the L1 finger to one side rather than lifting it suddenly when attempting a legato to the altissimo register (e.g. *a'' – d'''*).

Fingers flying

Often the player faced with seemingly insuperable technical passages is prone to panic. Try passages slowly when you are learning them.

Imaginative practice using alternative fingerings, different rhythmic groupings and variable accents is always useful. In technically awkward passages try overdoing the finger movement, then when the passage is more familiar, use as little movement as possible. Try to move as smoothly as possible. Grabbing and jerky movements will make legato more difficult. Particularly in the break area, an ergonomic combination of wrist, forearm and finger movement is essential for a rounded technique. Above all, remember that evenness of finger technique and evenness of sound are one and the same thing.

- Shostakovich, Symphonies Nos. 1, 9 and 10.
- Bartók, *Miraculous Mandarin* and *Concerto for Orchestra*: all parts (first, second/E♭ and bass) are worth learning.
- Barber, Violin Concerto, finale: think of fingering here in a rhythmic way.
- Ravel, *Daphnis et Chloé*, 1st and 2nd suites: first clarinet opening: keep L4 d♭' key down for the whole of the opening bar. Keep sound very soft and legato. Alternative fingerings come in very handy in the final 5/4 section!
- Ravel, *Tombeau de Couperin* and Piano Concertos: bear in mind side *c♯'''* and open *d'''* (rather flat but acceptable at speed).
- Tchaikovsky, Symphonies (e.g. finale of No. 4): the *tutti* passages are often worth looking at as well.
- Tippett, *Ritual Dances for Midsummer Marriage* and Symphony No. 4: the dances contain one of the repertoire's hardest passages for two clarinets in rhythmic unison.
- Schoenberg, *Chamber Symphony No. 1*: very tricky for E♭, B♭ and bass clarinets.
- Stravinsky, *Firebird*, *Petrouchka* (*tuttis* not in the passage books are more tricky than the solos), *Symphony in Three Movements*, *Symphony in C, Jeu des cartes* and *The Rake's Progress* have rhythmic intricacies and technical challenges.
- Dukas, *Sorcerer's Apprentice*, and Roussel, *Bacchus et Ariane*, are two particularly difficult examples from the French repertoire.
- Prokofiev, Piano Concertos Nos. 2 and 3.
- Balakirev, *Islamey*: if this crops up, have a good look at it!
- Richard Strauss, *Der Rosenkavalier*, *Ein Heldenleben*, *Till Eulenspiegel*, *Le Bourgeois Gentilhomme*, second Horn Concerto, *Don Juan*, *Die Frau ohne Schatten*, *Elektra*, *Salome* and *Ariadne auf Naxos*. Most Strauss is worth learning. Bits of *Rosenkavalier* and *Die Frau ohne Schatten* are terrifying!
- Borodin, *Polotsvian Dances*: Most performances seem to omit the opening movement, which contains some tricks.

- Rimsky-Korsakov, *Scheherazade* (timing the runs with the flute in the 3rd movement is often hard, and the 4th movement has a good finger twister!) and *Le Coq d'or* solo.
- Josef Suk, *Asrael Symphony* has a tricky scherzo with two clarinets playing in unison and *The Ripening* is demanding for all three players.

Tuning

It is generally useful to have a working knowledge of fingerings you can use to flatten sharp notes on the clarinet. This will include using R1–3 and L3 for sharper throat notes and using the RH rings (not R1) to flatten *c♯'* and *d'*. Bear in mind certain characteristics of the different members of the wind section when examining tuning:

- Sharpness of oboe and flute: to enhance audibility, certain instruments prefer to be heard than to blend.
- Sharpness at the lower end of the bassoon's range: the entire woodwind section depends on the second bassoonist's bass notes.
- Flatness at the lower end of the flute's range.
- Flatness at the bottom end of the clarinet's range; difficult to correct!
- Sharpness on clarinet's throat notes and above *g''* (e.g. Schubert 'Unfinished' Symphony: end of 2nd movement, or Beethoven Ninth Symphony, slow movement). Brahms's Piano Concerto No. 2 has a very tricky passage for both clarinets for breathing and tuning of the clarino register.

Changing clarinets

There are several instances where greasing the joints of the mouthpiece is rather essential in order to change quickly from B♭ to A or vice versa. Walton's *Façade* contains awkward quick changes from B♭ to A and to bass, especially if the movements segue into each other.

Staccato

Articulation is often hugely simplified by viewing it as an extension of legato, so that it becomes a passive rather than an attacking action. Progressing through a series of legato soft-tonguing exercises within one breath, starting with no gaps between the notes and gradually introducing more, keeps the emphasis on the proper formation of the notes, whatever their length. The tongue can then concentrate on clearing out of the reed's way and allowing it to vibrate.[3]

- Beethoven, Symphony No. 4, finale: fortunately, the tricky clarinet solo is in unison with the strings, unlike the earlier bassoon solo; articulating quickly over the break: try slurring to the grace note.
- Smetana, *Bartered Bride* Overture.
- Mendelssohn, *Midsummer Night's Dream* scherzo.
- Raff, Symphony No. 3, scherzo: here is a surprise for the connoisseur! The ability to double tongue would be very useful here!
- Tchaikovsky, *Overture Miniature* and *Marche* from *The Nutcracker*.
- Kodály, *Galánta Dances*: the *tutti* passages – many in unison with the flute and full orchestra – are hard.
- Beethoven, Symphony No. 7, slow movement; Prokofiev, Violin Concerto No. 2, slow movement: these have very taxing passages of slow tonguing.
- Benjamin Britten, *Building of the House* Overture: this is embarrassingly difficult for most mortal tongues!

Transposition

However strong one's advocacy of the C clarinet, it is necessary to be prepared to transpose its music, which ranges over a very wide repertoire from Beethoven and Rossini through Mendelssohn, Berlioz, Smetana, Tchaikovsky and Verdi to Suk and Schoenberg. For Mahler and Richard Strauss the C clarinet is generally indispensable.

Transposing by a semitone either way – from B♭ to A clarinet and vice versa – can overcome awkward passages (cf. remarks on page 37):

- Henry Wood, *Fantasy on Sea Songs*: the Hornpipe is in B major on the B♭ instrument!
- Brahms, Symphony No. 1, slow movement: changing for the solo avoids an awkward slur to top $c\sharp'''$.
- Tchaikovsky, Piano Concerto No. 1, slow movement: middle section $g\sharp'' - c\sharp'' - d\sharp''$ slurred is easier on the A clarinet.
- Dvořák, Symphony No. 7: in preparation for a passage that would otherwise be on a cold instrument, or at the opening of Brahms Symphony No. 3, where there is insufficient time to change instruments.
- Strauss, Oboe Concerto: in practice, this is often transposed for A clarinet, averting the need for extreme sharp keys.

Solo work

If the opportunity presents itself, recitals and chamber music make a more intimate alternative to orchestral playing. Personally I have always found the latter more difficult, partly because the range of responsibilities is so much wider. As a recitalist, you can let only yourself, your pianist and your audience down. In the orchestra, there are your colleagues and a conductor to think of as well! Playing recitals does provide the hidebound orchestral musician with opportunities for expressive freedom and a chamber music style, but despite an ever-growing repertoire of worthwhile pieces, merely playing recitals can be a very limiting existence for a clarinettist. Life as a soloist may seem more glamorous than as a member of a larger team, but the orchestral repertoire has many good tunes and regular opportunities for intimate playing within the orchestral context. In a recital or in chamber music, balance is an entirely different issue. It is often necessary to tone down the orchestral projection significantly. It may also be necessary to make allowances for the fixed pitch of a piano. A collection of slightly longer barrels and tuning rings will normally suffice.

Playing under the scrutiny of modern microphones is a discipline worth examining. As well as the ambience and resonance of the hall, microphone positioning and distance from the instrument are crucial if the recording is to sound natural. Listening back to broadcasts, it has always struck me that one needs to exaggerate elements such as tonal colour, vibrato and of course dynamic levels if they are to be heard at all over the air. On the other hand, most microphones are now so responsive that they will pick up less musical sounds like key noise, breaths and air leaking from the side of the mouth. On some recordings even the player's movements are audible. As a result clarinettists try to eliminate these intrusions as much as possible. Repairs to the instrument will normally deal with the problem of key noise, but leaking air – an inaudible habit of orchestral clarinettists – is more of a problem. Getting rid of this can involve changing the set-up in some way, though I have usually coped with it by painstaking long note practice prior to the recording. If the sound is still intrusive in the studio, some companies resort to noise reduction methods, which make the clarinet sound altogether duller.

10 The contemporary clarinet

ROGER HEATON

Why is the clarinet such a popular instrument among contemporary composers? Is it that, as a social group, clarinettists combine intellect, industry and experimentation with a happy disposition? Well, this may be a contributing factor, but a rather more probable hypothesis is that the instrument itself combines flexibility with a tonal palette ranging from woody, chuckling cosiness to seering, ear-splitting intensity. It is the clarinet's expressiveness, agility and richness of tone which has attracted composers and has led to the many close associations between composer and performer: a tradition which has resulted in the wealth of concertos and chamber music from the eighteenth and nineteenth centuries discussed in Chapter 5.

In the twentieth century this composer–player teamwork has blossomed, particularly in the post-Second World War period. Experimenting and researching together, composers have written pieces which could not have existed without the specific talents of certain instrumentalists. Each has influenced the other as the range of pitch and colour has been extended, multiphonics discovered and exploited, microtones played on orchestral instruments not built for them, circular breathing rediscovered, percussive, air and simultaneous vocal sounds all brought together to broaden the spectrum of sound possibilities.

The language and style of new music has become much more familiar to audiences during the last fifteen years or so and music by living composers is beginning to appear regularly in mainstream concert programming and recording. More performers are actively involved in playing new music alongside traditional repertoire and it is no longer a minority interest appealing only to the specialist. That's the good news. The bad news is that there is still an astonishing reluctance among many young players to play music written by living composers.

Musicians often have a depressingly conservative view of music supported by conservatoire training and its emphasis on the seventeenth to nineteenth centuries. New music demands a wide range of colour and expression which, of course, should be central to the performance of music from all periods, and many of the sounds discussed in this chapter require a flexibility both musically and technically. Young clarinettists rightly strive for their ideal tone and equality of production throughout the range of the instrument, but this is only one, albeit important, aspect of playing and can lead to a rather narrow view of the instrument's potential: a terrible blandness of tone and approach when applied indiscriminately to the already over-worked and overplayed clarinet 'core' repertoire from Mozart to Poulenc. One hears too often today yet another Brahms or Mozart played with facility but with this kind of dull, received utility musicality. It needs a kind of daring and imagination to push the instrument to its limits, to make sounds which might not be conventionally 'beautiful'. One needs to take on board the fact that this small area of Western, mostly European, classical art music is only part of a wider picture that also includes things like Eric Dolphy's bass clarinet solos or a Turkish folk clarinettist playing on a metal instrument pitched in G! New music today, more than ever before, is freer of accepted conventions. It is less inhibited, more open to dipping into all kinds of other musics, pinching and reworking ideas, sounds and rhythms from around the globe. Playing all these different kinds of new music can focus our attention on the nuts and bolts of playing the clarinet, the very fabric of the instrument itself. It forces us to use the instrument to try to express something vital and living rather than simply as a diverting salon entertainment. Some players are now looking to the past and working with copies of eighteenth- and nineteenth-century instruments in order to re-create the sound and 'feel' of an earlier performance practice. All of this, however rewarding and challenging for the player (and it is interesting to see that many of the clarinettists working in this field are also committed to new music), however much it changes our perspective and perhaps gets us closer to the music, is still museum work. Only by engaging with what is being created now, the new in all its many guises from pop to art, can we ensure a healthy future for music.

To put today's contemporary art music in context we must first look at some recent history. From the mid-1950s to the late 1970s the composer's research into extending the technique of traditional instruments was energetically matched by the then small band of committed new-music performer-specialists. The compositional basis for this extension of instrumental vocabulary was in the newly found freedom of musical language. Composers at the turn of the century had pushed at the edges of chromaticism within the boundaries of tonality. Schoenberg and his pupils went one step further, breaking with tonality and laying the foundations of both a free-atonal style and the new theory of composition with twelve notes: a system for organising and controlling free atonality equal to the theory of functional harmony for tonal composition. The post-Second World War composers took the work of the Second Viennese School, and the freedom of pitch and rhythm offered by atonality, with an energy and zeal which would inevitably lead to a reappraisal of the individual sounds themselves. The late works of Webern pointed Boulez and Stockhausen, among others, in the direction of a serial organisation not only of pitch but of rhythm and dynamics. This was a system which proved to be too restricting, but when it was discarded it left behind a still wider repertoire of sounds and materials and opened further doors to different ways of organising material, from the superficially purposefully disorganised Cage-inspired aleatoricism to the grand designs of Stockhausen's moment forms.

The natural next step in the search for greater expressive resources to fill these newly invented forms and structures was the parallel emergence of the infinite possibilities of electronics. Despite the recent huge advances in technology, electronics as a compositional medium for classical Western art music is still problematic. Some of the best works created on tape still remain the earliest: Stockhausen's *Gesang der Jünglinge* (1955/6), for example. There are a few fine works for electronics/tape alone and with instruments, but the main thrust of compositional work still remains within the acoustic domain. Now, with the computer, anyone can write and perform immense, mind-bogglingly complex symphonies in the comfort of their own home for relatively little cost. The crux of the problem is that much of this easily produced and readily available music uses sampled and synthesised versions of the existing old acoustic instruments.

The progress of art music in our century is a complex story with many subplots. When Schoenberg opened the floodgates the younger modernists – Berio, Nono, Maderna, Ligeti, Xenakis and others, together with Boulez and Stockhausen – inherited and continued a Western European language traceable back through Schoenberg to Wagner, Beethoven and beyond. While these heavyweights of the avant-garde are, of course, important and influential, they are only part of the story. There is also the parallel experimental movement whose equally influential ancestors include Satie and Charles Ives. This movement, with John Cage as its towering central figure, has progressed through the development of, among other things, indeterminacy, environmental and multimedia pieces, but an increasingly important movement within experimentalism is the rediscovery and reinterpretation of tonality, most apparent in the post-modern minimalist composers whose work during the last ten years has had a critical acclaim and popularity unprecedented in contemporary art music. Some critics consider that, as we come to the turn of another century, the modernist movement, culminating in the extreme complexities of a younger generation of composers led by Brian Ferneyhough, has run its course, and the way into the twenty-first century is populated by a new breed of composers concerned with consonance rather than dissonance. We shall see!

The final strand of this story lies with the traditionalists and conservatives. Sibelius, Britten and Shostakovich loom large over a breathtakingly diverse and rich body of work. Copland's *Concerto* and Poulenc's *Sonata* are two enduring and popular masterpieces picked at random from the clarinet repertoire; however, this particular story is covered elsewhere in this book.

Extended instrumental techniques from the 1950s to the 1970s were always the preserve of the specialist player. The great American jazz–classical clarinettist William O. Smith, who studied composition with Milhaud and Roger Sessions but is probably better known for playing with Dave Brubeck since the late 1940s, heard the flautist Severino Gazzelloni play Berio's *Sequenza I* (1958) for solo flute and began to experiment himself with multiple sounds, producing *Variants* (UE) for solo clarinet – a veritable catalogue of new sounds in six short movements with an excellent explanatory introduction – in 1963. In the early 1960s Smith was working in Rome and collaborated with Luigi Nono on his large-scale work for four voices, tape and solo clarinet (playing mostly multiphonics), *A floresta è jovem e cheja de vida* (Ricordi), composed between 1965 and 1966. Nono has always worked closely with players who do not simply perform but have a creative part in inventing the works themselves. Up to his death in 1990 he worked with a small group of Italian musicians including the clarinettist Ciro Scarponi. Italy seems to have been the melting pot for early instrumental experimentation: the composer Bruno Bartolozzi's pioneering *New Sounds for Woodwind* (Oxford, 1967, 2nd edn, 1982) was an early attempt to systematise and notate multiphonics, microtones and colour trills (different fingerings of the same pitch) which Bartolozzi had worked on with orchestral wind players in Milan and Florence in the early 1960s. The research on clarinet was continued by Giuseppe Garbarino whose own excellent *Method for Clarinet* appeared in 1978.

In Britain Alan Hacker's energy, imagination and extraordinarily individual technique resulted in many commissions, some of which have already been listed by Pamela Weston in Chapter 5. A handful of these pieces remain among the best in the repertoire – Peter Maxwell Davies's *Hymnos* (1967 BH) for clarinet and piano, Harrison Birtwistle's *Linoi* (1969 UE) for basset clarinet and piano (inside plucked strings), and Alexander Goehr's *Paraphrase* (1969) for solo clarinet. Incidentally, Bartolozzi's own *Collage* (1973 Edizioni Suvini Zerboni Milan) for solo clarinet was dedicated to Hacker.

In Germany Hans Deinzer gave the first performance of one of the most important works for clarinet of the last fifty years: Pierre Boulez's *Domaines* (1961–6 UE). Shortly afterwards, Alan Hacker played the first ensemble performances with Boulez conducting. *Domaines* exists as a piece for both solo clarinet and clarinet with ensemble. Its form shows Boulez's passing flirtation with aleatory techniques, with its choice of different routes through the material and freedom of order of the pages. This apparent randomness is always under control, not least in the unifying structure of the number 6. There are six pages of solo material which are then mirrored, in almost exact retrograde, by six more. On each page there are six different fragments of material and two possible ways of reading the page, either from top to bottom or side to side. The sixness is reflected in the notes themselves: rhythmic groups of six notes, segmentations of the twelve chromatic pitches, subdivisions and groupings of dynamics and rhythms. In the ensemble version there are six ensembles of one (a solo bass clarinet), then two, then three instruments through to six (a string sextet). Each of the soloist's pages is related to one of the groups, both physically, spaced out on the concert platform, and in the musical material itself. The soloist plays a page next to an associated group who then play their material as he/she walks away to choose another group with which to play, and so on until the six pages are finished and all six groups have played. Then, in the mirror version, the groups play first, with the conductor choosing the order, and the clarinettist following from group to group. The writing for clarinet is fascinating, wonderfully colourful and detailed in notation; almost every new technique is here with a particularly beautiful use of dynamics (sometimes a different one for every note) and multiphonics. This is a piece all clarinettists should know.

In France the trombonist Vinko Globokar – perhaps the most innovative and inventive of all the composers working with extended techniques and who became, albeit short-lived, head of instrumental research at Boulez's IRCAM in Paris – collaborated with clarinettist Michel Portal and with that other great composer–performer, the oboist Heinz Holliger, on a number of pieces including the *Discours* series. *Discours IV* (1974 Peters) for three clarinettists has, among other extraordinary sounds, three players blowing one clarinet (a mouthpiece at both ends and a cor anglais reed in the thumb-hole), two bass clarinets, with bells off, being played into a bowl of water, and three contrabass clarinets without mouthpieces being played with trombone embouchures. *Voix Instrumentalisée* (1973 Peters) for solo bass clarinet without mouthpiece is the best piece we have for a vocalising player. The four pages of score with twelve short sections of material mix graphic notation with precise pitch control for the fingerings, lip buzzing and vocal pitches. There is a text, in French, which is used phonetically: 'Art and science cannot exist without the possibility of expressing paradoxical concepts'. There are sections of extreme difficulty where singing, lip glissandi and key movement are to be executed simultaneously. Part of the energy of this music, which links it with the music of the British 'complex' composers, is in the striving for all the composer demands and also, sometimes, in an honourably improvised approximation. This is a piece with moments of great beauty, and great humour.

With the mouthpiece back on the instrument(!) the bass clarinet has become almost as important to composers as the clarinet. Since Schoenberg's *Pierrot lunaire* (1912) it has been a regular doubling instrument in new ensemble music. Two players in particular have worked for its acceptance as a solo instrument in its own right: Josef Horák has commissioned a huge amount of, mostly, Czechoslovakian music, and Harry Sparnaay's commissions range from Feldman's *Bass Clarinet and Percussion* (1981 UE) to Brian Ferneyhough's extraordinarily difficult and complex *Time and Motion Study I* (1977 Peters). Sparnaay is also a driving force for new music in his own native Holland. The stylistic range of music for the bass is as wide as that for the clarinet: from funky minimalist music, the two bass parts in Steve Reich's *New York Counterpoint* for solo and tape (ten other clarinets) (1985 BH) and the haunting lyrical beauty of a piece like Gavin Bryars's *Three Elegies for Nine Clarinets* (1993/4 Schott), to the altogether tougher atonal music of a fine solo piece like Isang Yun's *Monolog* (1983 Bote & Bock). Most composers demand an instrument which extends down to low c and the range of Yun's piece, and the Feldman among many others, is to high c''''. These high notes on the bass are easy to produce and have a full, clear ringing tone. I give some fingerings in the section at the end of this chapter.

The E♭ clarinet, on the other hand, has fared less well. The only solo piece of any note, the final brief section of Henze's concerto *Le Miracle de la Rose* (1981 Schott) apart, is the *Tre Studi* (1954 Salabert) by Giacinto Scelsi (1905–88), that astonishingly innovative and reclusive Italian composer whom Feldman once described as the 'Charles Ives of Italy'. As early as 1944 Scelsi had written a mature, richly free-atonal *First String Quartet*, but it is the later works – sonorous, sometimes microtonal, almost improvisatory, always concerned with the drama and beauty of sound – which reveal Scelsi's uniqueness. He wrote some major works for clarinet which are little known in Britain: the piece for E♭ clarinet, two solos for B♭ clarinet, the exquisite miniature *Ixor* (1956 Salabert) and the large-scale *Preghiera per un'ombra* (1954 Salabert), and the wild and folky concerto with an ensemble of seven instruments *Kya* (1959 Salabert). Scelsi's music uses exact quarter-tones as part of its orientally inspired language, but it is the use of notated wide vibrato, as well as the strange metal mutes for the strings, which gives the music its strangely rustic quality.

In contemporary music, as in pre-classical music, vibrato is used ornamentally as an effect placed on top of the basic sound for heightened expressivity, and is carefully notated when required, as in Stockhausen's *In Freundschaft* (1977 Stockhausen Verlag) or Boulez's *Domaines*. There are, of course, no hard and fast rules for its use, but with the clarinet a little vibrato goes a long way and too much wobbling on any wind instrument is tiresome; nevertheless there is room for a little warming at the peaks of phrases in the more romantic free-atonal pieces such as the last page of Berio's *Sequenza IX* (1980 UE) – another piece that should be in every clarinettist's library – or Penderecki's simple arch-shaped miniature *Prelude* (1987 Schott). Stockhausen asks for the accelerando of vibrato, from a single note into vibrato moving faster into a trill, so it is necessary to use jaw vibrato for exact control.

Moving on to tone, this can be changed in three different ways: the choice of the hardware itself (clarinet, mouthpiece and reed), by changes in the oral cavity and throat (the real source of a player's particular tone) and finally by alternative fingerings.

Alternative fingerings are a time-honoured method of changing the tone and intensity of specific notes ('voicing' particularly around the throat notes) as well as correcting intonation. Composers, including Boulez and Berio, have used them to change the colour on single held notes and on, for example, *subito piano* notes, and have used a variety of notations (Boulez uses + − + − above the written pitch) leaving the choice of fingerings to the player. As the alternative fingerings move further away from the original pitch they become quarter-tone fingerings. When used fast they become trills, called colour trills or *bisbigliando* or, as the French/Romanian composer Horatiu Radulescu calls them 'yellow tremoli'.

Horatiu Radulescu has created a unique soundworld based on the harmonic spectrum. His *The Inner Time* (1982 Lucero Press) for solo clarinet is a piece lasting twenty-eight minutes using only multiphonics, harmonics and 'yellow tremoli', where notes are split apart and the harmonics explored individually then built and layered on top of each other, much like the solo free improvisation of British saxophonist Evan Parker. It is a piece of immense activity and difficulty often sounding as though three or four clarinets are playing simultaneously and, like the Globokar bass piece, it is impossible to realise correctly as the composer intends. The graphic notation shows the rhythms to be articulated on all the numbered harmonics of the spectrum resulting from the split fundamental.

Changing tone by altering the shape of the oral cavity is generally rather vaguely notated, usually with wishy-washy descriptive words like 'flutey' or 'feathery'. It is much clearer in works which use predominantly air sounds, either air alone or air mixed with tone. Two of the best examples are Denis Smalley's *Clarinet Threads* (1985 MS) for clarinet and tape – which also uses key click noises, multiphonics and high teeth-on-reed pitches all carefully mixed with synthesised and sampled clarinet sounds on tape – and the leading German composer Helmut Lachenmann's *Dal Niente (Interieur III)* (1970 Edition Gerig) for solo clarinet. All Lachenmann's clarinet music – the concerto *Accanto* (1980 Breitkopf) and *Allegro Sostenuto* (1988) for clarinet, cello and piano – was written for the Swiss player Eduard Brunner (as were the clarinet quintets and concertos by Denisov and Yun).

Lachenmann uses air sounds with and without tone, key clicks, teeth-on-reed sharp accents and slap tongue in all his works. He explains,

The square note-heads are toneless sounds of blowing with prescribed fingerings through which the degree of brightness of the air-sound is differentiated. This action is to be performed with a narrow oral cavity, the sound, although relatively thin, should however be clearly perceptible ... in its different degrees of brightness. (Performance Instructions to *Dal Niente*).

This technique is a kind of filtering. Try pronouncing 'he' then 'you', now move smoothly in one breath from 'he-you', now do the same mouth shape and movement but with only a hissing breath sound. It is this kind of technique Lachenmann uses for changing the tonal colour. The same technique is used in Tibetan vocal harmonics. Hum a low pitch in the nose (as though saying 'ng') with the mouth shut then open the mouth slowly from an 'o' shape to an 'ah' shape to move up and down the harmonic series of the hummed pitch (good fun in the privacy of your own bathroom!).

Breathing and articulation are, of course, fundamental to wind technique and I will explain circular breathing later in this chapter. Some composers have examined note production in more detail than the basic technique of how to start and stop a note. The American composer Donald Martino (himself a clarinettist) and German Hans Joachim Hespos have designed notations for the differing attack and release of notes. Martino's 1966 article giving a new additional notation for stress and attack, 'Notation in general – articulation in particular' in the journal *Perspectives of New Music*, is reprinted in the excellent *Perspectives on Notation and Performance*, ed. Boretz and Cone (New York, 1976), pp. 102–13. Hespos's notation (Fig. 10.1) uses a slight modification of standard note-heads.

Hespos's two solo works – *Harry's Musike* (1972 Hespos Ed.) for bass clarinet, and *Pico* (1978 Hespos Ed.) for Eb or piccolo Ab or contrabass clarinet – like all his music, use the full gamut of new techniques, particularly vocal, and his music is often played by free-jazz improvisers.

◇ = air < = air with some tone
◯ = open attack, open release
◗ = open attack, clear release
◖ = clear attack, open release

Figure 10.1 Notation by Hans Joachim Hespos

To round up some of the remaining techniques: flutter-tongue and glissando are part of every player's technique and need no introduction here. Some of the sillier sounds – such as mouthpiece alone; mouthpiece on the lower joint of the instrument (forming a strange and exotic scale); blowing across the barrel (as one blows across the neck of a beer bottle); hitting the barrel with the palm of the hand (which does appear in Lachenmann's large ensemble piece *Mouvement*); muting (a cork in the bell which produces high harmonics with all fingers down and the register key open, and also produces a bad headache in the unfortunate player) – are all, thankfully, disappearing into obscurity.

Vocal effects, singing while playing, can produce some rich and interesting noises as can be found in Globokar's music, particularly the solo trombone pieces he writes for himself to play. Singing a semitone or quarter-tone away from a pitch, resulting in the difference tone beats, is also the last resort for those who cannot flutter-tongue.

The slap tongue is a percussive popping sound which appears in a great many pieces. It is created by the same process as clicking the tongue on the roof of the mouth but on the reed itself, using most of the tongue flat on the reed and pulling it away quickly, forming a vacuum.

Finally to electronics. More and more instruments are now being amplified, not only for large and outdoor spaces, but in the regular concert hall. The Kronos and Balanescu string quartets, among others, play with amplification as do the composer-led ensembles of Philip Glass, Gavin Bryars and Michael Nyman. It makes for more impact of sound and greater immediacy, as one would get from listening to a CD at home, and allows the possibility of adding reverberation to enhance the acoustic. When playing with tape or electronics it is necessary to be amplified so that the live sound can be mixed and balanced with the electronic sounds and placed in the same acoustic. For all these purposes good air microphones are used, and sometimes discreet clip-on radio microphones. Now there is a vast array of live treatments that can be made; gone are the days of just a foot pedal box-of-tricks with distortion, ring modulator and an octave divider. MIDI applications and the introduction of the wind synthesisers have opened up wider possibilities. The recent Yamaha digital wind system looks and feels like a clarinet with saxophone fingerings and has a range of seven octaves; it can be changed to sound like any instrument you choose, can transpose, play polyphonically and so on. These instruments, which have been around since the early 1980s, are good in jazz and pop, but have still to find a home in classical new music.

Today, happily, the list of players actively involved in new music, commissioning new work and playing in the many new music ensembles, is too long to include here. The American scene is well covered by what is still by far the best book on new clarinet techniques, Phillip Rehfeldt's *New Directions for Clarinet* (University of California Press, 1976, rev. edn 1994). This indispensable book covers all aspects of new technique. Most importantly the fingerings given for microtones and multiphonics are clear and correctly produce the notated pitches, unlike Bartolozzi's more problematic book which, like Garbarino's *Method*, uses the confusing number notation for fingerings. For bass clarinet the best book available is the recent one by the Dutch bass clarinettist Henri Bok (with composer Eugen Wendel), *New Techniques for the Bass Clarinet* (Salabert, 1989).

What follows is a selection of fingerings and suggestions for playing some of the recent techniques discussed here; I hope they will be helpful. Incidentally, no special equipment is required. I play on a standard set-up; mouthpieces with wider tip openings will make high notes difficult to play. The fingering notation I favour for the Boehm system, and used in the examples below, is clear and easily read without recourse to a separate diagram of the instrument. Complex new music already has a great deal of information on the page besides the notes themselves, and a simple graphic representation of a fingering can be read in an instant (Fig. 10.2).

High notes

All players should play scales and arpeggios to c'''' as part of their regular practice. Contemporary composers have written considerably higher than this, and some of the highest notes have been written for Hacker by Birtwistle and Maxwell Davies, particularly the latter's *The Seven Brightnesses* for solo clarinet (1975 BH) which finishes on g''''. $c\sharp''''$, d'''' and $e\flat''''$ are all good and usable notes with normal embouchure but above this the notes become unstable, thin and squeaky. Figure 10.3 gives fingerings from c'''' to g''''. Try using a 'short lip' (Fig. 10.4) where as little as possible of the lower lip damps the reed. Above g'''' you will probably need to use teeth on the reed, but if you use the short lip puffing out your cheeks seems to help up there!

Microtones

Microtones are becoming increasingly important to composers not simply as quasi-ethnic note-bending effects but as an integral part of

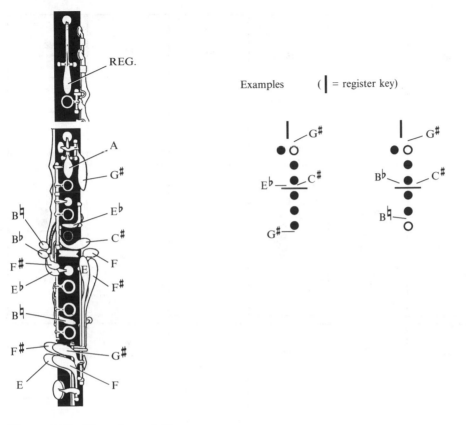

Figure 10.2   Fingering notation

the pitch language. The music of Xenakis and a younger generation of French composers who have taken the harmonic spectrum as a basis for their music (Grisey, Murail, Levinas, Radulescu) as well as the important British group of 'complex' composers (Ferneyhough, Dillon, Finnissy and others) all use microtones with facility and subtlety although for very different reasons. While the French group notate the exact tuning of the resulting harmonics of a chosen fundamental, the 'complex' group organise the quarter-tones as extra real pitches within the further saturation of the chromatic scale. Example 10.1 (page 176) shows the final few bars from the solo part of Brian Ferneyhough's *La Chute d'Icare* (1987 Peters) for solo clarinet and ensemble.

Quarter-tones can be articulated and heard very clearly, eighth-tones are much more approximate and rely on lip-bending. Figure 10.5 shows the notation for a quarter-tone scale from *c′* to *g′* with enharmonics and *c′* to *d′* in eighth-tones. Quarter-tones, in the main, use real fingerings but are often of poor quality. Always play them in context, in relation to the fixed chromatic notes. You may have to widen micro-intervals, depending on the voice-leading, so that the quarter-tone becomes a discernible pitch rather than sounding like bad

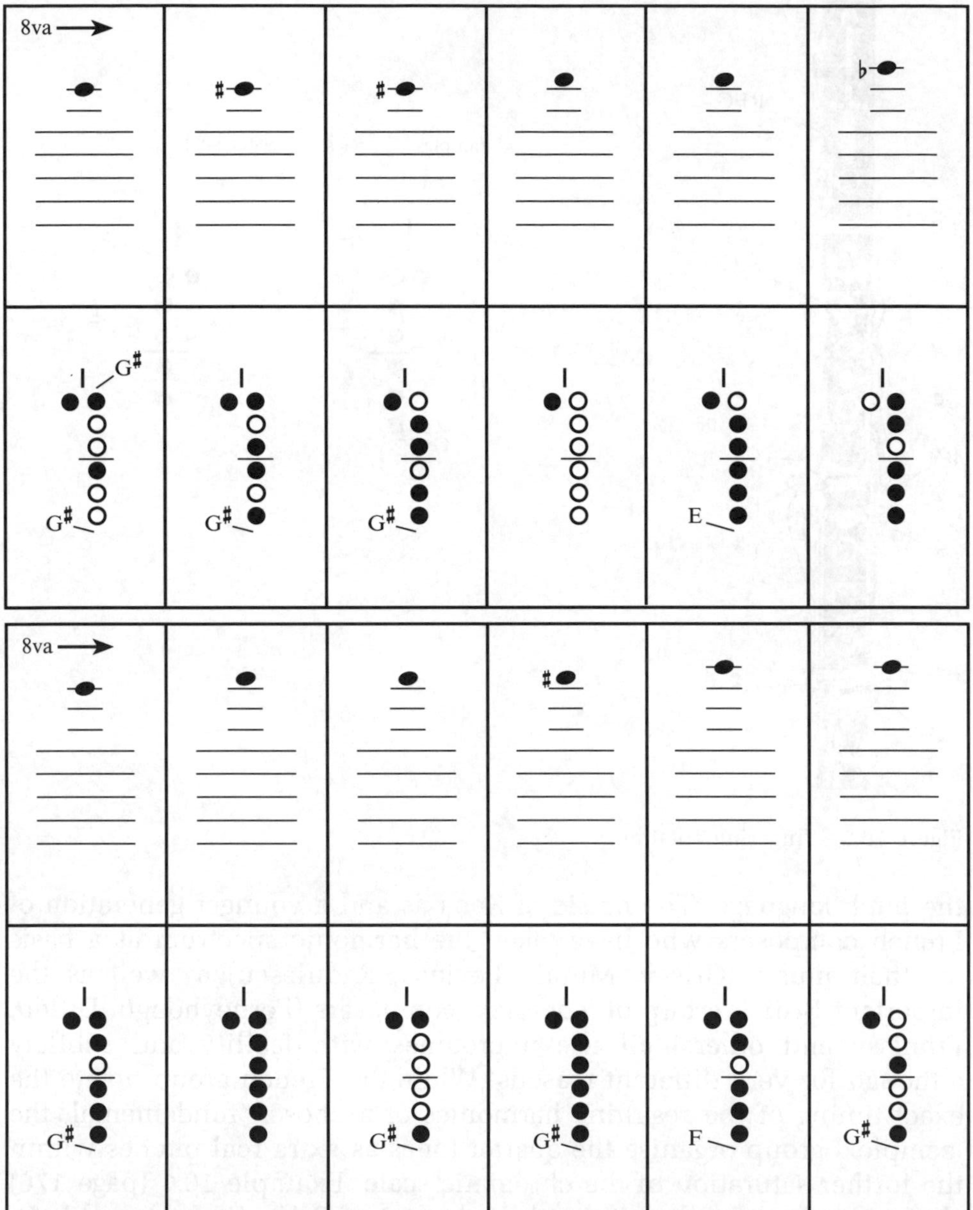

Figure 10.3   High notes for B♭ clarinet

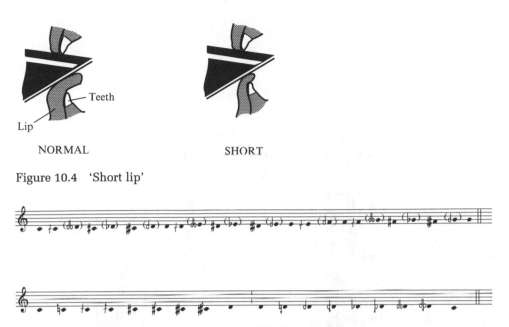

Figure 10.4   'Short lip'

Figure 10.5   Notation for quarter-tone and eighth-tone scales

intonation! Figure 10.6 is a selection of good standard fingerings, but tailor them to your own particular needs and instrument set-up.

Multiphonics

There are two types. Firstly, those produced by splitting a regular fingering in the low register by altering the embouchure so that a fundamental sounds simultaneously with a selection of its harmonics; similarly in the upper register regular notes can be lipped down to produce the undertones. Secondly, and more satisfactory, there is the type produced by a special fingering. The latter are used extensively in new music because of the accuracy with which the upper and lower notes can be pitched.

Splitting a regular note can be achieved in a number of ways. On low E or F try dropping the lower jaw by half an inch while still keeping the lower lip on the reed. Reapply pressure to move up the harmonics. There are many examples of this type of harsh, electronic-sounding multiphonic and also many different notations, from diamond-shaped note-heads to crosses above the notes. In Xenakis's music, for example, he gives a fundamental and then notates zones, low to high, of the resulting harmonics.

The second type of multiphonics is easier to produce but you need to practise balancing the upper and lower notes at an equal dynamic. One note, usually the upper one, will always come more easily, so you need to concentrate on the other. Tonguing can help to sound the two

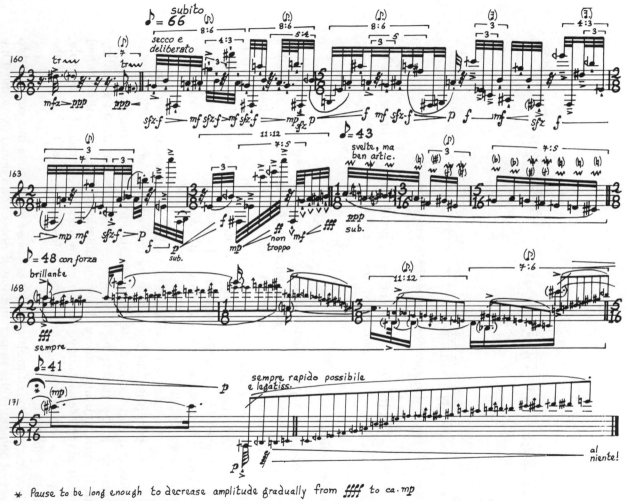

* *Pause to be long enough to decrease amplitude gradually from ƒƒƒƒ to ca. mp*

Example 10.1   the final bars of the solo clarinet part of *La Chute d'Icare* by Brian Ferneyhough

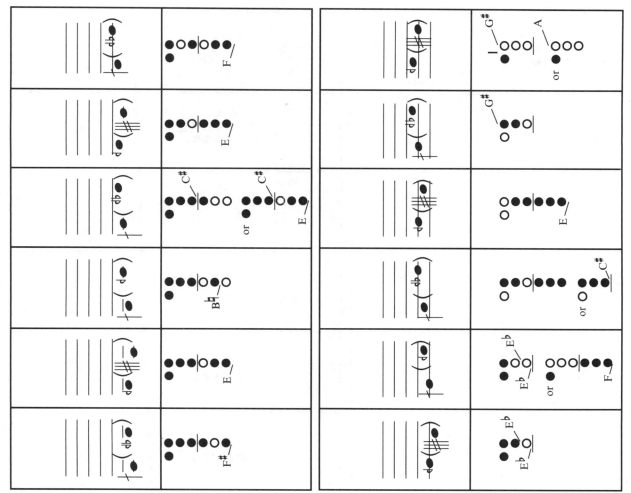

Figure 10.6   Quarter-tone fingerings for B♭ clarinet

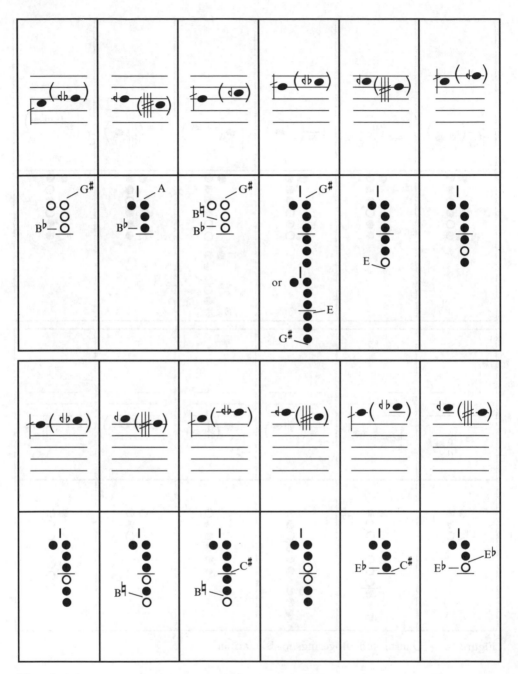

Figure 10.6

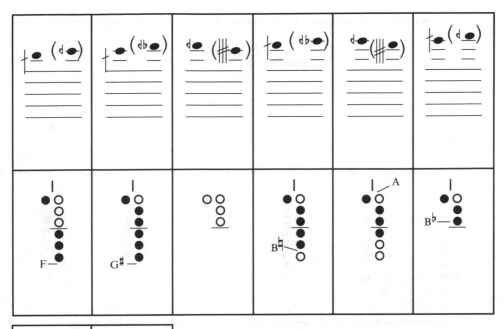

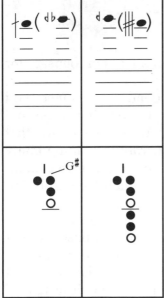

Figure 10.6

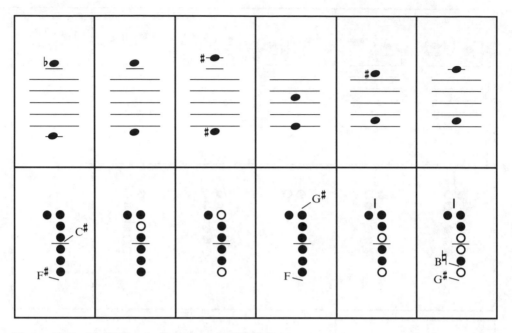

Figure 10.7   Multiphonic fingerings for B♭ clarinet

pitches together, and generally they need a lot of air to compensate for the resistance of the fingerings.

Figure 10.7 gives six fingerings of this second type. Once you understand that this type is simply achieved by playing a normal fingering, with or without register key, and then venting *above* that note (often in the left hand) then you are on the way to making many of your own. Note that, generally speaking, the right lower hand controls the upper harmonics, and the left upper hand controls the lower fundamental pitches.

Examples 10.2 and 10.3 are of multiphonic writing. The first is from Boulez's *Domaines* and the second from the German composer Robert H. P. Platz's *RAUMFORM* for solo clarinet (1982 Breitkopf). Boulez simply gives one pitch that the player can make a multiphonic with; I have chosen to take this as the top of the multiphonic which has an *f♯* as its lower pitch. The Platz was more problematic as he composed the two-part writing he wanted to hear and left it to the player to find a solution. Fortunately the fingerings proved very straightforward and the two parts are clearly heard.

Circular breathing

Circular breathing, or continuous breath, is an ancient technique used more and more by players and one being specifically asked for by composers: Stockhausen, *In Freundschaft*, and James Dillon, *Crossing*

Example 10.2   from Pierre Boulez, *Domaines*

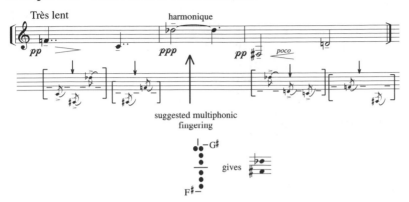

Example 10.3   from Robert H. P. Platz, *Raumform*, bar 28

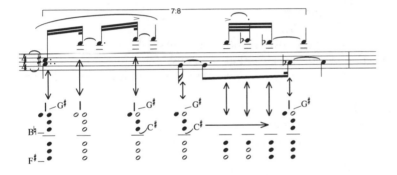

Over (1978 Peters). Here's how to practise it in three easy stages.

(1)   Fill your cheeks full of air; stop off the throat with the root of the tongue; push the air out slowly with the cheek muscles making a rude 'raspberry' noise!

(2)   Fill your cheeks as before; stop off the throat; hold the air in your cheeks and breathe in and out normally through the nose.

(3)   Fill your cheeks as before and breathe in through the nose slowly while simultaneously pushing the air slowly out of your cheeks in the 'raspberry' noise.

That's it. Now with the clarinet.

Practise playing notes with cheeks' air only, as in (1) above playing an open *g'* rather than a 'raspberry', then try sniffing in while pushing out. The difficulty is that, after breathing in, returning to normal breathing can give a bump in the air-flow when reopening the throat.

Bass clarinet fingerings

The bass clarinet, because of its covered keys, is much more limited in the control of multiphonics and microtones while being richer in harmonics because of the length of the tube. There isn't space here to notate the variations between clarinet and bass clarinet fingerings and those interested should refer to Henri Bok's book. You can use some of the clarinet fingerings given in Figure 10.3 and Figure 10.6 as a starting point. Figure 10.8 gives some high-note fingering suggestions.

Select list of some recent important pieces

LUCIANO BERIO: *Sequenza IX* (1980 UE) solo
   Lied (1983 UE) solo
HARRISON BIRTWISTLE: *Verses* (1966 UE) cl and pn
   Linoi (1969 UE) cl and pn
   Melancolia 1 (1976 UE) cl and orch
   Clarinet Quintet cl, st qt(1980 UE)
PIERRE BOULEZ: *Domaines* (1966 UE) solo/solo and ens
   Dialogue de l'ombra double (1986 UE) cl and electronics
GAVIN BRYARS: *Three Elegies for Nine Clarinets* (1993/4 Schott) solo cl/bass
   and tape
CORNELIUS CARDEW: *Mountains* (1988 Forward Music) solo bass
ELLIOTT CARTER: *GRA* (1993 BH) solo
PETER MAXWELL DAVIES: *Hymnos* (1967 BH) cl and pn
FRANCO DONATONI: *Clair* (1980 Ricordi) solo
MORTON FELDMAN: *Clarinet and String Quartet* (1983 UE) cl and st qt
BRIAN FERNEYHOUGH: *Time and Motion Study I* (1977 Peters) solo bass
   La Chute d'Icare (1987 Peters) solo and ens
VINKO GLOBOKAR: *Voix Instrumentalisée* (1973 Peters) solo bass
ALEXANDER GOEHR: *Paraphrase* (1973 Schott) solo
HANS WERNER HENZE: *Le Miracle de la Rose* (1981 Schott) solo B♭/bass/E♭ and
   ens
HELMUT LACHENMANN: *Accanto* (1980 Breitkopf) cl and orch
   Allegro Sostenuto (1989 Breitkopf) cl, vc, pn
STEVE REICH: *New York Counterpoint* (1985 BH) cl and tape
GIACINTO SCELSI: *Ixor* (1956 Salabert) solo
   Kya (1959 Salabert) cl and ens
WILLIAM O. SMITH: *Variants* (1963 UE) solo
KARLHEINZ STOCKHAUSEN: *In Freundschaft* (1977 Stockhausen Verlag) solo
TORU TAKEMITSU: *Waves* (1976 Schott) solo & ens
ISANG YUN: *Monolog* (1983 Bote & Bock) solo bass
   Concerto (1981 Bote & Bock) cl and orch
   Quintet (1984 Bote & Bock) cl and st qt
IANNIS XENAKIS: *Echange* (1989 Salabert) solo bass and ens

UE – Universal Edition   BH – Boosey and Hawkes

= half hole

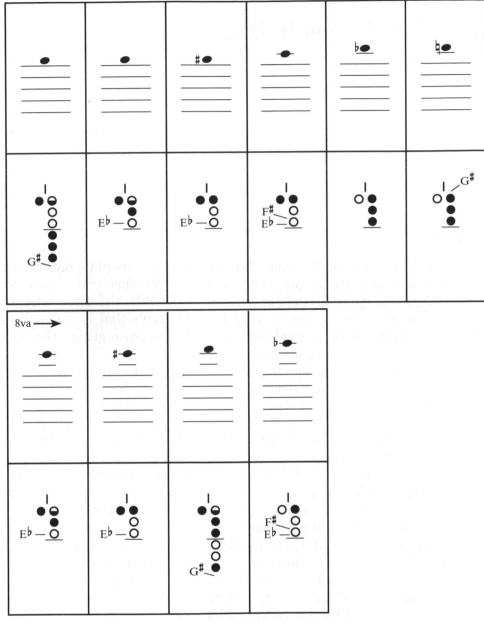

Figure 10.8   High notes for bass clarinet

11 The clarinet in jazz

JOHN ROBERT BROWN

Introduction

Listen to almost any performance from the first decade of recorded jazz and you will hear the sound of the clarinet. Whether you choose to listen to the Original Dixieland Jazz Band (ODJB), the King Oliver/ Louis Armstrong recordings or Jelly Roll Morton's Red Hot Peppers, you will hear every ensemble topped by upper-register clarinet, playing in harmony above the melody.

All the evidence about the origins of jazz points to the music having developed from vocal performances. Undoubtedly field hollers, work songs, religious music and the famous post-1817 New Orleans Congo Square dances were all part of the picture, as far as vocal music was concerned. After the end of the Civil War in 1865 the New Orleans blacks were able gradually to acquire the instruments of the military band, including the clarinet. Military (marching) bands were important in all-French settlements, and in New Orleans most of the early jazz players started their careers in such wind bands, playing marches, polkas, quadrilles and so on. From these two sources – the vocal folk/ dance music and the marching band – it is quite easy to understand how the five- or six-piece jazz bands evolved. Of course the evolution of jazz included the influence of many other musical styles, ranging from Ragtime and Klezmer to the Chopin waltzes from which stride piano (with its 'striding' left hand of a bass note on beats 1 and 3 and a chord on beats 2 and 4) was probably derived. But it is with these smaller 'marching bands', with their trumpet–trombone–clarinet front line, that jazz first appeared on gramophone recordings.

Jazz clarinet on record

It is not necessary for an aspiring jazz player to hear the whole of jazz history. One's favourite style and repertoire makes an entirely appropriate starting point. The following brief overview of important jazz clarinettists is presented chronologically for simplicity, and is not intended to imply that each decade represents an advance on the previous one.

The poor quality of early recordings seems to be a major barrier to appreciation for many younger listeners. Recent attempts to remaster early recordings, using digital techniques, have been very successful and have made listening a lot easier. A series of CD releases, *Jazz Classics In Stereo* (BBC Records) engineered by Robert Parker, is to be particularly recommended. Also worth acquiring is the CD *Clarinet Marmalade – 25 Great Jazz Clarinettists* (Living Era, AJA 5132, 1994), which contains examples of the work of many of the players mentioned in this chapter.

Thomas Edison devised the first sound-recording machine in 1877. The first playback machines were on sale in Germany by the late 1880s, and by 1893 similar machines were on sale in America. However, we have to wait until 1917 for the first jazz recordings, which were made by the Original Dixieland Jazz Band, a five-piece (cornet, clarinet, trombone, piano, drums) white band from New Orleans, that swept the world. In America they travelled first to Chicago. They then appeared in New York to great acclaim, and in 1919 spent nine months at the Hammersmith Palais in London. Thus the first jazz clarinettist to be recorded was the ODJB's Larry Shields (1893–1953). He was born in the same year as Lorenzo Tio, the first great teacher of jazz clarinet. Tio's most famous pupil was Duke Ellington's Barney Bigard (1906–80). Jazz clarinet playing began with these figures. The mystery of where they found their formative influences is one of the great and frustrating puzzles of twentieth-century wind playing.

The most striking aspects of Shields's contribution to these ODJB recordings are the maturity of the style (Shields was only twenty-four-years old), the outrageous quality of his two-bar breaks with their glissandi and whinnying effects, and the fact that – apart from the two-bar breaks – there are no solos. The players who came after Shields *can* be heard soloing. Leon Rappolo (1902–43) and Frank Teschemacher (1906–32) are the important white clarinettists of the 1920s, along with Jimmy Dorsey (1904–57) and Pee Wee Russell (1906–69). The New Orleans lineage begins with Alphonse Picou (1878–1961) whose famous *High Society* solo, with its resemblance to the piccolo solo in the military-band origins of jazz, and continues through George Lewis (1900–68), whose influence came to bear later, in the post World War Two New Orleans jazz revival. The three great New Orleans clarinet-tists were Johnny Dodds (1892–1940), Jimmy Noone (1895–1940) and Sidney Bechet (1897–1959). Dodds is to be heard on the seminal *Hot Five* and *Hot Seven* recordings with Louis Armstrong. Bechet's enduring fame lies in his great popularity in France, where he became a popular entertainer almost in the Maurice Chevalier class towards the end of his life. Indeed he is now remembered mostly for his soprano saxophone playing, with unmistakable vibrato. But his clarinet work in the earlier days should not be overlooked, such as *Blues In Thirds* (1940) with Earl Hines. Mention should also be made of the work of Albert Nicholas (1900–73) and Omer Simeon (1902–59).

Yet for the layman and casual observer of the jazz scene, all this was but a prelude to the swing era, the period in the late 1930s when jazz became the pop music of the day, the age of the big swing band fronted and led by a virtuoso instrumentalist. This was the heyday of Benny Goodman (1909–86), the 'King of Swing', and Artie Shaw (*b.* 1910), the 'King of the Clarinet'. Both musicians are well represented on recordings. Goodman made his first trio recordings when he was not yet eighteen. If you are seeking just one recording to represent Benny Goodman, then try the 1938 Carnegie Hall Jazz Concert. The concert took place on 16 January 1938, and it is undoubtedly easier to search for the recording by date than by record number, as it has been reissued many times in every format. Not only is the twenty-eight-year-old clarinettist at peak form, but the concert has the bonus of performances by many members of the Count Basie and Duke Ellington bands of the time. Goodman is the clarinettist's clarinettist, yet his failure to assimilate the developments of modern jazz, coupled with his serious involvement with chamber and orchestral music (in addition to commissioning the works from Bartók, Copland, Hindemith and others mentioned in Chapter 5, he gave the world première of the Poulenc Clarinet Sonata in 1963 with Leonard Bernstein), has meant that he has received an unfairly hostile treatment from jazz journalists and from some jazz historians. There was not even an authoritative biography until two excellent ones appeared in quick succession some time after his death, James Lincoln Collier's *Benny Goodman and the Swing Era* (Oxford, 1989), and Ross Firestone's *Swing, Swing, Swing* (London, 1993).

Artie Shaw also became briefly involved with what he called 'long-form music' before giving up the clarinet completely in his mid-forties. His subsequent autobiography, *The Trouble With Cinderella* (New York, 1952), included a vivid portrayal of the conflict between art and entertainment which is so familiar to many musicians. One of the many highlights of his career was the recording of *Any Old Time* (New York, 1938) by the singer Billie Holiday, a song for which the gifted Shaw had written both words and music, and scored the big-band arrangement! Notable Artie Shaw performances on record include his *Concerto for Clarinet* (Hollywood, 1938) and his hit records *Frenesi* (four million sold in 1940) and *Begin the Beguine* (1938). He too suffered his share of critical deafness. In a chapter on the clarinet in what is widely regarded as one of the best companions to jazz available, *The Jazz Book* by Joachim Berendt (Frankfurt, 1973), he is dismissed as a 'minor Benny Goodman of a sort'! In contrast, a video biography of Shaw – *Time Is All You've Got* (1984), by the brilliant Brigitte Berman – is well worth seeing.

Although, of course, jazz continued to develop after the Second World War there was (and is) a large group of excellent jazz clarinet players who chose to play in what could be described as a modified Benny Goodman style. Kenny Davern (*b.* 1935), Arne Domnerus (*b.* 1924), Pete Fountain (*b.* 1930), Edmond Hall (1901–1967), Peanuts Hucko (*b.* 1918), Ove Lind (*b.* 1926), Johnny Mince (*b.* 1912), Ken Peplowski (*b.* 1958), Dave Shepherd (*b.* 1929), Putte Wickman (*b.* 1924) and Bob Wilber (*b.* 1928) are all available on record and are well worth hearing. Indeed, although in the late 1940s and early 1950s jazz moved on quickly from Charlie Parker-inspired bebop, the clarinet was largely left out of the picture. The only substantial and enduring contributor was Buddy De Franco (*b.* 1923), who won the *Downbeat* poll ten years running. He has an outstanding fluency, a dazzling command of the high register, an understanding of the harmonic language of bebop, and a tone that suited the music well. His playing has a character that is sharply different from that of the swing-era clarinettists. His 1954 quartet recording with pianist Art Tatum is legendary, though some of his more recent work presents a happier and more cohesive overall result. The critical and popular neglect that Buddy De Franco has suffered in the latter part of his career is one of the scandals of post-war jazz.

Other clarinettists who made innovative contributions in the 1950s and 1960s include Jimmy Giuffre (*b.* 1921), Duke Ellington's Jimmy Hamilton (*b.* 1917), Abe Most (*b.* 1920) and Sam Most (*b.* 1930), Tony Scott (*b.* 1921), Bill Smith (*b.* 1926), the tragically short-lived Swedish clarinettist Stan Hasselgard (1922–48), the Australian Don Burrows (*b.* 1928), and British clarinettists Vic Ash (*b.* 1930), Sandy Brown (1929–75) and Tony Coe (*b.* 1934). As a result of the post-war revival of interest in traditional jazz, two British clarinettists, Monty Sunshine (*b.* 1928) and Acker Bilk (*b.* 1929), became household names when their simple (and not at all jazzy) recordings of *Petite Fleure* and *Stranger On The Shore* respectively climbed high into the top 40 record charts both in Britain and America in the early 1960s.

Jazz styles continued to evolve via the abstract and the free, but despite interesting performances from Roland Kirk (1936–77), John Carter (*b.* 1929) and Perry Robinson (*b.* 1938), the major clarinet contributions to the avant-garde seemed to be from players of the lower members of the clarinet family. Eric Dolphy (1928–64) used the bass to great effect, for example in Oliver Nelson's *The Blues And The Abstract Truth* (Impulse AS5, 1961); Anthony Braxton (*b.* 1945) made rare but fascinating use of the contrabass when he played Charlie Parker's

Ornithology on his LP *In The Tradition* (Steeplechase SCS 1015, 1974). David Murray (*b.* 1955) continues this trend; his *Murray's Steps* (Black Saint 0065, 1983) received impressive critical acclaim, both for his tenor saxophone playing and his work on bass clarinet.

In the mid-1970s jazz lovers began to be aware of the clarinet playing of the established New York saxophonist Eddie Daniels (*b.* 1941). His *Morning Thunder* (CBS 36290, 1980) presented jazz-rock clarinet performances with a top New York session band, the first of several such releases. Combining a very refined technique (one night in Munich recently I heard him turn in an elegant performance of the Mozart Concerto) with an instantly recognisable jazz sound, he has been a consistent and deserving poll winner throughout the 1980s and 1990s (Fig. 11.1). *To Bird With Love* (GRP Records, GRP 95442, 1987) or *Breakthrough* (GRP Records, GRPD 9533, 1986) make a useful introduction to his work.

With the recordings of Paquito D'Rivera (*b.* 1948) it began to look as though there was a possibility of a jazz-clarinet renaissance. Born in Cuba, Paquito was a child virtuoso on saxophone and clarinet – and a Benny Goodman fan. After his New York debut in 1980 the *New York Times* stated that he 'should be heard ... by anyone who likes jazz that's inventive, hot and heartfelt', but he did not come to worldwide attention until he toured with Dizzy Gillespie's United Nations band in the late 1980s. Hear *Tico Tico* (Chesky JD 34, 1989) or *Reunion* (Messidor 15805–2, 1991), the latter featuring fellow Cuban Arturo Sandeval on trumpet.

At the time of writing, the most frequently mentioned new names in the world of jazz clarinet are those of Don Byron and Marty Ehrlich. Don Byron aims to bring both Klezmer and Rastafarian elements to jazz. Marty Ehrlich has been voted number one clarinet player in the '*Talent deserving of wider recognition*' section of the *Downbeat* critics' poll, and was the subject of a recent article entitled '*Is Marty Ehrlich the future of jazz?*' in the *New Yorker* magazine.

It is heartening to be able to conclude this brief overview of jazz clarinet on record with the thought that the place of the clarinet in jazz is now as strong as at any time since the end of the swing era and the end of the hegemony of Benny Goodman and Artie Shaw. May the trend continue.

Equipment

Most jazz clarinettists play on standard B♭ Boehm-system wooden clarinets, and use standard commercial mouthpieces and reeds. However, there are some considerations peculiar to jazz which determine choices for some players; these are principally connected with tone and volume.

Figure 11.1　Eddie Daniels

It is important for a jazz clarinettist to sound like no one else, and to have a tone appropriate to the style in which he plays. For example, a clarinettist who is captivated by early jazz, and who enjoys the playing of Johnny Dodds, Omer Simeon or Albert Nicholas, will be likely to choose equipment to make it easier for him to capture that style. As these players all played on pre-Boehm instruments (Albert-system or similar) this probably accounts for the number of 'simple'-system clarinets still seen in bands emulating the New Orleans style today. Occasionally old metal clarinets are used in these bands. Other players may simply wish to heighten their own individualism, so as to be easily recognised. This quest for identity presumably accounts for the contemporary British clarinettist Tony Coe's unusual choice of a C clarinet in boxwood, for example.

The need to play at high volume levels also influences reed and mouthpiece choices, and this in turn affects the choice of tuning barrel. Clarinettists playing in the classic New Orleans trumpet–trombone–clarinet instrumentation usually find themselves at a disadvantage when trying to match volume levels with the much louder brass instruments, particularly when these are allied to the power of the modern rhythm section. If you don't like using a microphone, then being able to play louder probably means choosing a more open mouthpiece and slightly softer reeds, and maybe taking a little more mouthpiece into the mouth. This all conspires to make it difficult to play up to a′=440 on a standard-length instrument, and it is common to find clarinettists in these circumstances resorting to a very short barrel – sometimes as much as 6.5 mm or more shorter than standard, but this is an undesirable solution to the problem. Clarinets are not designed to function accurately with such distorted proportions, and there is inevitably the penalty of poor intonation. Incidentally, staccato becomes more difficult with more mouthpiece in the mouth, though a clean and fast staccato is not high on the list of stylistic requirements for the jazz clarinettist.

The instruments and reeds used by the major jazz clarinettists are reassuringly orthodox. *Downbeat* appears to be the only music magazine to have consistently listed the equipment used by its interviewees. Reading through *Downbeat* interviews of the last three decades every one of the famous clarinettists interviewed claimed to use one of the popular brands of clarinet and popular brands of reeds of middle strength, between two- and three-and-a-half.

What to play

For me, one of the pleasures of teaching in a large college jazz department is the contact one has with the regular flow of visitors who come to perform or teach, or merely drop in to have a look round. Naturally, some of the visiting teachers have been excellent, but it must be said that helpful teachers are uncommon amongst these world-class jazz performers. Of course it is unfair to expect that every great player will have the insight to understand both how he weaves his magic *and* the skill to be able to communicate that insight, though there have been moments when the thought occurred that it was a little cheeky of some musicians to accept payment for a kind of teaching that was little more than expert demonstration. In the 'most unhelpful' category was an unforgettable visit by a ten-piece band of eminent New York musicians who called on us during a British tour. Following a crop of highly-acclaimed CD releases, these musicians were all well-known to the more aware jazz students. After giving a brief but quite wonderful performance in the college recital room, the group separated to enable each instrumentalist to take a few students away to practice rooms to receive specialist help and advice. The drummer was a widely-respected writer and player, so I attached myself to his group. One of our drum students was beside himself with eager anticipation at having such close contact with one of his heroes. Unfortunately the excitement didn't last long. The session started with what I now recognise as the classic way in which *not* to begin a masterclass. 'Anyone got any questions?' asked one of the visiting heroes. An eager and very hip drum student was quick to respond. 'Yes. If you're playing with a bass player who isn't grooving, what do you do about it?' he asked. 'I say "Man, You ain't groovin'!"' What marvellous confirmation of the truth of the celebrated saying that there are no such things as stupid questions, but only dumb answers. I find myself constantly trying to avoid giving a dumb answer to a similarly fundamental question, 'How do you know what to play?'

In order to arrive at a helpful answer, two assumptions must be made. First, you must have some proficiency on your instrument. You don't have to be a conservatoire-trained virtuoso, but a moderate command of scales and arpeggios is essential. Contemporary jazz is not simple music. The more technique you have the better, though it should not be allowed to dominate the music. Remember the virtue of art concealing art.

Secondly, it is essential that you have a love of some aspect of jazz. It does not really matter which aspect, but love it you must. If you share the opinion of the educationalist A. S. Neill, that jazz is all 'noisy, quacking stuff',[1] you are never going to play it convincingly, any more than you could learn to speak German convincingly if you found the language to be ugly and harsh. Impossible – or perhaps I should say *unmöglich*! Whether you love the outrageous vibrato of Johnny Dodds, the wistful low register of Jimmy Giuffre, the exuberance of Benny Goodman, the melodic inventiveness of Artie Shaw, the harmonic skill of Buddy De Franco or the inscrutable waywardness of Pee Wee Russell, you simply have to be in sympathy with some aspect of jazz if you are going to make progress. If one's efforts are going to sound convincing and be taken seriously, then what one chooses to play must be part of, or at least built on, the jazz tradition. One's performance should carry a jazz accent. The playing should display some aspects of the jazz vocabulary. These include a personal tone-quality, jazz vibrato, note colourations (growls, swoops, bends, glissandi), the presence of a swing feel and so on. Otherwise – to pursue the analogy of learning German – there is a danger of communicating nothing at all. Imagine the impossibility of learning German out of a book, without ever hearing the language spoken. It may seem strange to place such heavy emphasis on having a love of jazz and doing lots of listening. Surely everyone who tries to play jazz will do so out of a love of the music, and after hearing some of the jazz greats? Unfortunately that is not the case. I strongly suspect that those orchestral players who casually ask a jazz musician 'How do you know what to play?' are simply trying to find a golden key that will save them a lot of trouble. They do not want to spend lots of time listening to music that they do not really like, and hope that a few words with a jazz-playing colleague will provide a handy short cut to jazz competence. The author Laurence Block puts the point vividly. In *Writing The Novel* (Cincinnati, 1985), page 47, he urges would-be novelists to read widely, and observes that 'An isolated tribesman who spontaneously invents the bicycle ... may be displaying enormous natural creativity, but one wouldn't expect the world to beat a path to his door'. The analogy for would-be jazz clarinettists is obvious. So one must emphasise two prerequisites for jazz study: a moderate amount of technical facility, and sufficient respect for the music to enable one to take a delight in doing a lot of listening. Given these two prerequisites, what else is required?

Without doubt those players who rely entirely on their ear are the most convincing improvisers and are, of course, comfortable in any context. By 'relying entirely on their ear' I mean that such players seem to be able to hear with outstanding accuracy the harmonic carpet laid out for them by the rhythm section, and can thus thread their way sure-fingeredly through any chord progression. Some of the greatest jazz players seem to have been able to do this, from Bix Beiderbecke to Chet Baker, from Scott Hamilton to Paul Desmond. Interestingly, there seems to be a penalty for such outstanding aural ability. Most of the players whom I've encountered who are able to accomplish such miracles of accurate hearing are not very good readers of music. But of course the two skills are not incompatible. The link is not axiomatic.

The crucial question is how to acquire such a refined hearing ability, and be able to react to what one is hearing. Unfortunately the only way to be absolutely certain of reaching the highest standards of aural awareness seems to be to start at a very young age. The research of Sergeant and Roche, 'Perceptual shifts in the auditory information processing of young children', *Psychology of Music*, 39 (1973), pp. 1–2, has shown that 95 per cent of musicians who possess perfect pitch took up music before the age of four. In a similar way most jazz players who rely on their ear seem to have begun early in life. Both they and the few late starters who are likewise outstandingly competent in this skill seem to have devoted a lot of time to playing along with recordings, as many authenticated accounts of great jazz players indicate. Cornettist Bix Beiderbecke is known to have learned the ODJB repertoire, and imitated Nick LaRocca's style, in this way. In a September 1982 *Downbeat* interview (p. 22) Benny Goodman claimed that he could still play Larry Shields's solo on St Louis Blues note-for-note as a result of learning it from a gramophone record as a youth. Saxophonist Charlie Parker is reputed to have taken a pile of Lester Young 78s along on his first summer-season job and 'played them white'. 78s turned white as they wore out, and Parker wore them out copying Lester's solos note-for-note. Speed up a Lester Young tenor solo and you'll see the connection with Parker's alto. Playing along with records worked as an educative device for all of these style-setting players, and it is still to be recommended today. Even if you are a late beginner, this is still an important activity to include in your practice routine.

A more lengthy but time-proven practice is to write down other people's solos. The arguments in favour of transcribing jazz solos are many, and follow from the reasons for playing along with records, which:

(1)   Give an insight into note choices.
(2)   Help the understanding of characteristic chord progressions.
(3)   Make excellent technical exercises.
(4)   Enable a repertoire of licks (favourite phrases) to be collected.
(5)   Promote awareness of form and development in solos.
(6)   Provide a basic repertoire of tunes and changes for beginner soloists.
(7)   Encourage concentrated listening, thus developing tone, vibrato and articulation in the jazz manner.

Although I have several books of transcribed solos in print I would be the first to emphasise that notwithstanding their usefulness players will achieve faster progress if they make their own transcriptions, particularly if they use their instrument in the process. Transcribing is not an armchair exercise, nor should it be treated merely as some sort of aural challenge. Do not regard the use of your clarinet when transcribing as cheating. Obviously, if you were doing an aural test then use of your clarinet would be inadmissible. But you are trying to improve your jazz playing, not doing an aural test, and therefore it is essential to play each phrase for yourself as you write it down. In fact, the playing is much more important than the notation, though of course writing the solo down does give you something permanent to retain. By means of the transcription, the recorded performance becomes palpable. Not only do the chosen notes become familiar to the transcriber but so do the tone, intonation, vibrato, rhythmic style and tonguing. The whole performance relates to the instrument. I have witnessed many young players rapidly undergo a magical transformation, particularly in the quality of their tone, as they work their way carefully note-by-note through several tracks by their favourite performer.

It would be helpful at this point to give some practical hints and tips concerning the methodology of transcription.

(1)   The recording must be made accurately at concert pitch. Even the best-recorded performance is likely to have some notes or phrases, or maybe some bass notes, that are going to be difficult to hear and to notate accurately. Couple this with an off-pitch recording and the task becomes impossible.

(2)   Use headphones if possible. These enable you to hear clearly, and also save wear and tear on the nerves of those within earshot as you constantly repeat those few difficult notes. If the headphones have individual volume controls you can sometimes gain some help by isolating a single channel.

(3)   Choose a method of reproduction that enables you to repeat passages quickly and accurately. A CD player with an A to B function (offering infinite repetition of a chosen fragment of the recording) is very helpful. For vinyl discs, repeated jabbing of the stylus is bad both for your favourite old record and your patience. It is better to transfer the recording to cassette and use a machine with a rewind/review facility. Best of all is to transfer the recording to open reel quarter-inch tape. This gives you excellent quality and enables you to locate and repeat single notes and phrases with accuracy.

(4)   Half- and double-speed versions of the recordings are helpful. Halving the speed of a recording drops the pitch of the music by an octave, whilst doubling the speed raises it an octave. This is easily done with a reel-to-reel machine, or a cassette deck with two speeds, pitch control and cue/review facilities. Dropping the music to half speed helps greatly with those rapid flurries of notes. It may seem that there is not much use for the double-speed facility, though it can be useful for difficult bass lines. What may sound a muddy or indistinct bass at normal speed becomes a clear and easily identified note in the middle register when the speed is doubled and the pitch raised an octave. Very few difficult bass lines remain obstinate when subjected to this treatment.

The bass part is very important. Some musicians seem content to write down the front-line part and disregard the accompaniment. Yet the meaning of the improvisation is lost unless it is put into a rhythmic and harmonic context. You need to know the chord progression in order to appreciate the note choices. As the harmonies have to be correct, it is not good enough to take the chords from a publisher's song copy, a play-along record or a fake book. (A fake book is a collection of jazz 'originals' and standard tunes, sometimes illegally published, with the music reduced to melody and chord symbols, and usually printed on one staff). It is unlikely that any professional jazz musician will use the chord changes *exactly* as found in such a publication.

To transcribe the harmonies is not as daunting as it sounds. For clarity, work on two staves, with the transcribed improvisation in the treble clef and the transcribed bass line in the bass clef below. With that duet, plus the guidance of the original chords from a fake book or similar, you will have a good idea where the harmonies on the recording match your fake book and where they deviate. Add to this any other clues you may be able to hear. You may spot an inner accompaniment line ('thumb line') or chord, or you may be able to transfer an easily identified harmony from another chorus. Remember that some of the great song-writers make different choices of harmony at each repetition of each eight bar phrase. Gershwin does this occasionally with delightful effect. However, for most performances you can assume that the harmonies are simply repeated. Put all of this together and you will have a very good idea of the chord progression, and the transcription should make good musical sense.

Now that you have a complete transcription, the chances are that after all that detailed work you will be able to play the solo without very much practice. Making the transcription yourself is far more educative than merely buying a book of clarinet transcriptions and treating them as sight-reading practice. Reading through a ready-made transcription is no more likely to bring you near to an understanding of how to play jazz than playing a Weber concerto will teach you how to compose! Ready-made transcriptions require careful study, but if they are intelligently used they do have a place in the jazz player's development (Fig. 11.2). They are most effective when used in conjunction with a copy of the recording from which they are taken.

Making transcriptions, and playing along with records, are not the only ways to approach jazz improvisation. However, they have been dealt with first here because of their acknowledged role in the formative process of some of the world's great jazz players. Other approaches to learning that can be considered are:

(1) Use of play-along records by Jamey Aebersold and others.
(2) Use of 'patterns for jazz' books.
(3) Use of improvisation-method text books.
(4) Attendance at jazz workshops or summer schools.
(5) One-to-one study.
(6) Enrolling on an advanced course.

Play-along records are specially produced as an aid to jazz improvisation. An accompaniment to tunes from the jazz repertoire is recorded by a rhythm section with the intention that the clarinettist (or any

April In Paris

Clarinet Solo by ARTIE SHAW

Words by E Y HARBURG
Music by VERNON DUKE

Figure 11.2 Artie Shaw recorded this version of Vernon Duke's *April in Paris* in Hollywood in May 1940. Though Shaw's interpretation respects the melody, this is nevertheless a jazz performance. The improvisation is concentrated at the phrase-endings and turn-rounds. From *Jazz Clarinet 2* arranged John Robert Brown.

other instrumentalist) plays along with the recorded accompaniment. A tuning note is provided at the start of the record, and there is a careful count-in recorded. The stereo is utilised so that the piano is recorded on one channel and the bass recorded on the other. This enables bass players to eliminate the recorded bass and enjoy the accompaniment of drums and piano, and a pianist can turn down the recorded piano and play to the accompaniment of bass and drums. The Aebersold play-along records are the best known, and there are now over sixty albums available in this series. The records are supplied with a booklet containing top line and chord symbols, and each tune on the record is printed at concert pitch, and in B♭ and E♭ transpositions, all in the treble clef. There is also a concert-pitch bass-clef version. Thus all of the common jazz instruments are catered for. These records are widely used by jazz students and jazz educators. The only criticism is that the piano accompaniment ('comping') is done in reaction to a real performer who was present at the recording session but is inaudible on the record. Such reactive playing is not necessarily going to fit well with your performance, though it is difficult to think of a better alternative.

'Patterns for jazz' are technical exercises written in a jazz style for any instrument, composed to fit over idiomatic jazz chord progressions. (Incidentally, jazz journalists, and others who should know better, frequently use the expression '*chord sequence*' – despite the fact that a sequence is a particular musical device – when what they mean is '*chord progression*'.) The best-known book of such patterns is *Patterns for Jazz* by Jerry Coker (Miami, 1970). This is available in both treble- and bass-clef versions. A typical basic pattern would be a quaver melody moving around a cycle of dominant-seventh chords (Ex. 11.1).

Ex. 11.1   Quaver melody moving round a cycle of dominant-seventh chords

Ideally, these patterns should be memorised – 'Meant to be played not read' as Coker's publisher suggests. Pattern books provide excellent study material for any clarinettist, not just the aspiring jazz player. Their great benefit is to help players of monophonic instruments to think harmonically, and to understand guitar chord symbols, the universal harmonic shorthand of the jazz musician. Confusion between, for example, F^7, F major^7 and F minor^7 is a constant difficulty for jazz students approaching the music from a background of traditional harmony. These patterns also introduce passing notes, higher extensions of the chords (ninths, thirteenths, etc.), auxiliary notes, chromatic side slips, pentatonicism, the blues' scale and all the other devices that go to make up the everyday vernacular of the seasoned jazz player. There is a useful discussion of devices commonly found in improvised solos in *The Teaching of Jazz* by Jerry Coker (Rottenburg, 1989).

Improvisation books are few in number, and not always accessible. At present the most comprehensive are *Improvising Jazz* by Jerry Coker (New Jersey, 1964), *Complete Method for Improvisation,* by Jerry Coker (Lebanon, 1980) and *How to Improvise* by Hal Crook (Rottenburg, 1991). Both Coker and Crook have impeccable playing credentials, and both teach in large American college jazz departments. The Crook method seems most appropriate for use as a course book for formal programmed study with a private teacher or in a college jazz department. The attention given to what *not* to play is particularly welcome. The chapter devoted to the use of silence has proved very helpful with my own students.

A good teacher can save one a lot of time. College jazz departments now offer full-time courses to degree and post-graduate level. In Europe there are advanced, large and long-established jazz courses in Cologne, Rotterdam and Leeds. The list of North American jazz courses at college level includes many universities, and the famous Berklee College in Boston, Massachusetts. The size and maturity of such a department is of some importance if one is to take advantage of a suitable variety of teachers and ensembles, not to mention the influence of a wide variety of fellow jazz students. At least one American department is large enough to claim no less than 800 first-study guitar students! The number of reed players is apparently not quite so great, but amounts to several hundred. Some musicians may find such numbers daunting. Nevertheless, in such departments there will certainly be plenty of helpful answers to the question 'How do you know what to play?'

12 The clarinet on record

MICHAEL BRYANT

Introduction

Recordings of clarinettists made at various times during the last hundred years or so chart some fascinating changes in attitudes to musical interpretation and offer an important glimpse into different national styles of playing. It is to these two main areas that this chapter will be primarily addressed, since in any event there can be no attempt to survey all currently available material within the confines of the space available.

Historic recordings have recently become the subject of much interest, and the evidence of performances on each of the various orchestral instruments through the twentieth century is indeed highly instructive in terms of performance styles. One writer has observed '... a trend towards greater power, firmness, clarity, control, literalness, and evenness of expression, and away from informality, looseness, and unpredictability'.[1] Most recorded performances from the earlier part of the century give a vivid sense of being projected as if to an audience, the precision and clarity of each note less important than the shape and progress of the music as a whole. In the late twentieth century the balance has shifted significantly, so that accurate and clear performance of the music has become the first priority and the characterisation of the music is assumed to be able to take care of itself. If pre-war recordings resemble live performance, many of today's concerts show a palpable influence of the recording session, with clarity and control an overriding priority.[2]

Today's literal interpretation of note-values, whilst allowing some flexibility, makes many early recordings seem almost casual in approach: 'The performances of the early twentieth century ... are volatile, energetic, flexible, vigorously projected in broad outline but rhythmically informal in detail. Modern performances are, by comparison, accurate, restrained, deliberate, and even in emphasis'.[3] Clarinet recorded history broadly reflects such general trends. In these circumstances, our own listening experience may well be enhanced if we can make some attempt to appreciate recordings in terms of their own time and place, taking into account priorities which may be different from our own; an awareness of technical developments in the studio can play a useful role in this learning process.

The effects of technical developments

Business sense, popular taste and technical developments have all governed the way in which recorded repertoire has been treated over the years. In the earliest days the duration and quality of cylinders and discs were both severe limitations. Recording quality improved with the introduction of laterally cut discs and of electrical rather than acoustic recording methods. Long playing records first made their appearance in 1948, whilst the advent of stereo ten years later brought about a temporary neglect of chamber music in favour of larger-scale works. The longevity of the cassette has been guaranteed by noise-reduction systems, whereas quadrophonic sound never really gained a foothold. The development of digital recording and the introduction of the compact disc in 1983 marked the beginning of a new era. LP sales have now virtually ceased, though they and 78 rpm discs can still be purchased from specialist dealers.

The early days, 1898–1925

As noted on page 85, correspondence published in *Musical Opinion & Music Trade Review* during 1893 established which composers were of interest to clarinettists at that time. Some light music is evident, but present in addition are Beethoven, Brahms, Gade, Gouvy, Heap, Mozart, Prout, Reinecke, Rietz, Schumann, Spohr, Stanford and Weber. This reflects a more serious concern for quality repertoire than early commercial recordings might imply. The reproduction of sound recordings in the home was at first a novelty. In the interest of sales the earliest instrumental recordings were usually designed to display the virtuosity of the player, while offering the listener familiar and popular tunes. Around 1900 the list of music recorded by clarinettists included such titles as *Auld Lang Syne*, *Bluebells of Scotland*, *Carnival of Venice*, *Coming through the Rye*, *Down on the Swanee River*, *My Old Kentucky Home*, *Turkey in the Straw*, *Plantation Echoes*, *Sally in our Alley*, *Home Sweet Home* and *Nellie Grey*. A. A. Umbach 'of [the] Trocadero Orchestra, London England', as he was announced on the etched centres of several Berliner discs, made his last recordings in February 1899. These included fantasies on *I puritani* and *Rigoletto*,

Mendelssohn's *Spring Song* and *Variations Brilliants* by Müller. These and several other themes from operas such as *Robert le Diable*, *Cavalleria rusticana*, *La forza del destino*, *William Tell*, *Mignon* and *La traviata* were recorded by such players as Henri Paradis (1901), Romolo Quaranta (1902) and Henri Lefèbvre (1904).

Gradually, music of greater intrinsic worth became available, such as the first movement of Weber's F minor Concerto, recorded by Carl Esberger for the Gramophone and Typewriter Company (GC 46055, 1907). Weber's Concertino was recorded by Charles Draper in a shortened form to fit on a single sided 12″ disc (HMV C 487; Gramophone Monarch 06000, 1906; Clarion 10006, 1909; Edison Bell 406–5730, c. 1905). Draper first recorded an abridged version of the first two movements of the Brahms Quintet in 1917, and it was left to the twenty-five-year-old Thurston in 1926 to record the complete work. Contemporary with this was Draper's Mozart Quintet; in the event, both records were rapidly deleted because of the introduction of electrical recording methods. Haydn Draper's acoustic recording of the Brahms Trio (Columbia L 1609–11, 1924) has so poor a balance that the clarinet is at times barely audible.

Electrical 78s, 1925–50

Charles Draper made a complete electrical recording of the Brahms Quintet in 1929 (reissued by Pearl, CD 9903, 1991). Brahms's Trio was recorded by Gaston Hamelin's American pupil Ralph McLane (1907–51) during his membership of the Boston Symphony Orchestra. Reginald Kell's version followed in 1941. The Brahms F minor Sonata was recorded by Luigi Amodio for Polydor, the E♭ by Thurston (Decca, 1937) and Benny Goodman (Columbia, 1945). On 2 November 1928 Draper recorded the Mozart Quintet with the Léner Quartet (reissued by the World Record Club SH 318, 1979). Here is an example of a disc where by modern standards the string playing seems casual at times, if not actually careless. Frederick Thurston gave the first performance of the Bliss Quintet at London's Wigmore Hall in February 1933 and subsequently recorded it with the Griller Quartet (Decca K 780/3, 1935). Though apparently satisfied with this recording, Thurston distrusted the medium, disliked taking part in recordings and as a result left fewer of them than his admirers might have wished.[4]

In the heyday of 78s Kell led the way with many fine recordings, his slow vibrato and expressive style appealing to many listeners. His recording of Schubert's *Der Hirt auf dem Felsen* with Elizabeth Schumann remains a benchmark for all who followed. The next year he made one of his best and most celebrated recordings – the Brahms Quintet with the Busch Quartet. This was preferred at the time to Draper's old recording on both musical and technical grounds and it has been reissued several times. Kell's other recordings from the period 1937–48 include the Mozart Concerto, Quintet and Trio, Beethoven and Brahms Trios, the Schumann *Phantasiestücke* (first complete version) and a further recording of the Schubert, with the soprano Margaret Ritchie.[5] An extrovert interpretation of Weber's Concertino had become customary, so that Kell's subtler, gentler and more expressive recording in 1940 came as something of a surprise.

Meanwhile the Italian clarinettist Amodio (1902–42) made a number of fine recordings. A pupil of Lugatti in Rimini and Bianchini in Bologna, he was invited by Toscanini to join the orchestra of La Scala Milan, where he remained until his death. Playing full Boehm clarinets with a crystal mouthpiece, his recordings in addition to Brahms included the Mozart Concerto, Quintet and Trio, Beethoven's Trio and Septet, Weber's *Grand Duo Concertant*, Schumann's *Phantasiestücke* Nos. 1 and 3 and Schubert's *Der Hirt auf dem Felsen*.

Into the LP era

One of the first clarinet LPs to appear was the *Duett-Concertino* by Strauss, with Gerald Caylor (clarinet), Don Christlieb (bassoon) and the Los Angeles Chamber Orchestra. Caylor served as solo clarinettist with the Portland Symphony Orchestra, the Janssen Orchestra of Los Angeles and the Hollywood Bowl Orchestra, and played for Twentieth Century Fox. Shortly after Kell's move to the USA in 1949 he made the first of his two recordings of the Brahms sonatas with Mieczyslaw Horszowski (Mercury MG 10016). Then with pianists Joel Rosen and Brooks Smith, Kell recorded seven LPs on the Decca Gold Label (USA), which were not widely distributed and remain scarce. Composers represented were Bartók, Brahms (both sonatas), Debussy, Hindemith, Milhaud, Saint-Saëns, Schumann, Stravinsky, Szałowski, Alec Templeton, Vaughan Williams and Weber, and there was also a collection of ten encore pieces. Kell played much light music during the war years, whose mood has been caught on some 10″ LPs issued in 1954, when he joined forces with Salvador Camerata and his orchestra (Brunswick AXL 2016 and LA 8632). The nostalgic idiom was almost a thing of the past even then, but Kell's clarinet playing is exquisite. In 1981 the Bruno Walter Society (USA) issued a heavily filtered LP (RR-485) of a Swiss radio recording of Kell and the Busch Quartet playing the Brahms Quintet. For LP Kell re-recorded the Mozart Concerto with the Zimbler Sinfonietta (without conductor) and with Horszowski the trios by Mozart, Beethoven (1953) and Brahms (1957). By the mid-1950s Kell's playing was becoming more artistically wayward and this is most noticeable on his late recordings of the Mozart and Brahms Quintets (Brunswick AXTL 1007 and 1008, and Saga XID 5151 and 1524).

The London Baroque Ensemble, already active on 78s, was among the first to issue wind music on LP in Britain in 1952. They recorded the E♭ Sonatina by Richard Strauss (Parlophone-Odeon PMA 1006 and HMV XLP 30016, Pye GSGC 14062 and Pye CCL 30119), the Octet, Rondino and Sextet by Beethoven (GSGC 14038) and the Gounod *Petit Symphonie* with the Dvořák Serenade on HMV XLP 30011. Their various clarinettists were not named on all record sleeves, but included Jack Brymer, Thomas Kelly, Walter Lear, Gervase de Peyer, Basil Tschaikov and Frederick Thurston. Bernard Walton and Stephen Waters were among the founding members, and they recorded Vivaldi's Concerto RV559 for two oboes and two clarinets on Pye CCL 30131. The Ensemble also recorded Mozart's rarely heard Nocturnes for three voices and three basset horns or two clarinets and basset horn, and this was reissued from 78s on Parlophone-Odeon PMB 1008.[6] Thurston can be heard in Haydn's Divertimento in C (Westminster WLP 5080); he also took part in the 1952 recording of the Dvořák Serenade on Parlophone R 0604/5 and PMB 1001. When he fell ill before its completion, Jack Brymer took his place in the second, third and fourth movements, with Gervase de Peyer as second clarinet. Thurston can be heard playing the cadenza in Sir Henry Wood's *Fantasia on British Sea Songs*, with the composer conducting the London Symphony Orchestra in 1939 (reissued on LP as HMV 33 SX 1524 and EMI STAMP 1, 1980).

Several of the British players mentioned above made important solo contributions on disc. Bernard Walton was a much admired player whose too few recordings (mostly of the standard repertoire) included the Mozart Concerto (1955) and Sinfonia Concertante (1953), the Mozart and Beethoven Piano Quintets (1955) and Schubert's *Der Hirt auf dem Felsen* (1969). Especially notable was his 1971 Unicorn recording of the Clarinet Quintet by Robert Simpson. One of Jack Brymer's first solo recordings (on 78s, HMV DB 211145–8) was the extended cadenza in Bantock's *Fifine at the Fair*, with Beecham. His discography continued in 1957 with Bartók's *Contrasts* and *Der Hirt auf dem Felsen* with Helga Mott. There followed three Mozart Concerto discs (1960, 1965 and 1973), the complete Mozart wind music as director of the London Wind Soloists (1963/4), recordings of the Mozart and Brahms Quintets, duo repertoire with piano, and a wonderfully executed disc of Elie Siegmeister's jazzy Clarinet Concerto (Turnabout TV-S 34640, 1973). Gervase de Peyer amassed a wide-ranging and highly influential solo discography, whilst also recording all the main chamber repertoire with London's Melos Ensemble during a period of almost twenty years from 1957. Some works were relatively unfamiliar at the time of their release, such as Berwald's Septet, Prokofiev's Quintet Op. 39, Janáček's *Mládí* and Concertino, and Schoenberg's Suite Op. 24 and Serenade Op. 29. His fine recording of the Bliss Quintet (WRC SCM 42, 1963) was only the second version of the work (after Thurston). He made a major contribution to contemporary music with virtuoso recordings of the peripatetic Concerto by Thea Musgrave (1974) and of concertos by Hoddinott (1972) and Matthias (1977). He was the first to record the Sonata for clarinet and cello by Phyllis Tate (1966), the Sonata by Hoddinott (1969) and the Sextet by John Ireland (1972).

The solo repertoire

Mozart

Mozart's Concerto has been recorded by more than one hundred players from around the world. Its first complete recording was by Haydn Draper in 1929 (Brunswick 20076–8), with an unnamed orchestra. It was also recorded by Luigi Amodio with the Berlin Municipal Orchestra, François Etienne with the Hewitt Chamber Orchestra and by Reginall Kell (1940) with Sargent and the London Philharmonic. Leopold Wlach recorded the work with the Vienna Philharmonic and Karajan on 7 December 1949 in the Brahmssaal, Vienna (78s, reissued on LP as Toshiba EMI EAC 30108). In 1969 Hans-Rudolf Stalder made the first recording of the Mozart Concerto using a basset clarinet of modern design and an edition prepared by Ernst Hess (Schwann Musica Mundi VMS 807). This has now become the accepted way to record this work, and Stalder's example has been followed by several others. The Concerto was first recorded on a basset clarinet of period design by Hans Deinzer in 1973 (BAC 3001 and IC 065–99829), and subsequently by several other players, including Alan Hacker, Eric Hoeprich, Colin Lawson and Antony Pay.

The Quintet K581 has also been recorded by over a hundred players, the 78 rpm era represented by Amodio (twice), Simeon Bellison, Benny Goodman, Charles Draper (twice) Louis Cahuzac, Philipp Dreisbach and Reginald Kell. Goodman recorded it again in 1957, Jost Michaels in 1962, Alfred Boskovsky in 1964 and Karl Leister in 1966, since which time there have been versions from most figures of international standing. Like the Concerto, the Quintet soon found exponents on the basset clarinet and has subsequently been recorded several times on the period basset clarinet. Mozart's Trio K498, whose inherent problems of balance can be solved more easily in the studio than the concert hall, has been recorded by about fifty players. Thurston, Amodio, Delécluse and Kell (1941, reissued on STB 1007, 1992) recorded it on 78s and from the LP era there are versions by Kell, Eugenio Brunoni and Boskovsky (1950s), Gervase de Peyer (two versions in the 1960s) and a host of other players since that time.

Weber, Spohr and Crusell

We have noted Charles Draper's shortened version of Weber's Concertino, *c.* 1905, issued by several recording companies and labels. Amongst other early versions were those by the Garde Républicaine (with the first clarinets playing the solo part en masse) and by Henri Paradis and Louis Cahuzac. The earliest version of either of the concertos was Carl Esberger's 1907 disc, already mentioned. Alois Heine's recordings (1952) of the two concertos are full of spirit, but with an over-leisurely finale to No. 2. The F minor work was recorded in the 1950s by Jacques Lancelot and by Heinrich Geuser and both concertos were recorded by Benny Goodman at the end of the following decade. Gervase de Peyer recorded the E♭ Concerto in 1961 and some eight years later added the F minor Concerto and Concertino to his substantial discography, his slow vibrato bringing an individual and magical character to the music. The LP era continued with a kaleidoscope of different nationalities, represented by Jozef Luptáčik (Slovakia), Bohuslav Zahradník (Czech Republic), Béla Kovács (Hungary), Serge Dangain (France), Oskar Michallik (East Germany) and Vladímir Sokolov (Russia). With the longer maximum duration of the compact disc it became more common practice to record all three works together. Sabine Meyer (1986) recorded the Weber Quintet in a transcription for string orchestra, an idea of which the composer himself might have approved, since it sits uncomfortably among better integrated works for the medium. Of special interest are the excellent recordings of all three works by Antony Pay (Virgin Classics, 1988), who plays a copy of a seven-keyed Simiot clarinet (with two added keys), made by Daniel Bangham in 1983. When the American clarinettist Jon Manasse recorded the complete clarinet works of Weber for XLNT Music in 1990, he included a new transcription of the *Andante e Rondo Ongroise* Op. 35, originally for viola but best known in the version for bassoon.

For many years Spohr and Crusell remained virtually unrepresented. The movement by Crusell entitled *Concert Piece*, recorded by O. L. Johannson on Favorite 84022 (1913), is an abridged version of the slow movement of Concerto No. 3. Following isolated broadcasts of Crusell's concertos, No. 2 became more widely known as a result of Gervase de Peyer's 1972 recording. However, it remained to Thea King to record all three (for Hyperion CDA 66708), and again it was Antony Pay who brought a period version to the studio, using a copy of a nine-keyed Grenser clarinet. Record companies were slow to realise that Spohr offers an excellent opportunity for the virtuoso. A welcome pioneering step was taken by Franz Hammerla, who acquitted himself well in a recording of the Concerto No. 3 with the Linz-Bruckner Symphony Orchestra conducted by Ludwig Georg Jochum (Urania URLP 7021).

Gervase de Peyer gave a wonderful performance of No. 1 in 1961 for L'Oiseau-Lyre (in a curiously dessicated and unsympathetic acoustic) to be followed by John Denman's No. 2 in 1973 (Oryx 1828) and Thea King's No. 4 (Meridian E 77022). Since that time No. 1 has proved most popular, though Antony Pay also recorded No. 2 (Argo, ZRG 920) and Karl Leister produced a very fine complete set of all four concertos (Orfeo, S 088–842H). The Swiss clarinettist Elizabeth Ganter coupled Nos. 1, 3 and 4 (Aurophon AU 34038, AU 34054, AU 34039),[7] while the Austrian Ernst Ottensamer has recorded Spohr's Concerto No. 1 for Philips and Nos. 1 and 3 for Naxos (8 550688).

Brahms

One cannot support the claim that Brahms's Trio has been neglected on record, since there have been more than forty versions. After the performances on 78s already detailed, there were LP versions by Leopold Wlach (1954) and Kell (a second recording in 1957), to be followed by many distinguished players, including Karl Leister (three times), George Pietersen and Peter Schmidl, as well as a number of British artists. The Quintet has been recorded by over fifty players. In the early years of LP there were four versions in 1953 and 1954, recorded by the American Alfred Gallodoro (dating from 1947 and transferred from 78s), Kell, Leopold Wlach and his pupil Alfred Boskovsky. This last won special praise from critics, as did Boskovsky's second version from 1962, a year in which there were also recordings by Kell, David Oppenheim and Jost Michaels. The following year the disc by Heinrich Geuser and the Drolc Quartet (Electrola STC 80449) won many friends, even in the face of later competition from de Peyer (1965) and Ríha (1966). During the next decade a fascinating variety of stylistic approaches were displayed by Brymer (1968), Leister (1969), Yona Ettlinger, Robert Gugolz and Oskar Michallik (1972). Herbert Stähr's 1973 recording is unmistakably one of the best performances on record. British players were prominent in the avalanche of interpretations which followed, but this is a corner of the repertoire where national styles of playing can be readily compared and contrasted, there being versions by Lux Brahn, Ulysse Delécluse, Henri Druart, Paul Druschler, Koji Fujika, David Glazer, Franz Klein, Dieter Klöcker, Igor Mosgovenko, David Shifrin, George Silfies, Vladímir Sorokin and Vladímir Sokolov, amongst others. Benny Goodman committed the Quintet to disc in 1986 and new recordings have continued to appear regularly since that time, displaying varying degrees of elegance and passion.

The sonatas have attracted more than sixty players. After the era of 78s, versions by Lancelot (1954) and Antoine de Bavier (1956) were followed by David Glazer (1965) and by Gervase de Peyer (1968) in a very free reading with Daniel Barenboim. Karl Leister has recorded the works as many as four times – in 1969, 1976, 1983 and 1984. As with the Quintet a variety of national performers has continued to be represented, including Hans-Rudolf Stalder (1971), Aurelian Octav Popa (1977), the distinguished Czech clarinettist Milan Kostohryz (1979) and the Lithuanian Algirdas Budrys (1982). In 1990 Keith Puddy recorded both sonatas on Mühlfeld's Bb clarinet at Schloss Elizabethanburg, Meiningen (Pickwick Allegro PCD 994). The imaginative orchestration of Brahms's F minor Sonata by Luciano Berio (1986) has been recorded by James Campbell (Cala CACD 1006, 1992).

Into the twentieth century

Debussy's masterly *Première rapsodie* has been recorded with piano and in the composer's orchestration in about equal numbers. It was first recorded in 1931, in the orchestral version, by Gaston Hamelin for HMV DB 4809; this performance has been reissued in both LP and CD formats. Benny Goodman, a consistent pioneer in the recording of mainstream repertoire, was next to record it in 1940 with Barbirolli and the New York Symphony Orchestra. Kell recorded the *Rapsodie* with piano in the 1950s, after which it remained neglected for a decade, with the exception of an undated recording (c. 1955) by the Dutch clarinettist Jos D'hondt. In the 1960s there were recordings of the orchestrated version by Gugolz, Drucker, Mikhailov, Boutard and Brymer, after which time the work has continued to attract an international array of performers, some of whom have also committed the piano version to disc.

The Clarinet Concerto by Nielsen was his last great orchestral work, completed in 1928 and written for Aage Oxenvad, a man of strong character from rural Jutland. It has been said that Nielsen expressed within the music some of Oxenvad's philosophy of life, an enigmatic mix of tenderness and aggression. Unrealised plans were laid for Oxenvad to record the Concerto, frustrated by the events of war; Louis Cahuzac made its first recording in Denmark in 1947 for Columbia LDX 7000/2, a version which has been reissued on several occasions. Cahuzac was a most marvellous player, of great clarity and sophistication. His recording, however, lacked the boldness and irascibility which is such an essential element in this work, so ably realised in the 1954 recording by Ib Eriksson, solo clarinettist of the Danish Radio Orchestra (Decca LXT 2979). It must be admitted that Benny Goodman's struggle with the Concerto can be plainly heard in his 1966 recording (RCA SBR 6701). Stanley Drucker recorded it the following year (CBS 72639, subsequently reissued by Sony). The number of recordings has since proliferated, including a suave and controlled 1971 version from John McCaw (Unicorn UNS 239), even more urbane than Cahuzac. Scandinavians have been increasingly represented, with an especially fine interpretation from Ole Schill, principal clarinet of the Gothenburg Symphony Orchestra (BIS CD 321, 1986).

The international perspective

As has already been suggested, recordings present a wonderful opportunity to become acquainted with different national styles of clarinet playing. For example, the distinctive musical personalities of Vienna and Prague, observed in Mozart's day, remain evident even today. In terms of the clarinet, Austrian conservatism is reflected both in a characteristically smooth style of playing and in the choice of recorded repertoire, though there has been a highly distinguished tradition of players, including after Wlach and Boskovsky the names of Alfred Prinz, Peter Schmidl and the period specialist Kurt Birsak. Alfred Uhl wrote several works for Wlach (see page 99), whilst as a member of the Vienna Octet Boskovsky ventured beyond Beethoven and Schubert to composers such as Henk Badings, Egon Wellesz and Hindemith. Franz Schmidt's Quintets in B♭ and in A have found a place in the discographies of Wlach, Prinz and Christoph Eberle; the first of these works has been recorded by Ernst Ottensamer, one of today's players maintaining the Austrian tradition.

By contrast, Czech clarinettists have continued to pursue a highly articulate style not dissimilar from that cultivated by players of period clarinets. The catalogues of Supraphon, Panton and Opus contain much music for large and small wind ensembles, as well as the classical and romantic solo repertoire and works by modern Czech and Slovak composers. Vladímir Ríha and Milan Kostohryz were among the first clarinettists to achieve solo status, and the field was later dominated by the late Bohuslav Zahradník and Jozef Luptáčik. Of special note are the many recordings by the solo bass clarinettist Josef Horák and pianist Emma Kovárnová of largely contemporary works, including commissions. Closely related in style are recordings of classical and contemporary repertoire by Hungarian artists, such as Béla Kovács, László Horváth, Kálmán Berkes and (of a younger generation) József Balogh.

The production of LPs in the former Soviet Union was extensive, though they were never exported in large numbers and remain difficult to trace. Concerto recordings include the Copland (Andrei Kazakov and Lev Mikhailov), Nielsen (Kalev Velthut), Lev Knipper (Raphael Bagda-sarian), Mozart (Hannes Altrov, Vladímir Sokolov and Vasili Zhel-vakov), Krommer, Weber Nos. 1 and 2 (Sokolov), Rimsky-Korsakov, Rakov (Mikhailov), Manevich (Isaac Roginsky) and Mercadante (Zhel-vakov). Recorded chamber music from Russia includes much of the standard repertoire, together with some native pieces, including Rakov's second Sonata, Glinka's *Trio Pathéthique*, and works by Rimsky-Korsakov, Prokofiev and Stravinsky. Elsewhere in Eastern Europe the Romanian Aurelian Octav Popa has won particular acclaim, his large solo discography including chamber music by native composers such as Tiberiu Olah, Myriam Marbe, Stefan Niculescu, Alexandru Hrisanide, Costin Miereanu, Octavian Nemescu, Liviu Dandara, Stefan Zorzor, Adrian Ratiu, Dumitru Bughici, Felicia Donceana and Matei Socor. Bulgarian recordings include the Clarinet Concerto Op. 70 (1966) by Lyubomir Pipkov, recorded by Petko Radev for Balkanton BCA 1012. Atanas Kolev recorded a solo disc for the same label (BCA 109809), including works by Hoffmeister, Marcel Dotremer and Tiberiu Olah. The clarinet was well represented in the catalogues of the former Yugoslavia, which included concertos by the Croatian Stjepan Šulek (performed by its dedicatee Ernst Ackun), the Slovenian Pavel Sivil (for Alojz Zupan) and the Serbian Aleksandar Obradovic (recorded by Milenko Stefanovic). The Croatian clarinettist Josip Nochta recorded for Jugoton LSY-61152 the Concerto (1952) by Bruno Bjelinski and the Clarinet Quintet (1940) by Boris Papandopulo. In Poland, the clarinettist Ludwik Kurkiewicz recorded the little-known Concerto by Karel Kurpinski (1785–1857), a work somewhat in the style of Weber, on an LP (Muza XL 0231) which has been transferred to CD (Concerto/Fidelio DP 25014).

Scandinavian clarinettists have continued to record prolifically, showing a particular affinity with native contemporary repertoire, which includes important concertos by (amongst others) Poul Ruders and Olav Berg. The extrovert Danish clarinettist Jens Schou has recorded trios by Emil Hartmann and Per Nørgård, as well as the Concerto by Bo Holten. Recordings by the gifted Swedish clarinettist Kjell-Inge Stevensson include besides Nielsen and Messiaen a recital with piano and second clarinettist Kjell Fagéus, and music by Swedish composers such as Karl-Birger Blomdahl and Anders Eliasson. Finland has also produced some remarkable recordings. An opportunity to hear the Concerto (1925) by Aare Merikanto for violin, clarinet, horn and string sextet should not be missed, in view of its strange mixture of impressionism, expressionism and nationalism. It was recorded by Love records (LRLP 228) in 1976 and has also been issued on CD by Ondine on ODE 703. A recital recorded by Jarmo Munter (Ponsi PEALP 10, 1978) includes the Clarinet Sonata by Pekka Kostiainen, a stylistic blend reminiscent of both Poulenc and Shostakovich. On the Finlandia and Ondine labels the avant-garde virtuoso clarinettist Kari Kriikku has recorded trios by Bruch and Zemlinsky, quartets by Crusell and Debussy's *Rapsodie*, in addition to contemporary music. The Finnish Clarinet Ensemble of nearly fifty professional players has recorded a CD for Finlandia

FACD 931 (1990) of music by contemporary Finnish and other composers.

Within Western Europe the long-standing dichotomy of French and German styles of playing is consistently evident. Until recently the many French clarinettists have perhaps tended not to produce records commensurate with their talent, a situation attributable to the policies and preferred repertoire of the record companies. In the 1950s Decca produced a series of discs under the auspices of the maker Selmer. The six discs devoted to the clarinet included original and transcribed music for clarinet sextet and recital works played by Ulysse Delécluse. After Cahuzac, Jacques Lancelot was the first player to record on a large scale, including the first version of the Françaix Concerto (RTF Inédit 995 019). Other important recording artists since have been Guy Deplus, Serge and Guy Dangain, Maurice Gabai, Philippe Cuper and Michel Portal. Recordings from Germany have been numerous and distinguished, featuring such performers as Alfred Bürkner, Heinrich Geuser, Jost Michaels and Herbert Stähr. The Swiss clarinettist Eduard Brunner has made many recordings whilst based in Munich, including music by Isang Yun, Aare Merikanto, Josef Suder, Prokofiev (transcription of the Sonata Op. 94), Vassily Lobanov, Krystof Meyer and Augustyn Bloch. The remarkably prolific Dieter Klöcker has developed a great interest in forgotten classical and romantic repertoire to be found in libraries and private collections, and has been unusually successful in persuading record companies to promote his findings, many of them for the first and only time. Karl Leister and Sabine Meyer have also made many important recordings which maintain the highest possible standards of technical proficiency, illustrating the great strengths of the German clarinet largely within a conservatively chosen repertoire.

In Holland the Netherlands Wind Ensemble won many friends for its recordings of the complete wind music of Mozart and Strauss, among other composers. There have been other enterprising areas of Dutch activity. Piet Honingh was a member of the Danzi Wind Quintet and one of the first clarinettists to play on period instruments, as on his 1969 recording of the Beethoven Trio Op. 11; his discography on modern instruments includes such rarities as the Rheinberger and Lachner nonets. Amongst other important Dutch artists are George Pietersen and the avant-garde bass clarinettist Harry Sparnaay. Another important centre of excellence has proved to be Switzerland, represented by such players as Robert Gugolz, Antony Morf, Lux Brahn, Elizabeth Ganter, Eduard Brunner, Thomas Friedli, Hans-Rudolf Stalder, Heinz Hofer, Elmar Schmid and several ensembles such as the Swiss Clarinet Players and the Philharmonic Clarinet Quintet. Stalder's discography is substantial, including such rarities as the Rolla Basset Horn Concerto, various recitals and chamber music, and with Thomas

Friedli the Concerto for two clarinets by Schnyder von Wartensee (Ex Libris CD 6039).[8] Among Stalder's recordings with period instruments is *Das Chalumeau: ein Portrait* (EMI 1C 065 16 9568), which includes the D minor Concerto for two chalumeaux by Telemann. Thomas Friedli's recordings include concertos by Pleyel, Mercadante, Molter, Mozart, Franz Tischhauser (*The Beggar's Concerto*, a humorous work of great technical difficulty), Sándor Veress and Krommer.[9]

Fifty years ago, many leading American clarinettists did not make any solo recordings and few were made at all. Simeon Bellison (1883–1953) of the New York Philharmonic Orchestra was an almost exact contemporary of Charles Draper, recording the Mozart Quintet (1937) and the Khachaturian Trio. Kálmán Bloch was for twenty-five years solo clarinettist of the Los Angeles Philharmonic and left recordings of the Milhaud Suite, the Ives Largo and Adolf Weiss's Trio with cello and piano. Gino Cioffi arrived in 1937 from his native Naples, played in the NBC Symphony under Toscanini and became solo clarinettist in Boston in 1950, recording a number of chamber works. In contrast Robert Marcellus, celebrated first clarinet at Cleveland, scarcely recorded at all, though his Mozart Concerto of 1967 has been greatly admired. The first American to make a substantial contribution to the catalogue was David Glazer, who pursued a mainly solo career and was a member of the New York Woodwind Quintet. Other widely recorded figures have been Harold Wright (Boston) and Larry Combs (Chicago). Stanley Drucker (New York) was the dedicatee of the Concerto by John Corigliano, which he recorded in 1981. Clarinettists David Shifrin, Mitchell Lurie, Arthur Bloom and Elsa Ludewig-Verdehr have all played a significant part in creating a substantial contemporary American repertoire for the instrument, whilst at the same time variously recording mainstream classical works. Richard Stoltzman has become one of the most conscientious and productive clarinettists in the studio, playing standard repertoire, transcriptions (including Schubert's 'Arpeggione' Sonata and Mozart's Bassoon Concerto) and various styles of contemporary music. He is one of a number of Americans to have recorded the Copland Concerto, first committed to disc by Benny Goodman in 1964. The Canadian James Campbell has a number of successful solo and chamber recordings to his credit. Of special note is his recording of Gary Kulesha's *Mysterium Coniunctionis* for clarinet, bass clarinet and piano, a rewarding work of almost nineteen minutes' duration (Centrediscs CMC CD 4392, 1992), with bass clarinettist David Bourque.

The British tradition has been continued by Colin Bradbury, Georgina Dobrée, Janet Hilton, Antony Pay and Keith Puddy, amongst many others. Thea King's partnership with Hyperion began with a recording of concertos by Stanford and Finzi, and subsequently featured rarely heard and otherwise unavailable music by British composers such as Blake, Cooke, Frankel, Jacob, Maconchy, Raws-thorne, Somervell and Stanford, as well as earlier significant figures from abroad such as Heinze, Rietz, Romberg and Tausch. Alan Hacker's individual contribution both to the period scene and to the avant-garde is reflected in his discography, with pioneering accounts of Mozart, Weber and others for the L'Oiseau-Lyre Florilegium label in the 1970s, contemporary with an account of *Hymnos* by Maxwell Davies (1972) and a recital entitled *Hymn to the Sun* (1977), including music by Birtwistle and Goehr. He is one of a number of players also to have recorded the Finzi Concerto, a piece which apparently does not travel well, though it is an especial favourite amongst British clarinettists. Amongst pre-eminent younger exponents of the work are Emma Johnson and Michael Collins, whose distinctive solo careers have already been widely reflected within the catalogues.

As this selective chapter reveals, a galaxy of different styles of playing and little-known repertoire awaits the enthusiast. The age of CD brings a steady stream of new versions of familiar pieces, but also an increasing number of opportunities to observe the sheer versatility of our instrument in new repertoire and in different playing styles from all corners of the world.[10]

Notes

1 Single reeds before 1750

1 Albert Rice, *The Baroque Clarinet* (Oxford, 1992), pp. 1–2.
2 *Ibid.*, p. 10.
3 Mersenne's illustrations are reproduced by Rice, p. 9.
4 Ekkhard Nickel, *Die Holzblasinstrumentenbau in der freien Reichsstadt Nürnberg* (Munich, 1971), p. 214.
5 Rice, p. 15.
6 Heinz Becker, 'Das Chalumeau bei Telemann', *Konferenzbericht der 2. Magdeburger Telemann-Festtage* (Magdeburg, 1969), p. 69.
7 Adrien Fauchier-Magnan, *The Small German Courts in the Eighteenth Century* (London, 1980), pp. 26–9, cited by Rice, p. 16.
8 Nickel, pp. 203–5.
9 Rice, p. 29.
10 From more sceptical writers there have been various recent suggestions that Jacob Denner continued to use his father's stamp after his death, that Jacob added his own initials to instruments made and stamped by his father, or even that all instruments were stamped by a Nuremberg official.
11 'The mock trumpet', *Galpin Society Journal*, 6, pp. 35–40.
12 See, however, the extracts in Jack Brymer, *Clarinet* (London, 1976), pp. 20–1.
13 Thurston Dart, 'The earliest collections of clarinet music', *Galpin Society Journal*, 4 (1951), pp. 39–41.
14 For example, see Colin Lawson, *The Chalumeau in Eighteenth-Century Music* (Ann Arbor, 1981).
15 Colin Lawson, 'The chalumeau in the works of Fux', in *Johann Joseph Fux and the Music of the Austro-Hungarian Baroque*, ed. H. White (Aldershot, 1992), pp. 78–94.
16 E. F. Schmid, 'Gluck–Starzer–Mozart', *Zeitschrift für Musik*, 104 (1937), pp. 1198–209.
17 Even later mention of the chalumeau occurs in J. V. Reynvaan's *Musijkaal Kunst-Woordenboek* (Amsterdam, 1795).
18 Colin Lawson, 'Graupner and the chalumeau', *Early Music*, 11 (1983), pp. 209–16.
19 Colin Lawson, 'Telemann and the chalumeau', *Early Music*, 9 (1981), pp. 312–19.
20 Pamela Weston, *Clarinet Virtuosi of the Past* (London, 1971), p. 20.
21 Michael Talbot, 'Vivaldi and Rome: observations and hypotheses', *Journal of the Royal Musical Association*, 113, (1988), pp. 28–46.

2 The development of the clarinet

1 Albert Rice, *The Baroque Clarinet* (Oxford, 1992).
2 Clarinet in B♭ by Thomas Collier, London, 1770: Keighley, Cliffe Castle Museum, No. 9110.
3 Peter Gradenwitz, 'The beginnings of clarinet literature: notes on a clarinet concerto by Johann Stamitz', *Music and Letters*, 17 (1936), pp. 145–50.

4 University of California, Berkeley, Department of Music No. 19.

5 Nicholas Shackleton, 'The earliest basset horns', *Galpin Society Journal*, 40 (1987), pp. 2–23.

6 Heinrich Grenser, 'Bermerken über eine neue Erfindung zur Vervollkommung der Flöte', *Allgemeine musikalische Zeitung*, 13 (1811), pp. 775–8.

7 Boston, Museum of Fine Arts, 38.1750.

8 Eric Halfpenny, 'Early English clarinets', *Galpin Society Journal*, 18 (1965), pp. 42–56.

9 Belgian Patent 1560 (5034), (1840).

10 British Patents 2806 (1861) and 1308 (1862).

11 French Patent 1943 (1854).

12 Carl Baermann, *Vollständige Clarinett-Schule* (Offenbach, 1864–75).

13 Rendall, plate 6; Kroll, plate 15; E. Elsenaar, *De Klarinet* (Hilversum, 1927), p. 30. The basset horn by A. & M. Mayrhofer is pitched in G and is now in the Oberhausmuseum, Passau. The remainder are pitched in F (except for the Strobach in A), divided between the Museum für Kunstgewerbe and the Museum für Hamburgische Geschichte, both in Hamburg.

14 Pamela Poulin discovered in Riga, Latvia, three concert programmes of performances presented by Anton Stadler in February and March of 1794 as part of a five-year concert tour throughout northern Europe and as far afield as St Petersburg. These programmes include an engraving of an unusual extended clarinet (with angled globular bell), which together with a letter from Stadler commissioning a basset clarinet (which he describes) provide us with sufficient information about its hitherto unknown design. Repertoire performed at Riga included concertos for the newly invented clarinet by Mozart (here given its first documented performance), Süssmayr (a work previously believed incomplete) and Stadler himself (a work otherwise unknown). This wealth of important evidence was first presented at the 1994 International Clarinet Congress in Chicago.

15 Hessiches Landesmuseums, Darmstadt, Inv. Nr. Kg61:116; illustrated in *Musikinstrumente an dem Hessisches Landesmuseum 16–19. Jahrhundert* (Darmstadt: Hessisches Landesmuseum, 1980), p. 51.

16 The locations of surviving basset horns by these makers are given by P. T. Young, *4900 Historical Woodwind Instruments: an Inventory of 200 Makers in International Collections* (London, 1993).

3   The clarinet family: clarinets in B♭, A and C

1 *The New Grove*, article 'Clarinet' tabulates the entire family, with a brief indication of the role and provenance of each instrument.

2 Valentin Roeser, *Essai d'Instruction à l'usage de ceux qui composent pour la clarinette et le cor* (Paris, 1764), p. 2

3 *Neue-Mozart Ausgabe X: 30/1, Attwood-Studien* (Kassel, 1965), pp. 156ff.

4 See Eric Halfpenny, 'The Boehm clarinet in England', *Galpin Society Journal*, 30 (1977), pp. 2–7.

5 But see the recommendation of the B♭ rather than the A clarinet for the solo in the third movement of Brahms's First Symphony in Rosario Mazzeo, 'The congenial clarinet family', *Selmer Bandwagon*, 40 (1979), p. 29.

6 John Warrack in *Chamber Music*, ed. Alec Robertson (Harmondsworth, 1957), p. 317.

7 See R. M. Longyear, 'Clarinet sonorities in early Romantic music', *Musical Times*, 124 (1983), pp. 224–6, and Colin Lawson, 'The authentic clarinet: tone and tonality', *ibid.*, pp. 357–8.

8 A rare appearance of the bass clarinet in C occurs in Liszt's symphonic poem *Mazeppa*.

The high clarinets

1 These are Badische Landesbibliothek, Karlsruhe, MSS 304, 334, 302, 337 (Becker's nos. 1–4, respectively in A, D, G and D majors), 328 and 332. These library numbers do not indicate a chronological order of composition. As noted in Chapter 5, these six concertos were probably written in the 1740s for Johann Reusch, then employed as a flautist and clarinettist in the Durlach court band of musicians at Karlsruhe, where Molter was Kapellmeister.

2 An example of this early style can be heard on Keith Puddy's recording of MS 332 (Capriole cassette, CAPT 1004) where he plays on a reconstruction of the two-keyed clarinet made by Zencker. Although the tone is beautifully pure and bright, it is rather louder and more 'clarino' than when today's instruments are used.

3 Colin Bradbury has included this virtuoso E♭ solo on his record *The Italian Clarinettist* ASV ALH942 (1983)

4 *Capriccio on Verdi's Foscari*; *Paraphrase on the quartet from Rigoletto*; *Fantasia on La Traviata*; *Piccolo Mafaico on Gounod's Faust*; *Fantasia on Ruy Blas*. It is rumoured that there are more E♭ solos to be found in the Milan Conservatoire, awaiting discovery by an enthusiastic devotee of the *piccolo clarinetto*.

5 John Bruce Yeh and the Chicago Pro Musica; William Neil, Concerto for Piccolo Clarinet, Newport Classic NPD 85537 (1992).

6 George Lewis playing in Bunk's Brass Band and Dance Band; CD American Music Records AMCD-6 (recorded 1945, issued 1992). George Lewis leading the Eureka Brass Band, Melodisc MLP 12–101 (recorded 1951).

7 John Casimir's Young Tuxedo Jazz Bands, Jazzology Records, JCE 21 (1962). A more recent recording *Getting to Know Y'All* (MPS 15269, (1969)) is by William Breuker. There is an interesting interview with Chris Blount in *Clarinet & Saxophone*, 14 (1989), pp. 28–9. He is continuing the marching-band tradition and style in Britain.

8 Klassisches Wiener Schrammelquartett Decca SLK 16397–P and Österrichische Phonethek ÖPH 10022.

9 Baines, p. 125, states that there is a G clarinet in the stage-band parts of *Norma and La traviata*. The publisher Ricordi states that there is no stage band in *Norma* and that *La traviata* requires an A♭ clarinet in the stage band.

The basset horn

1 There was formerly a clarinet in F which was known as the tenor clarinet – used in military bands – which was indeed much more similar to the E♭ alto, since it too had no lower extension notes.

2 This was the instrument chosen by E. L. Gerber in *Historisch-biographisches Lexicon der Tonkünstler* (Leipzig, 1790–92) to illustrate the range of the basset horn.

3 J. G. Albrechtsberger, in *Gründliche Anweisung zur Composition* (Leipzig, 1790), p. 427, lists basset horns in G, F, E, E♭ and D.

4 *Letters of Clara Schumann and Johannes Brahms 1853–1896*, ed. Berthold Litzmann (London, 1927), p. 56.

5 See Michael Whewell, 'Mozart's basset horn trios', *Musical Times*, (1962), p. 19.

6 Daniel N. Leeson and David Whitwell, 'Concerning Mozart's Serenade in B♭ for thirteen instruments, KV 361 (370ᵃ)', *Mozart-Jahrbuch* (1976–7), pp. 97–130, incline towards a date of composition of 1783–4, coinciding with the presence in Vienna of the Bohemian basset horn virtuosi Anton David and Vincent Springer. Previously the work was thought to have been written in 1780–1 for players of the Munich orchestra.

7 At the head of the orchestration of Op. 113, Mendelssohn prefers the rarer spelling *Concertstück*.

The bass clarinet

1 Meyerbeer's *Les Huguenots* (1836) contains the first major bass clarinet solo, following various developments in design during the preceding years. See Nicholas Shackleton's observations in Chapter 2; also Rendall, pp. 141–8, and Kroll, p. 114.

4   The development of the clarinet repertoire

1 C. F. Whistling and F. Hofmeister, *Handbuch der musikalischen Literatur* (Leipzig, 1817, ten supplements, 1818–27; *R* New York, 1975); compilation by Jo Rees-Davies entitled *The Clarinet Repertoire in Whistling & Hofmeister* (Brighton, 1988).
2 F. J. Fétis, *Biographie universelle des musiciens* (2nd edn, Paris, 1873/*R* Brussels, 1963); extracts translated by Jo Rees-Davies as *Fétis on Clarinettists and Clarinet Repertoire* (Brighton, 1988).
3 Letter to his father from Munich, 3 October 1777, translated by Emily Anderson and quoted in the *New Grove* article 'Fiala'.
4 E. Hanslick, *Geschichte des Concertwesens in Wien: aus dem Concertsaal (Kritiken und Schilderungen aus dem letzte 20 Jahren des Wiener Musiklebens)* (Vienna, 1870/*R* Farnborough, 1971), vol. II, p. 397. The passage quoted by Oskar Kroll in *The Clarinet*, taken out of context, gives a slightly misleading view and should not be taken as a criticism of Orsi's playing; the preceding sentences state that Hanslick had not heard the Italian clarinettist perform, but had merely heard him praised, adding further that Orsi's fellow countrymen had an historical tradition of virtuosity on woodwind instruments.
5 G. Lowe, *Josef Holbrooke and his Works* (New York, 1920).

7   Teaching the clarinet

1 K. Swanwick, *Music, Mind and Education* (London, 1988), p. 14.
2 For more discussion on this topic see A. Sigel, *Clarinet Articulation* (New Jersey, 1987).
3 See especially C. Flesch, *The Art of Violin Playing* (New York, 1930).
4 See for example *The Cambridge Clarinet Tutor* by Paul Harris (Cambridge, 1981), or *Enjoy Playing The Clarinet* by Ruth Bonetti (Oxford, 1984, rev. edn, 1991).
5 For her ideas and concept of 'developing practice' and other suggestions, the author wishes to thank Melanie Ragge.
6 C. Baermann, *Vollständige Clarinett-Schule* Offenbach, André, 1864–75; H.-E. Klosé, *Méthode* (English Edition: London, Lafleur, 1874); H. Lazarus, *New and Modern Method* (London, Lafleur, 1881).
7 Swanwick, p. 36.

8   Playing historical clarinets

1 *The Interpretation of the Music of the Seventeenth and Eighteenth Centuries* (London, 1915), p. 471.
2 *A Comprehensive Performance Project in Clarinet Literature with an Organological Study of the Development of the Clarinet in the Eighteenth Century*, DMA thesis (University of Iowa, 1985), p. 205.
3 *The Early Flute* (Oxford, 1992), p. 72.
4 'Oiling the wood', *Clarinet & Saxophone*, 8/1 (1983), pp. 9–11.
5 *Literarische Fragmente* (Grax, 1785), p. 286.
6 In Chapter 1 we have already noted this author's enthusiasm for the chalumeau.
7 J. F. B. C. Majer, *Museum musicum* (Schwäbisch Hall, 1732), p. 39, reproduced by Albert Rice, *The Baroque Clarinet* (London, 1992), p. 65.

8 J. P. Eisel, *Musicus Autodidaktos* (Erfurt, 1738), following p. 78, reproduced in Rice, p. 69.

9 Within the *Buch* just above the metal bell at the foot of the instrument is contained an S-bend of extra tubing to produce written *c* and *d* (see Chapter 2). To this design the Stadlers added *c♯*, and also the *e♭* required by Mozart in his Serenade K361, notes which are, however, unavailable on all surviving specimens.

10 The precise relationship of the basset horn in G (for which part of the concerto was originally sketched) and the basset clarinet in A continues to remain elusive.

11 As Nicholas Shackleton has remarked in Chapter 2, the Strobach basset clarinet in Hamburg may in fact be the closest to Stadler's own design.

12 J. Joachim and A. Moser, *Violinschule* (Berlin, 1905).

9   The professional clarinettist

1 Several trusts and foundations offer the chance to audition for funds to continue studies, together with opportunities to be seen and heard by musical decision-makers. For further information refer to books such as the *British Music Yearbook* and *Musical America*, or write to the *Fédération des Concours Internationaux de Musique* in Geneva, which is merely a channel for information about international competitions, not a watch-dog.

2 However, Jack Brymer observes that 'Within a few minutes the really fine artist is obvious and after an hour the satisfactory orchestral worker has so settled in that it seems a shame to move him'. *In the Orchestra* (London, 1987), p. 27.

3 Tonguing speed, length of note and quality of sound are all influenced by the speed with which the tongue rebounds on to the reed. In fact, the ability to tongue also depends on the length of one's tongue (shorter tongues find fast staccato easier). Some French clarinettists seem to articulate the reed with the middle of the tongue rather than the tip. See also Antony Pay's remarks on articulation in Chapter 6.

11   The clarinet in jazz

1 A. S. Neill, *Summerhill* (London, 1926), p. 226.

12   The clarinet on record

1 Robert Philip, *Early Recordings and Musical Style* (London, 1992), p. 229.

2 *Ibid.*, pp. 232–3.

3 *Ibid.*, p. 234.

4 Thurston's discography also includes the Beethoven Septet and the Bax Nonet. Unfortunately his recording of the Finzi Concerto with Sir Adrian Boult and the BBC Symphony Orchestra at Oxford's Sheldonian Theatre (for the BBC transcription service) has been lost.

5 In 1939 Kell recorded one of the two clarinet quintets by his father-in-law Josef Holbrooke (reissued by Testament, SBT 1002, 1991).

6 The basset horn players on this disc were Bernard Bree, Richard Temple-Savage and Michael Whewell.

7 Elizabeth Ganter's discography also includes Crusell's Concerto No. 2 (Aurophon 34 054).

8 This record also provides an excellent performance of the Sinfonia Concertante Op. 80 by Krommer, for flute, clarinet and violin.

9 Amongst other important Swiss projects should be mentioned a unique recording (Gallo 3900418, 1984) of the Quintet by Constantin Regamey mentioned on page 88. At its first performance in a private house in Warsaw in 1944, the Quintet was immediately recognised in musical circles (as Lutosławski later recalled) as a

revelatory work of great maturity, close in mood to Messiaen's *Quatuor pour le fin du temps*.

10 Some important developments have not been mentioned in the main text, such as the flourishing Australian scene, ranging from the 1958 recording of the Brahms E♭ Sonata (Australian Columbia 330S 7560) by Clive Amadio, through the discography of Donald Westlake (for many years first clarinet in Sydney) to recordings of contemporary native composers performed by his son Nigel Westlake. The majority of Japanese recordings, such as those by the former principal clarinet of the NHK Symphony Orchestra Kohichi Hamanaka, unfortunately rarely find their way to Europe. Japanese record companies have promoted both European and indigenous clarinet repertoire, as well as reissues of chamber music featuring Draper, Kell, Lancelot and Sorokin, amongst others. Other areas of the world (such as Italy) have become markedly more active since the beginning of the era of CD. Belgium is another country which has offered a small but varied selection of recordings. Most prolific has been Walter Boeykens, largely within mainstream repertoire and also as director of his own clarinet choir.

Appendices

1 Sources and tutors for the early clarinet in modern edition or facsimile

Backofen, J. G. H., *Anweisung zur Klarinette, nebst einer kurzen Abhandlung über das Bassett-Horn* (Leipzig, c. 1803); facsimile, Moeck (Celle, 1986)

Blasius, F., *Nouvelle méthode de clarinette* (Paris, c. 1796); facsimile, Minkoff (Geneva, 1972)

Eisel, J. P., *Musicus Autodidaktos, oder der selbst informirende Musicus* (Erfurt, 1738); facsimile, Zentralantiquariat der DDR (Leipzig, 1976)

Francoeur, L-J., *Diapason général de tous les instrumens à vent* (Paris, 1772); facsimile, Minkoff (Geneva, 1972)

Lefèvre, J. X., *Méthode de clarinette* (Paris, 1802); facsimile, Minkoff (Geneva, 1974)

Majer, J. F. B. C., *Museum Musicum Theoretico Practicum* (Schwäbisch Hall, 1732); facsimile, Bärenreiter (Cassel, 1954)

Roeser, V., *Essai d' instruction à l'usage de ceux qui composent pour la clarinette et le cor* (Paris, 1764); facsimile, Minkoff (Geneva, 1972)

Vanderhagen, A., *Méthode nouvelle et raisonnée pour la clarinette* (Paris, 1776); facsimile, Minkoff (Geneva, 1972)

2 A select list of tutors

Compiled by Paul Harris

pre 1000

Baermann, C., *Vollständige Clarinett-Schule* (André, 1864-75)

Berr, F., *Traité complet de la clarinette à quatorze clefs* (Duverger, 1836)

Klosé, H., *Méthode pour servir à l'enseignement de la clarinette à anneaux mobiles* (Meissonnier, 1843)

Lazarus, H., *New and Modern Method for the Clarinet* (Lafleur, 1881)

Müller, I., *Méthode pour la nouvelle clarinette et clarinette-alto* (Gambaro, 1825)

post-1900

Bonetti, R., *Enjoy Playing the Clarinet* (Oxford University Press, 1984; rev. 1991)

Draper, G., *Introduction to the Clarinet* (Oxford University Press, 1962)

Harris, P., *The Cambridge Clarinet Tutor* (Cambridge University Press, 1981)

Jettel, R., *Klarinetten Schule* (Doblinger, 1949)

Langenus, G., *Modern Clarinet Playing* (Fischer, 1913)

Thurston, F., and Frank, A., *The Clarinet: a Comprehensive Tutor* (Boosey and Hawkes, 1939; rev. edn 1979)

Wastall, P., *Learn as you Play* (Boosey & Hawkes, 1978)

3   Recommended studies

A select list compiled by Paul Harris, which is intended to guide clarinet teachers towards publications of particular interest and value

Balassa, G., *Collection of Studies* (Editio Musica Budapest, 1973)

Davies, J., and Harris, P., *80 Graded Studies* (Faber, 1986)

Demnitz, F., *Elementary School* (Peters)

Gabucci, A., *60 Divertimenti* (Ricordi, 1957)

Jeanjean, P., *Vade Mecum du clarinettiste* (Leduc, 1927)

Jettel, R., *The Accomplished Clarinettist* (Weinberger, 1952)

Kell, R., *17 Staccato Studies* (International Music Company, 1958)

Kroepsch, F., *416 Studies* (International Music Company, 1957)

Müller, I., *30 Studies in All Keys* (Ricordi, 1832)

Rose, C., *32 Studies* (Leduc, 1913)

Stark, R., *Arpeggio Studies, Op. 39* (International Music Company)

Uhl, A., *48 Studies* (Schott, 1940)

Weidemann, L., *75 Etuden für Klarinette* (Kalmus)

Weston, P., *50 Classical Studies* (Fentone, 1976)

Zitek, F., *16 Modern Etudes, Op. 14* (Rubank, 1966)

4   Orchestral excerpts and studies

Compiled by Paul Harris

Bartholomey, P., *Mahler – Orchestral Studies* (Zimmerman)

Bonade, D., *Orchestra Studies* (Leblanc)

Caillet, L., *Orchestral Passages from Modern French Repertoire* (Durand)

Drapkin, M., *Symphonic Repertoire for Bass Clarinet* (Roncorp)

Drucker, S., *Orchestral Excerpts Vols. 5–8* (International Music Corporation)

Giampieri, A., *Orchestral Studies* (2 vols.) (Ricordi)

Hadcock, P., *Orchestral Excerpts for E♭ Clarinet* (Roncorp)

Heyneck, E., *Orchestral Studies* (10 vols.) (Merseburger)

Hinze, F., *Orchestral Studies* (2 vols.) (Breitkopf)

Hinze, F., *Wagner – Orchestral Excerpts* (International Music Corporation)

McGinnis, R., *Orchestral Excerpts vols. 1-4* (International Music Corporation)

Temple-Savage, R., *Difficult Passages from the Symphonic Repertoire* (Boosey and Hawkes)

Waln, G., *Clarinet Excerpts from the Orchestral Literature* (Belwin Mills)

Select bibliography

Adlung, J., *Anleitung zu der Musikalischen Gelahrtheit* (Erfurt, 1758/R1953)

Albrechtsberger, J. G., *Gründlicher Anweisung zur Composition* (Leipzig, 1790)

Altenburg, W., *Die Klarinette* (Heilbronn, 1904)

Antolini, F., *La retta maniere di scrivere per il clarinetto ed altri instromenti da fiato* (Milan, 1813)

Bach, C. P. E., *Versuch über die wahre Art das Clavier zu spielen*, 2 vols. (Berlin, 1753–62); tr. W. J. Mitchell as *Essay on the True Art of Playing Keyboard Instruments* (New York, 1949)

Baines, A., *European and American Musical Instruments* (London, 1966)
Woodwind Instruments and their History (London, 1957; 3rd edn, 1967)

Baron, S., *Benny: King of Swing* (New York, 1979)

Bartolozzi, B., *New Sounds for Woodwinds* (London, 1967; 2nd edn, 1982)

Becker, H., 'Das Chalumeau bei Telemann', *Konferenzbericht der 2. Magdeburger Telemann-Festtage* (Magdeburg, 1967), pp. 68–76
'Das Chalumeau im 18. Jahrhundert', *Speculum musicae artis: Festgabe für Heinrich Husmann* (Munich, 1970), pp. 23–46
'Zur Geschichte der Klarinette im 18. Jahrhundert', *Die Musikforschung*, 8 (1955), pp. 271–92

Benade, A. H., *Fundamentals of Musical Acoustics* (New York, 1976)

Berendt, J., *The Jazz Book* (Frankfurt, 1973)

Berg, L. N., *Den første Prøve for Begyndere udi Instrumental-Kunsten* (Christiansand, 1782)

Berlioz, L. H., *Grand Traité de l'instrumentation et d'orchestration modernes Op. 10* (Paris, 1843); tr. M. C. Clarke as *A Treatise on Modern Instrumentation* (London, 1858)

Birsak, K., *Die Holzblasinstrumente im Salzburger Museo Carolino Augusteum* (Salzburg, 1973)
Die Klarinette: Eine Kulturgeschichte (Buchloe, 1992, tr. G. Schamberger, 1994)
'Salzburg, Mozart und die Klarinette', *Mitteilungen der Internationalen Stiftung Mozarteum*, 33 (1985), pp. 40–7

Block, L., *Writing the Novel* (Cincinnati, 1985)

Boese, H., *Die Klarinette als Soloinstrument in der Musik der Mannheimer Schule* (Dresden, 1940)

Bok, H. and Wendel, E., *New Techniques for the Bass Clarinet* (Paris, 1989)

Bonade, D., *The Clarinetist's Compendium* (Kenosha, 1962)

Bonanni, F., *Gabinetto armonico* (Rome, 1722)

Boretz, B., and Cone, E. T., *Perspectives on Notation and Performance* (New York, 1976)

Brixel, E., *Klarinetten-Bibliographie* (Wilhelmshaven, 1978)

Brown, H. M., and Sadie, S. (eds), *Performance Practice*, 2 vols. (London, 1989)

Brymer, J., *Clarinet* (London, 1976)
  From Where I Sit (London, 1979)
  In the Orchestra (London, 1987)

Burney, C., *A General History of Music*, 4 vols. (London, 1776–89/*R* 1935)

Carse, A., *The Orchestra in the Eighteenth Century* (Cambridge, 1940)
  The Orchestra from Beethoven to Berlioz (Cambridge, 1948)
  The History of Orchestration (London, 1925/*R*1964)
  Musical Wind Instruments (London, 1939/*R*1965)

Charlton, D., 'Classical clarinet technique: documentary approaches', *Early Music*, 16 (1988), pp. 396–406

Chatwin, R. B., 'Handel and the clarinet', *Galpin Society Journal*, 3 (1950), pp. 3–8

Coker, J., *Complete Method for Improvisation* (Lebanon, 1980)
  Improvising Jazz (New Jersey, 1964)
  Patterns for Jazz (Miami, 1970)
  The Teaching of Jazz (Rottenburg, 1989)

Collier, J. C., *Benny Goodman and the Swing Era* (Oxford, 1989)

Crook, H., *How to Improvise* (Rottenburg, 1991)

Crow, E. J., 'Remarks on certain peculiarities in instruments of the clarinet family', *Proceedings of the Musical Association*, 11 (1884–5), pp. 19–33

Cucuel, E. J., *Etudes sur un orchestre au XVIIIe siècle* (Paris, 1913)

Dangain, G., *A propos de la clarinette* (Paris [1978])

Dart, R. T., 'The earliest collections of clarinet music', *Galpin Society Journal*, 4 (1951), pp. 39–41
  The Interpretation of Music (London, 1954)
  'The mock trumpet', *Galpin Society Journal*, 6 (1953), pp. 35–40

Dazeley, G., 'The original text of Mozart's Clarinet Concerto', *Music Review*, 9 (1948), pp. 166–72

Diderot, D., and D'Alembert, J. (eds), *Encyclopédie, ou Dictionnaire raisonné des sciences, arts et métiers*, vol. 3 (Lausanne and Berne, 1753)

Dolmetsch, A., *The Interpretation of the Music of the Seventeenth and Eighteenth Centuries* (London, 1915; 2nd edn, London, 1946/*R*1969)

Donington, R., *The Performer's Guide to Baroque Music* (London, 1973)
  The Interpretation of Early Music (London, 1963; 3rd rev. edn, London, 1974)

Doppelmayr, J. G., *Historische Nachricht von den Nürnbergischen Mathematicis und Künstlern* (Nuremberg, 1730)

Druschler, P., *The Altissimo Register: a Partial Approach* (Rochester, NY, 1978)

Eberst, A., *Klarnet od A do Z* (Cracow, 1970)

Elsenaar, E., *De Clarinet* (Hilversum, 1927)

Eppelsheim, J., 'Bassetthorn-Studien', *Studia organologica: Festschrift für John Henry van der Meer zu seinem fünfundsechzigsten Geburtstag*, ed. F. Hellwig (Tutzing, 1987), pp. 69–125

'Das Denner-Chalumeau des Bayerischen Nationalmuseums', *Die Musik-forschung*, 26 (1973), pp. 498–500

Fauchier-Magnan, A., *The Small German Courts in the Eighteenth Century* (London, 1980)

Fétis, F. J., *Bibliographie universelle des musiciens* (Paris, 1860)

Finson, J. W., 'Performing practice in the late nineteenth century, with special reference to the music of Brahms', *Musical Quarterly*, 70 (1984), pp. 457–75

Firestone, R., *Swing, Swing, Swing* (London, 1993)

Fitzpatrick, H., 'Jacob Denner's woodwinds for Göttweig Abbey', *Galpin Society Journal*, 21 (1968), pp. 81–7

Flesch, C., *The Art of Violin Playing*, 2 vols. (Eng tr., New York, 1930)

Forsyth, C., *Orchestration* (London, 1914; 2nd edn, London, 1935)

Fröhlich, J., *Vollständige Theoretisch-praktische Musikschule* (Bonn, 1810–11)

Gabucci, A., *Origine e storia del clarinetto* (Milan, 1937)

Galpin, F. W., *European Musical Instruments* (London, 1937)

Gallwey, T., *The Inner Game of Tennis* (New York, 1974)

Gandolfi, R., *Appunti intorno al clarinetto compilati ad uso delle scuole del R. Istituto musicale di Firenze* (Florence, 1887)

Garbarino, G., *Method for Clarinet* (Milan, 1978)

Garsault, F. A. P. de, *Notionaire, ou mémorial raisonné* (Paris, 1761)

Gee, H. R., *Clarinet Solos de Concours, 1897–1980* (Bloomington, 1981)

Gerber, E. L., *Historisch-biographisches Lexicon der Tonkünstler* (Leipzig, 1790–2)

Gigliotti, A., 'The American clarinet sound', *Woodwind Anthology* (Evanston, 1972), pp. 341–2

Gilbert, R., *The Clarinetist's Discography III* (New York, 1991)

The Clarinetist's Solo Repertoire (New York, 1972)

Gillespie, J. E., *Solos for Unaccompanied Clarinet* (Detroit, 1973)

Gradenwitz, P., 'The beginnings of clarinet literature: notes on a clarinet concerto by Johann Stamitz', *Music and Letters*, 17 (1936), pp. 145–50

Grenser, H., 'Bermerken über eine neue Erfindung zur Vervollkommung der Flöte', *Allgemeine musikalische Zeitung*, 13 (1811), pp. 75–8

Hacker, A., 'Mozart and the basset clarinet', *Musical Times*, 110 (1969), pp. 359–62

Hadcock, P., 'Unkinking the E-flat clarinet', *The Clarinet*, 9 (1982), pp. 30–4

Haine, A., *Adolphe Sax, sa vie, son œuvre, ses instruments de musique* (Brussels, 1980)

Halfpenny, E., 'Castilon on the clarinet', *Music and Letters*, 35 (1954), pp. 332–8

'Early English Clarinets', *Galpin Society Journal*, 18 (1965), pp. 42–56

'The Boehm clarinet in England', *Galpin Society Journal*, 30 (1977), pp. 2–7

Haskell, H., *The Early Music Revival* (London, 1988)

Hawkins, J. A., *A General History of the Science and Practice of Music*, 5 vols. (London, 1776/R1963)

Helistö, P., *Klanetti* (Klaustinen, 1988)

Hess, E., 'Anton Stadler's "Musik Plan" ', *Mozart-Jahrbuch*, (1962), pp. 37–54
'Die ursprüngliche Gestalt der Klarinettenkonzerts KV622', *Mozart-Jahrbuch* (1967), pp. 18–30

Heyde, H., *Historische Musikinstrumente im Bachhaus Eisenach* (Eisenach, 1976)

Hoeprich, T. E., 'A three-key clarinet by J. C. Denner', *Galpin Society Journal*, 34 (1981), pp. 21–32
'Clarinet reed position in the 18th Century', *Early Music*, 12 (1984), pp. 49–55
'Finding a clarinet for the three concertos by Vivaldi', *Early Music*, 11 (1983), pp. 60–4
'The L. C. Denner [*sic*] clarinet at Berkeley', *Galpin Society Journal*, 37 (1984), p. 114

Horwood, W., *Adolphe Sax 1814–1894: his Life and Legacy* (Bramley, 1980)

Jaffrey, K. S., *Reed Mastery* (Summer Hill, 1956)

Joachim, J., and Moser, A., *Violinschule* (Berlin, 1905)

Kappey, J. A., *Military Music: a History of Wind-Instrumental Bands* (London, c. 1894)

Karp, C., 'Baroque woodwind in the Musikhistoriska Museet, Stockholm', *Galpin Society Journal*, 25 (1972), pp. 80–6
'The early history of the clarinet and chalumeau', *Early Music*, 14, (1986), pp. 545–51

Kastner, G., *Traité général de l'instrumentation* (Paris, 1837; suppl. 1844)

Klosé, H. E., *Méthode pour servir à l'enseignment de la clarinette à anneaux mobiles, et de celle à 13 clés* (Paris, 1843)

Koch, H. C., *Musikalisches Lexicon* (Offenbach, 1802)

Köchel, L. R. von, *Johann Joseph Fux* (Vienna, 1872)

Kodály, Z., *The Selected Writings of Zoltan Kodály* (Budapest, 1974)

Kolneder, W., *Antonio Vivaldi* (London, 1970)
'Die Klarinette als Concertino-Instrument bei Vivaldi', *Die Musikforschung*, 4 (1951), pp. 185–91

Kroll, O., 'Das Chalumeau', *Zeitschrift für Musikwissenschaft*, 15 (1932–3), pp. 374–8
Die Klarinette (Cassel, 1965; tr. H. Morris, ed. A. Baines, London, 1968)

Kronthaler, O., *Das Klarinettenblatt: Eine Bauanleitung* (Celle, 1988)

Langwill, L. G., *An Index of Musical Woodwind Makers* (Edinburgh, 1960, rev., enlarged 6th edn, 1980), rev. W. Waterhouse as *The New Langwill Index* (London, 1993)

Lawson, C., 'Beethoven and the development of wind instruments', in *Performing Beethoven*, ed. R. Stowell (Cambridge, 1994), pp. 70–88
'Graupner and the chalumeau', *Early Music*, 11 (1983), pp. 209–16
'Telemann and the chalumeau', *Early Music*, 9 (1981), pp. 312–19
'The authentic clarinet: tone and tonality', *Musical Times*, 124 (1983), pp. 357–8
'The basset clarinet revived', *Early Music*, 15 (1987), pp. 487–501
'The chalumeau: independent voice or poor relation?' *Early Music*, 7 (1979), pp. 351–4

The Chalumeau in Eighteenth-Century Music (Ann Arbor, 1981)

'The chalumeau in the works of Fux', in *Johann Joseph Fux and the Music of the Austro-Italian Baroque*, ed. H. White (Aldershot, 1992), pp. 78–94

'The early chalumeau duets', *Galpin Society Journal*, 27 (1974), pp. 125–9

Leeson, D. N., and Whitwell, D., 'Concerning Mozart's Serenade for thirteen instruments, KV 361 (370ª)', *Mozart-Jahrbuch* (1976–7), pp. 97–130

Litzmann, B. (ed.), *Letters of Clara Schumann and Johannes Brahms 1853–1896* (London, 1927)

Longyear R. M., 'Clarinet sonorities in early Romantic music', *Musical Times*, 124 (1983), pp. 224–6

Lowe, G., *Josef Holbrooke and his Works* (New York, 1920)

Lyle, A., 'John Mahon's clarinet tutor', *Galpin Society Journal*, 30 (1977), pp. 52–5

MacGillivray, J. A., 'The woodwind', in *Musical Instruments through the Ages*, ed. A. Baines (Harmondsworth, 1961)

Mahillon, V. C., *Catalogue du Museé instrumentale de Conservatoire de Bruxelles* (Ghent, 1893–1912)

Malot, J.-F., *L'Art de bien faire une anche de clarinette* (Avallon, 1820)

Maramotti, R., *Il clarinetto* (Bologna, 1941)

Martino, D., 'Notation in general – articulation in particular', *Perspectives on Notation and Performance*, ed. B. Boretz and E. T. Cone (New York, 1976), pp. 102–13

Mattheson, J., *Das neu-eröffnete Orchestre* (Hamburg, 1713)

Mazzeo, R., *The Clarinet: Excellence and Artistry* (Sherman Oaks, 1981)

'The congenial clarinet family', *Selmer Bandwagon*, 40 (1979), p. 29

Mersenne, M., *Harmonie universelle* (Paris, 1636)

Meyer, J., *Akustik der Holzblasinstrumente in Einzeldarstellungen* (Frankfurt am Main, 1966)

Mozart, L., *Versuch einer gründlichen Violinschule* (Augsburg, 1756/R1976; tr. E. Knocker, 1948)

Müller, I., *Méthode pour la nouvelle clarinette et clarinette-alto* (Paris, 1825)

Murr, C. G., *Beschreibung der vornehmsten Merkwürdigkeiten in Nürnberg* (Nuremberg, 1778)

Neill, A. S., *Summerhill* (London, 1926)

Neumann, F., *Ornamentation and Improvisation in Mozart* (Princeton, 1986)

Newhill, J. P., *The Basset-Horn and its Music* (Sale, 1983; rev. edn, 1986)

'The contribution of the Mannheim School to clarinet literature', *Music Review*, 10 (1979), pp. 90–122

Nickel, E., *Die Holzblasinstrumentenbau in der freien Reichsstadt Nürnberg* (Munich, 1971)

Opperman, K., *Handbook for Making and Adjusting Single Reeds* (New York, 1956)

Repertory of the Clarinet (New York, 1960)

Orff, C., *Orff-Schulwerk: Past and Future* (London, 1964)

Paynter, J., and Aston, P., *Sound and Silence* (Cambridge, 1970)

Peyser, J. (ed.), *The Orchestra: Origins and Transformations* (New York, 1986)

Philip, R., *Early Recordings and Musical Style* (Cambridge, 1992)

Picken, L., *Folk Music Instruments of Turkey* (London, 1975)

Pino, D., *The Clarinet and Clarinet Playing* (New York, 1980)

Pisarowitz, K. M., '"Müasst ma nix in übel aufnehma . . .", Beitragsversuche zu einer Gebrüder-Stadler-Biographie', *Mitteilungen der Internationalen Stiftung Mozarteum*, 19 (1971), pp. 29–33.

Planas, E., 'Oiling the wood', *Clarinet & Saxophone* , 8/1 (1983), pp. 9–11

Poulin, P. L., 'A report on new information regarding Stadler's concert tour of Europe and two early examples of the basset clarinet, *Mozart-Jahrbuch* (1991), pp. 946–55

  'The basset clarinet of Anton Stadler', *College Music Symposium*, 22 (1982), pp. 67–82

Previn, A., *Orchestra* (London, 1979)

Quantz, J. J., *Versuch einer Anweisung die Flöte traversiere zu spielen* (Berlin, 1752; 3rd edn, 1789/R1953); tr. E. R. Reilly as *On Playing the Flute* (London and New York, 1966)

Rees-Davies, J., *Bibliography of the Early Clarinet* (Brighton, 1986)

  Clarinet and Saxophone Periodicals Index (Brighton, 1985)

  The Clarinet Repertoire in Whistling and Hofmeister 1817–26 (Brighton, 1988)

  Fétis on Clarinettists and Clarinet Repertoire (Brighton, 1988)

Rehfeldt, P., *New Directions for Clarinet* (Berkeley and Los Angeles, 1976; rev. edn, 1994)

Reid, R. H., *The Gramophone Shop Encyclopaedia* (New York, 1936; 3rd edn rev. R. D. Darrell, 1948)

Rendall, F. G., 'A short account of the clarinet in England', *Proceedings of the Musical Association*, 68 (1941–2), pp. 55–86

  The Clarinet (London, 1954; rev. 3rd edn by P. Bate, 1971)

Rice, A. R., 'Clarinet fingering charts, 1732–1816', *Galpin Society Journal*, 37 (1984), pp. 16–41

  'Garsault on the clarinet', *Galpin Society Journal*, 32 (1979), pp. 99–103

  The Baroque Clarinet (Oxford, 1992)

  'The clarinette d'amour and basset horn', *Galpin Society Journal*, 39 (1986), pp. 97–124

Richardson, E. G., *Acoustics of Orchestral Instruments* (London, 1929)

Richmond, S., *Clarinet and Saxophone Experience* (London and New York, 1972)

Ridenour, T., *The Annotated Book of Altissimo Clarinet Fingerings* (Longwood, 1986)

Robertson, A., *Chamber Music* (Harmondsworth, 1957)

Rosenblum, S. P., *Performance Practices in Classic Piano Music* (Bloomington and Indianapolis, 1988)

Ross, D., *A Comprehensive Performance Project in Clarinet Literature with an Organological Study of the Development of the Clarinet in the Eighteenth Century'*, DMA thesis (University of Iowa, 1985)

Russianoff, L., *Clarinet Method* (London and New York, 1982)

Saam, J., *Das Bassethorn* (Mainz, 1971)

Sachs, C., *Handbuch der Musikinstrumentenkunde* (Leipzig, 1920; 2nd edn, 1930)

Savo, G., *Cenni storici sull' origine del clarinetto* (Salerno, 1939)

Schafer, R. M., *The Rhinoceros in the Classroom* (London, 1975)

Schmid, E. F., 'Gluck–Starzer–Mozart', *Zeitschrift für Musik*, 104 (1937), pp. 1198–209

Schönfeld, J. F. von, *Jahrbuch der Tonkunst von Wien und Prag* (Vienna, 1796/R1976)

Schubart, C. F. D., *Ideen zu einer Ästhetik der Tonkunst* (Vienna, 1806/R1969)

Selfridge-Field, E., *Venetian Instrumental Music from Gabrieli to Vivaldi* (Oxford, 1975)

Shackleton, N., 'The earliest basset horns', *Galpin Society Journal*, 40 (1987), pp. 2–23

Shaw, A., *The Trouble with Cinderella* (New York, 1952)

Sigel, A., *Clarinet Articulation* (New Jersey, 1987)

Snavely, J., 'Clarinet literature available on recordings', *National Association of College Wind and Percussion Instructors*, 19/2 (1971) pp. 35–8; 19/3 (1971), pp. 12–14; 19/4 (1971), pp. 12–16

Solum, J., *The Early Flute* (Oxford, 1992)

Spratt, J., *How to Make Your Own Clarinet Reeds* (Stamford, 1956)

Stark, R., *Die höhe Schule des Clarinett-Spiels* (Mannheim, 1900)

Stein, K., *The Art of Clarinet Playing* (Evanston, 1958)

Street, O. W., 'The clarinet and its music', *Proceedings of the Musical Association*, 42 (1915–16), pp. 89–115

Stowell, R., *Violin Technique and Performance Practice in the Late Eighteenth and Early Nineteenth Centuries* (Cambridge, 1985)

Strunk, O., *Source Readings in Musical History* (New York, 1950)

Stubbins, W. H., *The Art of Clarinetistry* (Ann Arbor, 1965)

Swanwick, K., *Music, Mind and Education* (London, 1988)

Talbot, M., *Vivaldi* (London, 1978)

   'Vivaldi and Rome: observations and hypotheses', *Journal of the Royal Musical Association*, 113 (1988), pp. 28–46

   'Vivaldi e lo chalumeau', *Rivista italiana di musicologia*, 15 (1980), pp. 153–81

The Clarinet, journal of The International Clarinet Association

The Clarinet & Saxophone, journal of the Clarinet & Saxophone Society of Great Britain

The New Grove Dictionary of Music and Musicians, ed. S. Sadie (London, 1980)

The New Grove Dictionary of Musical Instruments, ed. S. Sadie (London, 1984)

Thurston, F. J., *Clarinet Technique* (Oxford, 1956; 3rd rev. edn, 1977)

Tromlitz, J. G., *Ausführlicher und gründlicher Unterricht die Flöte zu spielen* (Leipzig, 1791); tr. A. Powell as *The Virtuoso Flute-Player* (Cambridge, 1991)

Türk, D. G., *Klavierschule* (Leipzig and Halle, 1789), tr. Raymond H. Haggh as *School of Clavier Playing* (Lincoln, Nb, and London, 1982)

Van der Meer, J. H., *Johann Joseph Fux als Opernkomponist* (Bilthoven, 1961)

Walther, J. G., *Musicalisches Lexicon* (Leipzig, 1732)

   Praecepta der musicalischen Composition (1708 (MS)/R1960)

Warner, T. E., *An Annotated Bibliography of Woodwind Instruction Books, 1600–1830* (Detroit, 1967)

Weigel, J. C., *Musicalisches Theatrum* (Nuremberg, *c.* 1722; facsimile, Cassel, 1961)

Weston, P., *Clarinet Virtuosi of the Past* (London, 1971)

  Clarinet Virtuosi of Today (Baldock, 1989)

  More Clarinet Virtuosi of the Past (London, 1977)

Whewell, M., 'Mozart's basset horn trios', *Musical Times*, 103 (1962), p. 19

Whistling, C. F., and Hofmeister, F., *Handbuch der musicalischen Literatur* (Leipzig, 1817, with ten supplements, 1818–27/*R*1975)

Willaman, R., *The Clarinet and Clarinet Playing* (Salt Point, 1949)

Willman, T. L. A., *A Complete Instruction Book for the Clarinet* (London, *c.* 1825)

Young, P. T., *The Look of Music; Rare Musical Instruments 1500–1900* (Vancouver, 1980)

  2500 Historical Woodwind Instruments: an Inventory of the Major Collections (New York, 1982)

  4900 Historical Woodwind Instruments: an Inventory of 200 Makers in International Collections (London, 1993)

  'Woodwind instruments by the Denners of Nürnberg', *Galpin Society Journal*, 20 (1967), pp. 9–16

Index